Introduction to wxMaxima
for Scientific Computations

By
Dr. M Kanagasabapathy

BPB PUBLICATIONS
20 Ansari Road, Daryaganj, New Delhi-110002

Distributors:

BPB PUBLICATIONS
20, Ansari Road, Darya Ganj
New Delhi-110002
Ph: 23254990/23254991

BPB BOOK CENTRE
376 Old Lajpat Rai Market,
Delhi-110006
Ph: 23861747

COMPUTER BOOK CENTRE
12, Shrungar Shopping Centre,
M.G.Road, Bengaluru–560001
Ph: 25587923/25584641

DECCAN AGENCIES
4-3-329, Bank Street,
Hyderabad-500195
Ph: 24756967/24756400

MICRO MEDIA
Shop No. 5, Mahendra Chambers,
150 DN Rd. Next to Capital Cinema,
V.T. (C.S.T.) Station, MUMBAI-400 001
Ph: 22078296/22078297

Published by Manish Jain for BPB Publications, 20, Ansari Road, Darya Ganj, New Delhi-110002 and Printed at Repro India Pvt Ltd, Mumbai

PREFACE

It is with great pleasure that I write this preface. The continued growth of the Maxima user community is very encouraging to me as a developer. I am proud to say that Maxima has continued to grow as a project over the years that I have been involved, and several related projects have been successfully developed, including the wxMaxima user interface. It is gratifying to see that Maxima and wxMaxima are useful to many people around the world, and with the support of the world-wide user community I am inspired to seek continued success with the Maxima project.

I first became involved with the Maxima project in 2003, when I was hoping to calculate some integrals related to the branch of statistics called survival analysis. I began to participate in the Maxima mailing list, and my first contribution to the code was the numericalio package to read and write data files. At some point I began creating releases, beginning with Maxima 5.9.3 or was it 5.9.2? which I continued for several years. I fixed many bugs, and addressed many messages to the mailing list. Through it all I have always enjoyed the easy-going camaraderie of my fellow developers. I have never met any of them in person, yet I feel that I know them well from our daily interactions.

I have often conceptualized the Maxima project as a sort of virtual workshop. The workshop has been standing for many years, and there are still a few old-timers around, although many workers have come and gone over the decades. The workers labor mostly on their own projects, as they decide are useful and appropriate, using the tools which are there in the workshop for anyone to use. Before embarking on a new project, often a worker will raise the issue and discuss different approaches with others on the mailing list. A discussion usually brings some consensus or general agreement about a task, before a worker begins to work on it. Or there may be no discussion. Tasks which are minor may be carried out without discussion; there may be discussion only after the fact, and sometimes even disagreement, leading to some work being undone. This too, is part of the overall picture of loosely-organized efforts in the workshop. We are all marching in more or less the same direction, but sometimes there are disagreements as to exactly where to go.I have to say that I find such an atmosphere very conducive to doing good work, and I believe this is a good model for software development in general.

Fundamental functions are methodically organized in this book in an articulate style, which might be absolutely useful for the beginners to understand the basics of Maxima. I hope that the readers of this fine contribution by Dr. M Kanagasabapathy will be inspired and may join us in the forthcoming Maxima project workshops. There is always more work to be done, and perhaps in times to come, future users of Maxima will thank the efforts of this author.

Robert Dodier
Developer & Project Administrator of Maxima
Portland, Oregon, USA

Author's Note

Scientific computing is an indispensable technique for physical, chemical and biological sciences or even for financial estimations to simulate the technical data through mathematical models. It plays a vital role from research and development to industrial processes optimization. Though many packages are available for numerical computations, very few packages are available for symbolic computations like Mathematica, Maple, MATLAB, FriCAS, Sage, Scilab, Axiom, Euler, SymPy, etc. Among these, Maxima is an open sourced free ware and has user friendly interface, yet capable of executing persuasive symbolic as well as numerical computations.

Though Maxima has copious, built-in computational and graphical functions with steep learning curve, this book is a beginner's guide and outlines the fundamental functions and algorithm of coding with simple examples. Basic functions are arranged alphabetically for quick reference.

I am sincerely indebted to **Dr. Robert Dodier**, USA, Developer & Project Administrator of Maxima and **Dr. Roland Salz**, Bochum, Maxima Module Developer for peer-reviewing the book manuscript, and for their suggestions despite their busy schedule.

I express my gratitude to our President, Secretary and college governing council members, Rajapalayam Rajus' College for granting consent to publish this book.

I am grateful to **Dr. V. Venkatraman**, Principal, Rajapalayam Rajus' College for his motivation to publish this work.

I extend my sincere appreciations to **BPB Publications,** India for formatting my work into book.

Table of Contents

Chapter 1

Introduction

Basics of cell structure

Each input command or text entered in wxMaxima workspace consistsof'cells'. Cells are the basic building blocks and each cell has a square bracket in the left side. Cells are of different types such as 'title cell', 'text cell', 'section cell' and 'input cell'. Input values in the cell can be denoted after→. There is a triangle at the top of the bracket. If the triangle is clicked, it will turn into solid and the cell contents can be hidden. Cell contents can be edited, deleted, selected, copied, divided and new cell can also be inserted within the existing cells by using mouse or keyboard controls or from the menu bar.

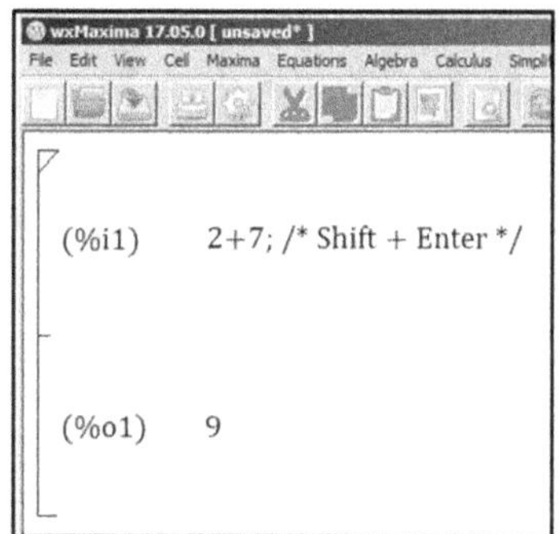
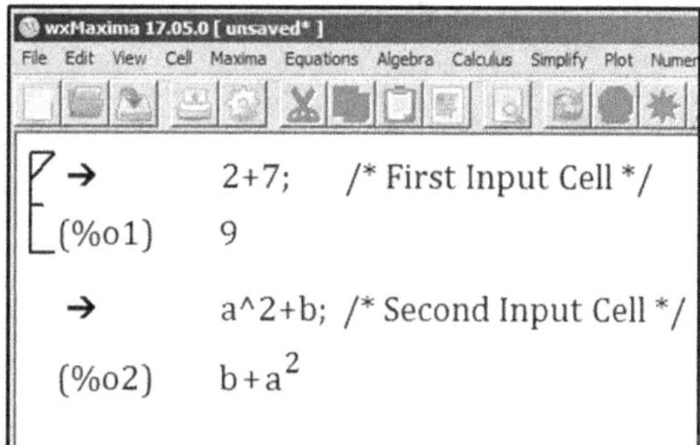

Annotations

Any command or function written inside /* ... */ or after /* is ignored and is not executed and comments are quoted with this.

Input and Output

Each input in the cells can be executed by entering values followed by semicolon (;) and evaluated by keyboard shortcuts (Shift + Enter) or from menu bar →Cell → Evaluate cells command, to get the output. wxMaxima can also be used as a calculator. For example, arithmetic numerical calculations can be performed as shown above.

If '$' is used instead of ';'then output will not be displayed and this is called quiet mode. Each input (i) and output (o) are recorded successively as

(%i1) and (%o1), (%i2) and (%o2) ...and so on. These input and output tags

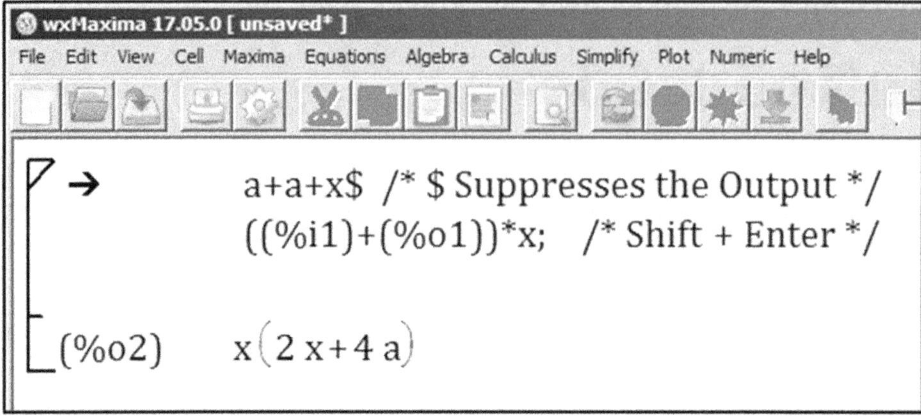

can be referred later for execution as shown below. The last output is referred just through **%**.

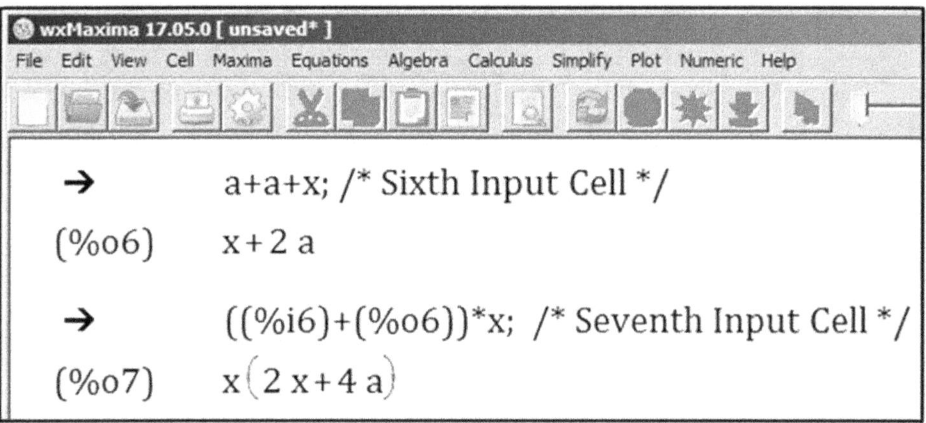

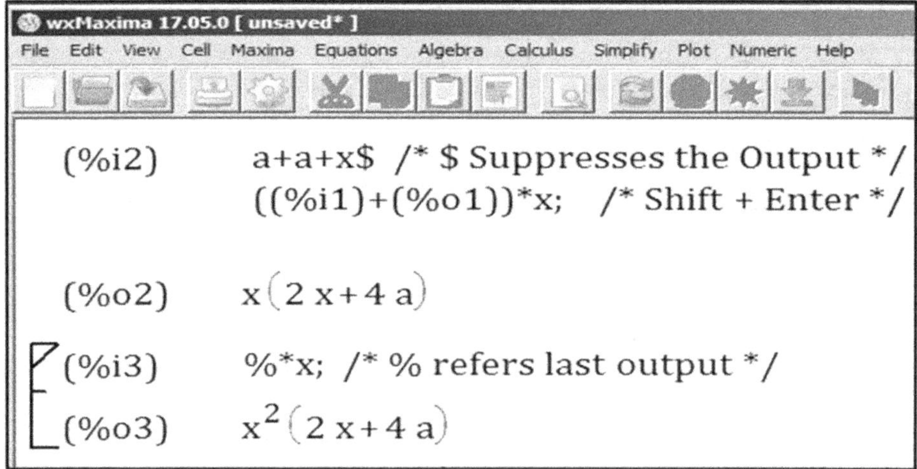

Graphical User Interface (GUI)

From the menu bar, all tools or functions can be easily accessed. For instance, Math or statistical tools and symbols can be directly accessed from the menu bar. View → History, lists the operations performed.

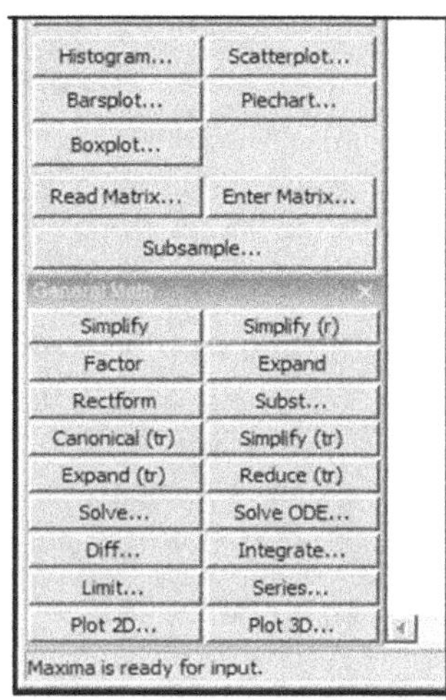

Math tools such as ODE, polynomial equations solver, algebra, calculus, simplifying expressions, 2D, 3D graph plotting, numerical precision, help topics etc., are accessed from relevant tabs in the main menu bar. Executions can be interrupted or memory can be cleared, or can be restarted or functions can be displayed or removed through the Maxima tab in the menu bar and it is embedded with many functions.

LaTex and MathML format

Contents in the cells can be selected, copied and saved as LaTex or MathML (word processor) or text or Image formats with Edit tab.

Configuring the interface

wxMaxima cell structure, appearance, fonts, number formats, worksheet style, execution methodology etc., can be altered from the default mode through Edit → Configure function as per users' choice.

Menu bar

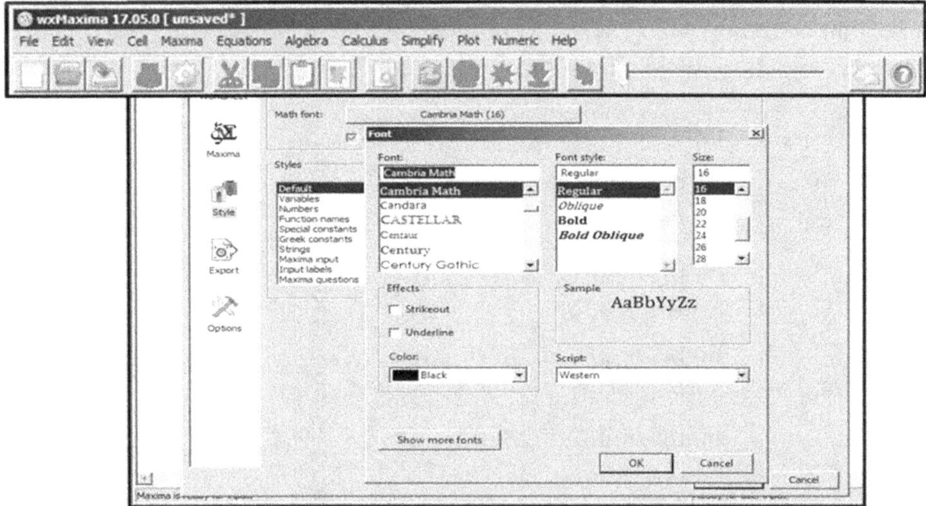

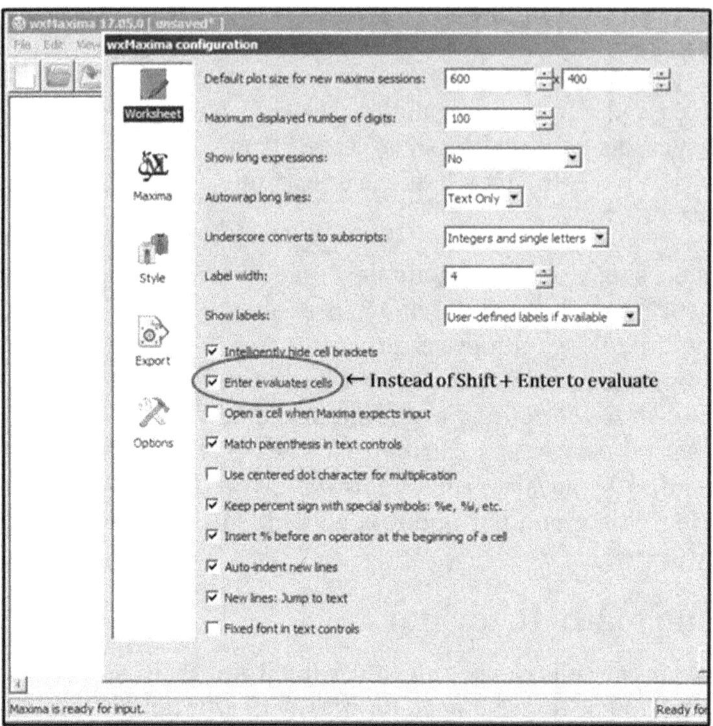

File formats

Worksheets can be saved and viewed as .wxmx or wxm (input without images). Maxima (.mac) and Lisp (.lisp) packages can be loaded through the file menu. Worksheet contents can also be saved as .html web page by, File → Export → HTML file option and hence the execution phases can be displayed, where wxMaxima is not installed.

Basic operators

Some of the basic math operators are:

+	addition
−	subtraction
*	multiplication
/	division
^or **	exponentiation
.	matrix multiplication
!	factorial

increasing precedence order

Operations within the parentheses ( ) are getting higher priority.

Example:

```
(%i1)    x+x*a;
(%o1)    ax + x
(%i2)    (x+x)*a;
(%o2)    2 a x
```

To assign a value to a variable, colon (:) is used.

Example: a:n;   /*assignsn for a*/

Rational and irrational numerical output

If the input is rational then the output is also rational, whereas if the input is irrational then the output is also irrational.

Example:

```
(%i1)        a:1/3;
(a)              1
                 ─
                 3
(%i2)        b:1.0/3;
(b)              0.3333333333333333
```

Using 'numer' function, rational input can be converted to irrational.

```
(%i3)        c:(1/3), numer;    /*numer –> converts to number*/
(c)              0.3333333333333333
```

Combined alphanumeric output can also be obtained.

```
(%i1)        a:2.58;
             b :a+c;      /* Shift + Enter */
(a)          2.58
(%o2)        b=c+ 2.58/* Note:  output is obtained after final input */
```

Symbolic computations

wxMaxima can execute both numeric as well as symbolic computations and this is one of the key facet required for scientific and engineering computations.

Example:

(%i1)	a : x^b*x^b+(x^b+x^b);	
	x:2;	
	b:3;	
(a)	$x^{2b}+2x^b$	/* Symbolic output */
(x)	2	
(b)	3	
(%i4)	a, numer;	/* to convert into numerical value */
(%o4)	80;	/* Numerical output */

Chapter 2

Basic Functions

f(variable)   := assignment operator

evaluates the given function for variable with assignment operator,

(%i4)   f(x):=4*x*y;
                 f(a);f(2);
                 f(b*2);
(%o1)   f(x):=4xy
(%o2)   4ay
(%o3)   8y
(%o4)   8by

!   or   factorial (...)

returns the factorial value

(%i1)   6!;
(%o1)   720

!!

double factorial of 'n' evaluates the product n × (n–2) × (n–4) × (n–6) × ....(n–m) where 'm' is largest integer and m ≤ n.

(%i1)   10!!
(%o1)   3840   /* 10 × (10–2) × (10–4)×(10–6)× (10–8) */

%e

represents exponential, the base of natural logarithm or Euler's number and is equals to 2.718281828459045.

%i

represents the imaginary number, $\sqrt{-1}$.

%phi

value of golden ratio, $\frac{1+\sqrt[2]{5}}{2}$ and is equals to 1.618033988749895.

%pi

value of π, and is equals to 3.141592653589793.

'

single quote operator prevents evaluation.

(%i1)	x:2;y:3;	
	a:(x+y)^2;	
	'a;	/* Shift + Enter */
(x)	2	
(y)	3	
(a)	25	
(%o4)	a;	/* not evaluated */

::   **assignment operator**

double colon is an assignment operator and evaluates both right-hand as well as left-hand side unlike single colon (:) operator.

(%i5)	a:[x,y,z];
	a ::[10,20,30];
	x;y;z;
(a)	[x,y,z]
(a)	[10,20,30]
(%o3)	10
(%o4)	20
(%o5)	30

::=   Refer: macro function definition operator

Some relational operators

<	less than	<=	less than or equal
>	greater than	>=	greater than or equal

(%i8)	[a,b]:[10,20];
	[c,d] : [20,30];
	if b>=c then 1 else 0;
	if a<b then yes else no;
(%o5)	[10, 20]
(%o6)	[20, 30]
(%o7)	1

(%o8)   yes

[ ] square brackets are used to enclose a list.

(%i3)   a:[x,y,z];   b:[1,2,z];
                a*b;
(a)   [x,y,z]
(b)   [1,2,z]
(%o3)   [x,2y,z^2]
(%i4)   a[3]: i;
(%o4)   i   /* List can be edited */
(%i5)   a;
(%o5)   [x,y,i]

_   underscore returns the last input, just as %.

{elements} to denote a set of elements.

abs(value)
returns the absolute value
(%i1)   a:−x$
(%i2)   b:abs(%);
(b) |x|

absolute_real_time ()
returns number of seconds from January 1, 1900, 0.00 AM to till now.
(%i1)   absolute_real_time ();
(%i2)   3731323672   /* as on 29th March 2018 */
                /* It can be used to trigger the computation schedule */

allbut
neglects the quoted and works with 'part' commands.
(%i3)   a:[x,y,z,m,n];
                part (a,[2,5]);
                part (a, allbut (2,1));
(a)   [x,y,z,m,n]

(%o2) [y,n]
(%o3) [z,m,n]

append(list1, list2, list3...)

returns a single list by combining in order, from the multiple lists.

(%i5)   a:[x,2*y];b:[2*x,y];c:[x^3,z,n];d:[z^2,a];

               append (a, b, c, d);

(a)   [x,2y]
(b)   [2x,y]
(c)   [x^3,z,n]
(d)   [z^2,[x,2y]]
(%o5)   [x,2y,2x,y,x^3,z,n,z^2,[x,2y]]

apply(expression)

constructs and evaluates an expression.

(%i3)   a:[2.4,4.6,7.8,−1.0,0.1,0.9];

               apply (max, a);apply (min,a);

(a)   [2.4,4.6,7.8,-1.0,0.1,0.9]
(%o2)   7.8
(%o3)   −1.0

it also convert a nested list into a matrix.

(%i2)   x:[[a,b],[y,c*d],[z,2*f]];apply(matrix, x);

(x)   [[a,b],[y,cd],[z,2f]]

(%o2)
$$\begin{bmatrix} a & b \\ y & cd \\ z & 2f \end{bmatrix}$$

apply1 (expression, condition1, condition2...)

repeatedly applies condition1 to expression until it fails. Then condition2 is applied in the same fashion.

args (...)

returns a list of arguments from the given expression.

(%i1)   nx+y/z−m*z;

(%o1) $-mz+\frac{y}{z}+nx$

(%i2)	args(%i1);
(%o2)	$[-mz,\frac{y}{z},nx]$ /* converted into list */

arithmetic (a,x,n)

returns the n_{th} value of series a, (a+x), (a+2x), ...,(a+(n–1)x).

To use this function first call, **load(functs)** function.

(%i1)	load(functs);
(%o1)	"C:\maxima-5.38.1\share\maxima\5.38.1_5_gdf93b7 b_dirty\share\simplification\functs.mac"
(%i2)	arithmetic (6, 2, 5);
(%o2)	14 /* 6, (6+2), (6+4),(6+6), (6+8) */
(%i3)	arithmetic (a,x,n);
(%o3)	(n–1)x + a

arithsum (a, x, n)

returns the sum of the series a, (a+x),(a+2x),....,(a+(n–1)x).

To use this function use first call, **load(functs)** function.

(%i1)	load(functs);
(%o1)	"C:\maxima-5.38.1\share\maxima\5.38.1_5_gdf93b7 b_dirty\share\simplification\functs.mac"
(%i2)	arithsum (6,2,5);
(%o2)	50 /* 6 + (6+2) + (6+4) + (6+6) + (6+8) */
(%i3)	arithsum (a, x, n);
(%o3)	$n\left(\frac{(n-1)x}{2} + a\right)$

ascii (int)

returns the character (char) for the US-ASCII integer (int).

int	= (0 to 127).
(%i1)	b:ascii(36);
(b)	$

related function is 'cint'

cint("char")

returns the US-ASCII integer for the character (char).

(%i2)	c:cint("#");
(c)	35

asympa

package for asymptotic analysis.

(%i1)   load(asympa); /* many such packages are used */

(%o1)   "C:\maxima-5.38.1\share\maxima\5.38.1_5_gdf93b7b_dirty\share

atom (expression)

returns true if expression is a number, name or string. Thus atom (5) or atom (a) or atom(5*4) is true while atom(5*x) is false.

augcoefmatrix (...)

returns augmented coefficient matrix forsystem of linear equations.

(%i2)   a : [x*2+3*y=9, x*3+y=9];

                augcoefmatrix (a, [x, y]);

(a)   [3y + 2x = 9, y + 3x = 9]

(%o2) $\begin{pmatrix} 2 & 3 & -9 \\ 3 & 1 & -9 \end{pmatrix}$

background [background, color]

sets the color of the graphics background and default is black. It accepts names or # followed by hexadecimal red-green-blue (RGB) strings.Valid names are red, green, blue, magenta, cyan, yellow, orange, violet, brown, gray, black, white, # hexadecimal RGB.

\\ backslash

literally refers \

belln (n)

returns the nth Bell number. Bell number gives the number of ways the set of elements can be arranged into non-empty subsets.

(%i2)   belln(5);   /* 5 elements can be arranged in 52 ways*/

(%o2)   52

bern (n)

returns the nth Bernoulli number for integer 'n'.

(%i1)   bern(8);

(%o1) $-\dfrac{1}{30}$

bernpoly (x,n)

returns the nth Bernoulli polynomial for the variable 'x'.

(%i1)   bernpoly (a, 3);

(%o1) $a^3 - \dfrac{3a^2}{2} + \dfrac{a}{2}$

bfloat (n)

converts all numbers or functions of numbers 'n' to big float numbers.
The number of significant digits in the resulting big floats is specified
by **fpprintprec** function.   (For details refer: **float(n)**)

binomial (x,y)

returns binomial coefficient x! / (y!(x–y)!). If x and y are integers, then the
numerical value of the binomial coefficient is computed.

(%i1)   binomial (x,x–5);

(%o1) $\dfrac{(x-4)\,(x-3)\,(x-2)\,(x-1)\,x}{120}$ /* 5 ! = 120 */

(%i2)   binomial (7,5);

(%o2)   21

bit_length (int)

determines how many bits of a positive integer (int) are there.
To use this, first call **load("bitwise")** function.

(%i1)   load("bitwise");

(%o1)   "C:\maxima-5.38.1\share\maxima\5.38.1_5_
               gdf93b7b_dirty\share\contrib\bitwise\bitwise.lisp"

(%i2)   bit_length(16);

(%o2)   5   /* binary 10000 */

block (variables, expressions, conditions) /* program function*/

allows to make the variables to be local for commands in expressions. If these variables are bound, block saves the current values of the variables for conditions upon entry to the block, then unbinds the variables so that they evaluate themselves.

(%i1)   block (do (a:read("Do you want to continue, type yes to continue?"), if(a=yes) then (x:read("Enter value of x"), print (x, b:5*x)) else return()))$

Do you want to continue, type yes to continue? yes;   /* type yes */

               Enter value of x3;   /* type any value */

               3   15

Do you want to continue, type yes to continue? no;   /* no quits*/

blockmatrixp (matrix)

returns true for a matrix and every entry of the matrix.

bug_report ()

prints Maxima and Lisp version numbers, and gives a link to the Maxima project bug report web page, similar to **build_info** function.

build_info ()

prints a summary of the parameters of the Maxima build structure.

(%i1)   build_info ();

(%o1)   build_info(version="5.38.1_5_gdf93b7b_dirty",

               timestamp="2016-05-13 22:33:49",host="i686-

               w64-mingw32",lisp_name="CLISP",lisp_version="2.49

               (2010-07-07) (built on toshiba [192.168.43.3])")

cardinality ({set})

returns the number of distinct elements of the set a.

(%i1)   cardinality ({b,a,b,c,d});

(%o1)   4   /* 4 distinct elements in the set*/

cartesian_product ({...})

returns a set of lists of Cartesian product.

(%i1)   cartesian_product ({b, –x}, {–1, 2*m, x});

(%o1)   {[b, –1], [b, 2m], [b, x], [–x, –1], [–x, 2m], [–x, x]}

charat (string, n)

returns the nth character of string.

(%i1)   charat("Its wxMaxima",7);

(%o1)   M

charlist (string)

returns the list of characters in string.

(%i1)   charlist("Its wxMaxima");

(%o1)   [I,t,s, ,w,x,M,a,x,i,m,a]

(%i2)   charlist("2x7im");

(%o2)   [2,x,7,i,m]

chebyshev_t (n, x)

Chebyshev polynomial of the first kind of degree n.

(%i1)   chebyshev_t (2, x);

(%o1) $-4(1-x) + 2(1-x)^2 + 1$

(%i2)   chebyshev_t (2, x);

(%o2) $-9(1-x) - 4(1-x)^3 + 12(1-x)^2 + 1$

chebyshev_u (n, x)

Chebyshev polynomial of the second kind of degree n.

(%i1)   chebyshev_u (2,x);

(%o1) $3\left(-\dfrac{8(1-x)}{3} + \dfrac{4(1-x)^2}{3} + 1\right)$

closefile ()   Refer: writefile

closes the transcript file opened by write file or append file.

coeff (expression, x, n)

returns coefficient of expression, in the polynomial term in x.

(%i1)   coeff (x^3*n*a–b*x^2+y*c*x–i, x^3);

(%o1)   an

(%i2)   coeff (x^3*n*a–b*x^2+y*c*x–i, x);

(%o2)   cy

(%i3)   coeff (x^3*n*a–b*x^2+y*c*x–i, i);
(%o3)   –1

col (matrix, m)

returns the mth column of the matrix.

(%i1)   M: matrix ([–a,3*y,u], [2*y,e,i*t],[n*c,v,m*e]);

(%o1) $\begin{bmatrix} -a & 3y & u \\ 2y & e & it \\ cn & v & em \end{bmatrix}$

(%i2)   col (M, 2);

(%o2) $\begin{bmatrix} 3y \\ e \\ v \end{bmatrix}$

row (matrix, n)

returns the nth row of the matrix.

(%i1)   M: matrix ([–a, 3*y,u], [2*y,e,i*t],[n*c,v,m*e]);

(%o1) $\begin{bmatrix} -a & 3y & u \\ 2y & e & it \\ cn & v & em \end{bmatrix}$

(%i2)   row (M, 2);
(%o2)   [2y e it]

combination (n,r)

returns the number of combinations of 'n' objects taken 'r' at a time.
To use this function first call, **load(functs)**.

(%i1)   load(functs);
(%o1)   "C:\maxima-5.38.1\share\maxima\5.38.1_5_gdf
               93b7b_dirty\share\simplification\functs.mac"
(%i2)   combination (4, 2);
(%o2)   6
               /* From a list of 4 members such as x, y, z & i, select only 2and
               the combination (4, 2). The possibilities are '6' as: (x, y), (x, z),
               (x, i), (y, z), (y, i), (z, i) */
               related function permutation

permutation (n,r)

returns the number of permutations of 'r' objects selected from a set of 'n' objects. To use this function first call, **load(functs)**.

(%i1)	load(functs);
(%o1)	"C:\maxima-5.38.1\share\maxima\5.38.1_5_gdf
	93b7b_dirty\share\simplification\functs.mac
(%i2)	permutation (4, 2);
(%o2)	12

From a list of 4 members such as x, y, z & i, select any 2 at a time and hence the permutation (4, 2). The possibilities are '12' as: (x, y), (y, x), (x, z), (z, x), (x, i), (i, x), (y, z), (z, y) (y, i), (i, y), (z, i), (i,z).

combine (expression)

simplifies the sum expression by combining the terms with the same denominator into a single term.

(%i1)	b:(x*t/3)+(y*i/4)–(e*x/(2*r))–(z*n/2);

$$(b) \qquad -\frac{nz}{2} + \frac{iy}{4} + \frac{tx}{3} - \frac{ex}{2r}$$

(%i2)	combine (b);

$$(\%o2) \qquad \frac{-6nz + 3iy + 4tx}{12} - \frac{ex}{2r}$$

compare (x, y)

returns a comparison operator such as <, <=, >, >=, =, # by comparing 'x' and 'y' . If can't compared, returns unknown.

(%i3)	m:(i–j)^3; n:i^3–(3*i^2*j)+(3*j^2*i)–j^3;
	compare (m,n);
(m)	$[i-j]^3$
(m)	$-j^3+3ij^2-3i^2j+i^3$
(%o3)	= /* m = n */
(%i3)	m:(i–j)^3; n:(j–i)^3;
	compare (m,n);
(m)	$[i-j]^3$
(n)	$[j-i]^3$
(%o3)	unknown

(%i3)	m:(2–3)^3$	n:(3–2)^3$
	compare (m,n);	
(%o3)	<	/* m = –1; n = +1 */

concat (arguments)

concatenates arguments. Single quote ' prevents the evaluation.

(%i4)	i:6.3;j:8.6;
	a:concat (i, j/2);
	b:concat ('i, j/2);
(i)	6.3
(j)	8.6
(a)	6.34.3
(b)	i4.3

cons (expression, list)

constructs a new list with expression as its first element, followed by the elements of list.

(%i1)	cons(b*x,[a,c,d/i]);
(%o1)	$[bx,a,c,\frac{d}{i}]$
(%i2)	%/(c*i);
(%o2)	$[\frac{bx}{ci},\frac{a}{ci},\frac{1}{i},\frac{d}{ci^2}]$

constvalue (x)

returns the physical constants valueswith its units. To use this first call, **load ("physical_constants")**.

(%i1)	load ("physical_constants");
(%o1)	"C:\maxima-5.38.1\share\maxima\5.38.1_5_gdf93b7b_
	dirty\share\ezunits\physical_constants.mac"
(%i2)	float(constvalue (%F)); /*F = Faraday's constant*/
(%o2)	$96485.3399\,\frac{C}{mol}$

(%i3)   float(constvalue (%R));

(%o3) $8.314472\,\dfrac{J}{K\,mol}$ /* Rfor Gas constant */

cont2part (f, [x, y, z])

returns the partitioned polynomial associated with contracted form f.

(%i1)   f: a*x^5+b*y^2–c*z^3;

(f) $-c\,z^3 + b\,y^2 + a\,x^5$

(%i2)   cont2part (f, [x, y,z]);

resolvante

generale

NOTE: To compile the system do load("sym/compile");

0 errors, 0 warnings

(%o2)   [[a,5,0,0],[b,2,0,0],[–c,3,0,0]]

content ()

returns a list with first element as the greatest common divisor of the coefficients of the polynomial terms.

(%i1)   i*x*y – j*x^2+k*x*m;

(%o1) $ixy – jx^2+kmx$

(%i2)   content(%);

(%o2)   [x,iy – jx+km]

continuous_freq(list, n)

returns the divided range with 'n' equal intervals between the minimum and the maximum values and counts the number of values.

To use this function first call, **load (descriptive)**.

(%i1)   load (descriptive);

(%o1)   "C:\maxima-5.38.1\share\maxima\5.38.1_5_gdf93

               b7b_dirty\share\descriptive\descriptive.mac"

(%i2)   a: [–3,2,3,7,9,13];

(a)   [–3,2,3,7,9,13]

(%i3)   continuous_freq (a, 8);

               /* 8 equal intervals stating from –3to 13*/

(%o3)   [[–3,–1,1,3,5,7,9,11,13],[1,0,2,0,1,1,0,1]]

convert(expression, [list])

converts one unit into other unit which is expressed as list. For inexact calculations "rat" warnings will be shown.

To use this function first call, **load("unit")**

(%i1)   load("unit")$

****

* Units version 0.50*
* Definitions based on the NIST Reference on*
* Constants, Units, and Uncertainty*
* Conversion factors from various sources including*
* NIST and the GNU units package*

****

Redefining necessary functions

Initializing unit arrays...

Done.

(%i2)   convert(4*kg/m/s, [g,inch,s]);

rat: replaced 39.37007874015748 by 5000/127 = 39.37007874015748

$$(\%o2) \qquad \frac{508}{5}\frac{g}{\%in\ s}$$

$$4\ kg = 4000\ g;\ 1m = \frac{100}{2.54}\ inch;\ so\ \frac{4000 \times 2.54}{100} = \frac{508}{5}\frac{g}{inch.sec}$$

(%i3)   convert(2*dA/inch^2,[A,m]);   /* A for Ampere */

rat: replaced 0.0254 by 127/5000 = 0.0254

rat: replaced 0.0254 by 127/5000 = 0.0254

$$(\%o3) \qquad \frac{5000000}{16129}\frac{A}{m^2} \quad /\text{*current per area = current density */}$$

$$2dA = 0.2\ A;\ (1\ inch)^2 = \left(\frac{2.54}{100}\right)^2 = \left(\frac{6.4516}{10000}\right) m^2$$

$$or\ \left(\frac{0.2 \times 10000}{6.4516}\right) = \frac{5000000}{16129}\frac{A}{m^2}$$

copy(x)

returns copy of the expression 'x'and is useful for a list or a matrix.

(%i2)	a : [i,j,k];	
	b : a;	
(a)	[i,j,k]	
(b)	[i,j,k]	
(%i3)	b[1] : x;	
(%o3)	x	
(%i4)	a;	
(%o4)	[x,j,k]	
(%i5)	b;	
(%o5)	[x,j,k]	
(%i2)	a : [i,j,k];	/* with copy function */
	b : copy(a);	
(a)	[i,j,k]	
(b)	[i,j,k]	
(%i3)	b[1] : x;	
(%o3)	x	
(%i4)	a;	
(%o4)	[i,j,k]	
(%i5)	b;	
(%o5)	[x,j,k]	

copy_file (file1, file2)

copies file located as file1 to file2.

cor (matrix)

returns the correlation matrix. To use this function first call, **load("descriptive");**

(%i1)   load ("descriptive");
             /* use $ instead of; to suppress this output */

Loading file C:\Users\M Kanagasabapathy\maxima\binary\
5_38_1_5_gdf93b7b_dirty\clisp\2_49__2010_07_07___built_
on_toshiba__192_168_43_3__\share\draw\grcommon.fas   ...
             ... /* load ("descriptive") calls */ ...
             0 errors, 0 warnings

(%o1)   "C:\maxima-5.38.1\share\maxima\5.38.1_5_
gdf93b7b_dirty\share\descriptive\descriptive.mac"

(%i2)   x: matrix([i,j],[k,l]);

(x) $\begin{bmatrix} i & j \\ k & l \end{bmatrix}$

(%i3)   cor (x);

(%o3)

$$\begin{bmatrix} \dfrac{\frac{k^2+i^2}{2}-\frac{(k+i)^2}{4}}{\frac{k^2+1}{2}-\frac{(k+1)^2}{4}} & \dfrac{\frac{kl+ij}{2}-\frac{(k+i)(l+j)}{4}}{\sqrt{\frac{k^2+1}{2}-\frac{(k+1)^2}{4}}\sqrt{\frac{l^2+j^2}{2}-\frac{(l+j)^2}{4}}} \\[4ex] \dfrac{\frac{kl+ij}{2}-\frac{(k+i)(l+j)}{4}}{\sqrt{\frac{k^2+1}{2}-\frac{(k+1)^2}{4}}\sqrt{\frac{l^2+j^2}{2}-\frac{(l+j)^2}{4}}} & 1 \end{bmatrix}$$

(%i4)   float(%);

(%o4)

$$\begin{bmatrix} \dfrac{0.5(k^2+i^2)-0.25(k+i)^2}{0.5(k^2+1.0)-0.25(k+1.0)^2} & \dfrac{0.5(kl+ij)-0.25(k+i)(l+j)}{\sqrt{0.5(k^2+1.0)-0.25(k+1.0)^2}\sqrt{0.5(l^2+j^2)-0.25(l+j)^2}} \\[4ex] \dfrac{0.5(kl+ij)-0.25(k+i)(l+j)}{\sqrt{0.5(k^2+1.0)-0.25(k+1.0)^2}\sqrt{0.5(l^2+j^2)-0.25(l+j)^2}} & 1.0 \end{bmatrix}$$

cos (x)
returns cosine value for angle 'x' expressed in radians.
(%i1)   float(cos(30));
(%o1)   0.154251449887584

cosh (x)
returns hyperbolic cosine.
(%i1)   float(cosh(2));
(%o1)   3.762195691083631

cot (x)
returns cotangent of 'x'.
(%i1)   float(cot(30));
(%o1)   −0.1561199521616592

coth (x)

returns hyperbolic cotangent of 'x'.

(%i1)   float(coth(30));

(%o1)   1.0

csc (x)

returns cosecant of 'x'.

(%i1)   float(csc(30));

(%o1)   −1.012113353070178

csch (x)

returns hyperbolic cosecant of 'x'.

(%i1)   float(csch(2));

(%o1)   0.2757205647717832

cspline (list)

returns the cubic spline interpolation polynomial for the given list.

To use this function first call, **load (interpol)\$**.

(%i1)   load(interpol)\$ /* output suppressed */

(%i2)   a:[[0,1],[1,2],[2,33],[3,244]]\$ /* [x, y] list */

(%i3)   cspline(a);

(%o3) $(-4x^3 + 5x + 1)\text{charfun } 2(x, -\infty, 1) + (-46x^3 + 414x^2 - 985x + 715)\text{charfun } 2(x, 2, \infty) + (50x^3 - 162x^2 + 167x - 53)\text{charfun } 2(x, 1, 2)$

/* find 'y' by interpolation from 'x' values*/

  Conditions

$(-4x^3+5x+1)$	$x_1 \leq x \leq x_2.$	$(0 \leq x \leq 1)$
$(50x^3-162x^2+167x-53)$	$x_2 \leq x \leq x_3$	$(1 \leq x \leq 2)$
$(-46x^3+414x^2-985x+715)$	$x_3 \leq x \leq x_4$	$(2 \leq x \leq 3)$

cv (list) or   cv (matrix)

returns the variation coefficient from the standard deviation and the mean for the given list or matrix.

$$/* \; cv = \frac{\text{standard deviation}}{\text{average}} \; */$$

To use this function first call, **load (descriptive)\$**.

(%i1)	load (descriptive) \$
(%i2)	a:[15.6, 17.5, 36.6,43.8, 58.2, 61.6, 65.2, 72.6, 98.9];
(a)	[15.6, 17.5, 36.6, 43.8, 58.2, 61.6, 65.2, 72.6, 98.9];
(%i3)	cv (a), numer;
(%o3)	0.483928113663802

days360 (year1, month1, day1, year2, month2, day2)

returns the days between 2 dates, by assuming 360 days per year, 30 days per month. To use this function first call, **load (finance)   \$**.

(%i2)	load(finance)\$
	days360(2017,7,1,2017,8,31);
(%o2)	60

deactivate (contexts)

deactivates the specified context from a series of context.

debugmode()

default value is false. If an error occurs, wxMaxima commences the debugger, if debug mode is set to true. User can enter commands to examine the error, through suitable commands.

declare (a, property)

assigns the property to 'a'and declare function returnables done.

declare recognizes many properties affirmed for a function. Some of them are given below:

- **additive:** simplify 'd_i' expression by the substitution $d\_i(a + b + c)$ into $d\_i(a) + d\_i(b) + d\_i(c)$.
- **alphabetic:** for alphabetic characters (which must be a string).
- **constant:** for symbolic constant.
- **even, odd:** for even or odd integer variable.
- **evenfun, oddfun:** for odd or even function.

- **integer, noninteger:** for an integer or non-integer.
- **posfun:** declares a positive function.

(%i1)   declare(a, integer, b, integer);

(%o1)   done

(%i3)   a:-2*1.75$ b:-2*a$

(%i5)   askinteger(a); askinteger(b);

rat: replaced -3.5 by -7/2 = - 3.5

(%o4)   no

rat: replaced 7.0 by 7/1 = 7.0

(%o5)   yes

declare_constvalue (constant, value)

declares the value of constant to be used in units. To use this function first call, **load (ezunits).**

(%i1)   load ("ezunits")$

(%i2)   declare_constvalue (p, 10 ` m / sec);

(%o2) $10 \grave{} \dfrac{m}{sec}$ /* Note: ` is prefixed */

(%i3)   time:(600 ` m)/ p;

(time) $\dfrac{600 \grave{}}{p} m$

(%i4)   constvalue (%);

(%o4)   60 ` sec

declare_dimensions ([list of values] dimensions)

declares dimensionsto the respective list of values. To use this function first call, **load (ezunits)$.**

(%i1)   load ("ezunits")$

(%i2)   declare_dimensions ([x, y, z], s, A, V);

(%o2)   done

(%i3)   C (x*y);   /* Here 'C' for Coulomb */

(%o3)   C(xy)   /* C = Ampere (A) × second (s) */

(%i4)   fundamental_units (C);

               0 errors, 0 warnings

(%o4)   fundamental_units(C)

(%i5)   load("unit")$

****

* Units version 0.50*
* Definitions based on the NIST Reference on*
* Constants, Units, and Uncertainty*
* Conversion factors from various sources including*
* NIST and the GNU units package*
****

Redefining necessary functions...

Initializing unit arrays...

Done.

(%i6)   convert(40*C/20,[A]);

(%o6)   2(As)

remove_dimensions ([list of values] dimensions)

removes the previously declared dimensions assigned to the respective list of values. To use this function first call, **load(ezunits).**

declare_fundamental_units (units, dimension)

this function declares fundamental units to respective dimensions.

Function 'remove_fundamental_units' reverts the previously assigned fundamental units.To use this function first call, **load (ezunits)$.**

(%i1)   load ("ezunits")$

(%i2)   fundamental_dimensions;

(%o2)   [length, mass, time, current, temperature, quantity,
                luminous_intensity]

(%i3)   declare_fundamental_dimensions (dollar, rupee);

(%o3)   done

(%i4)   fundamental_dimensions;

(%o4)   [length, mass, time, current, temperature, quantity,
                luminous_intensity, dollar, rupee]

(%i5)   declare_fundamental_units (rupee, dollar);

(%o5)   [rupee]

(%i6)   dimensions (70 ` rupee/dollar);

(%o6) $\dfrac{\text{rupee}}{\text{dollar}}$

Other such related functions are:

declare_qty, declare_units, declare_weights, declare_translated, declare_unit_conversion, etc.

decreasing increasing

to recognize the function 'f' as an decreasing or increasing function.

(%i1)	assume(x>y);
(%o1)	[x>y]
(%i2)	is(f(x) > f(y));
(%o2)	unknown
(%i3)	declare(f, decreasing);
(%o3)	done
(%i4)	is(f(x) > f(y));
(%o4)	false
(%i5)	is(f(x) < f(y));
(%o5)	true /* similarly the function increasing is also used */

define (f (x) expression)

defines a function, 'f' with argument 'x' for the given expression.

(%i1)	a : sin(y);
(a)	sin(y)
(%i2)	define (F (y), a);
(%o2)	F(y):=sin(y)
(%i3)	F(30);
(%o3)	sin(30)

defint (expression, x, a, b)

returns the definite integral for 'x', when lower (a) and upper (b) limits are specified for the expression.

| (%i1) | defint (x^4, x, a, b); |
| (%o1) | $\dfrac{b^5}{5} - \dfrac{a^5}{5}$ |

del

on differentiation returns an expression 'del', if an independent variable is not specified.

(%i1)	diff(x^3,x);
(%o1)	$3x^2$
(%i2)	diff(x^3);
(%o2)	$3x^2$del(x)

delete(value, [list] or {set})

removes the value from the given list or set.

(%i1)	a:[x,2*x,3*x,4*x,y,2*y,3*y,4*y];
(a)	[x,2x,3x,4x,y,2y,3y,4y]
(%i2)	delete (3*x, a);
(%o2)	[x,2x,4x,y,2y,3y, 4y]
(%i3)	delete(log(x), log(x)+cos(y));
(%o3)	cos(y)
(%i4)	n:{x,2*x,3*x,4*x,y,2*y,3*y,4*y};
(n)	{x,2x,3x,4x,y,2y,3y,4y}
(%i5)	delete (3*x, n);
(%o5)	{x,2x,4x,y,2y,3y, 4y}

delete_file (file)

deletes the specified file.

denom (expression)

returns the denominator from a rational expression.

(%i1)	denom ((z*i)/(i*sin(z)*r));
(%o1)	r sin(z)

depends ([f] x)

declares functional dependencies for variables for differentiation. In the absence of declared dependence, diff (f, x) yields zero. If depends (f, x) is declared, diff (f, x) yields a symbolic derivative.

(%i1)	z:depends ([a, b], x);
z	[a(x),a(x)]

(%i2)   diff (z);

(%o2) $[(\frac{d}{dx} a(x)) \, del(x), (\frac{d}{dx} b(x)))del(x)]$

(%i3)   diff ((a,b),x);

(%o3) $\frac{d}{dx} b$

describe (string)   describe (string, exact)   describc (string, inexact)

It is a help function and it displays documented details for the function, entered as string(case-insensitive).

describe(string, inexact) displays all the documented details for the function. If there is more than one such item, wxMaxima asks the user to select an item from the listed items to display.

(%i1) describe (del, exact);

 -- Function: del (<x>)

   'del (<x>)' represents the differential of the variable x.

   'diff' returns an expression containing 'del' if an independent

   variable is not specified. In this case, the return value is the so-called "total differential".

   Examples:
   (%i1)   diff (log (x));
                del(x)
   (%o1)   -----
                x
   (%i2)   diff (exp (x*y));
                x y   x y
   (%o2)   x %e   del(y) + y %e   del(x)
   (%i3)   diff (x*y*z);
   (%o3)   x y del(z) + x z del(y) + y z del(x)

There are also some inexact matches for `del'.

Try `?? del' to see them.

(%o1)   true

(%i1) describe(List, exact);

No exact match found for topic `List'.

Try `?? List' (inexact match) instead.

(%o1) false   /* ?? List → input further details for this topic */

(%i2)   **?? List**

0:                Lists
1:    %rnum_list (Functions and Variables for Equations)
2:    charlist (String Processing)
3:    copylist (Functions and Variables for Lists)
4:    create_list (Functions and Variables for Lists)
5:    derivlist (Functions and Variables for Differentiation)
6:    dimensions_as_list (Functions and Variables for ezunits)
7:    full_listify (Functions and Variables for Sets)
8:    infolists (Functions and Variables for Command Line)
9:    List delimiters (Functions and Variables for Lists)
10: listarith (Functions and Variables for Lists)
11: listarray (Functions and Variables for Arrays)
12:   listconstvars (Functions and Variables for Expressions)
13: listdummyvars (Functions and Variables for Expressions)
14: listify (Functions and Variables for Sets)
15: listoftens (Functions and Variables for itensor)
16: listofvars (Functions and Variables for Expressions)
17: listp (Functions and Variables for Lists)
18: listp <1> (Functions and Variables for linearalgebra)
19: list_correlations (Functions and Variables for descriptive statistics)
20: list_matrix_entries   (Functions and Variables for Matrices and Linear Algebra)
21: list_nc_monomials (Functions and Variables for Affine)
22: makelist (Functions and Variables for Lists)
23: maplist (Functions and Variables for Program Flow)
24: poly_normalize_list (Functions and Variables for grobner)
25: poly_return_term_list (Functions and Variables for grobner)
26: read_binary_list (Functions and Variables for binary input and output)
27: read_list (Functions and Variables for plain-text input and output)
28: read_nested_list   (Functions and Variables for plain-text input and output)
29: sublist (Functions and Variables for Lists)
30: sublist_indices (Functions and Variables for Lists)

(%i3) describe(diff, exact);

0: diff   (Functions and Variables for Differentiation)

1: diff <1> (Functions and Variables for Differentiation)

2: diff <2> (Functions and Variables for itensor)

Enter space-separated numbers, `all' or `none': 1;

-- Function: diff

   diff (<expr>, <x_1>, <n_1>, ..., <x_m>, <n_m>)

   diff (<expr>, <x>, <n>)

   diff (<expr>, <x>)

   diff (<expr>)

Returns the derivative or differential of <expr> with respect to some or all variables in <expr>.

   `diff (<expr>, <x>, <n>)' returns the <n>'th derivative of <expr> with respect to <x>.

   `diff (<expr>, <x_1>, <n_1>, ..., <x_m>, <n_m>)' returns the mixed partial derivative of <expr> with respect to <x_1>, ..., <x_m>. It is equivalent to `diff (... (diff (<expr>, <x_m>, <n_m>) ...), <x_1>, <n_1>)'.

   `diff (<expr>, <x>)' returns the first derivative of <expr> with respect to the variable <x>.

   `diff (<expr>)' returns the total differential of <expr>, that is, the sum of the derivatives of <expr> with respect to each its variables times the differential `del' of each variable. No further simplification of `del' is offered.

   The noun form of `diff' is required in some contexts, such as stating a differential equation. In these cases, `diff' may be quoted (as `'diff') to yield the noun form instead of carrying out the differentiation.

   When `derivabbrev' is `true', derivatives are displayed as subscripts. Otherwise, derivatives are displayed in the Leibniz notation, `dy/dx'.

Examples:

(%i1)   diff (exp (f(x)), x, 2);

                      2
                f(x) d   f(x) d   2
(%o1)   %e   (--- (f(x))) + %e   (-- (f(x)))
                      2   dx
                     dx

(%i2)   derivabbrev: true$

(%i3)   'integrate (f(x, y), y, g(x), h(x));

                  h(x)
                   /
                   [
(%o3)   I   f(x, y) dy
                   ]
                   /
                  g(x)

(%i4)   diff (%, x);

                h(x)
                 /
                 [
(%o4)   I   f(x, y) dy + f(x, h(x)) h(x) - f(x, g(x)) g(x)
                 ]   x   x   x
                 /
                g(x)

For the tensor package, the following modifications have been incorporated:

(1) The derivatives of any indexed objects in <expr> will have the variables <x_i> appended as additional arguments. Then all the derivative indices will be sorted.

(2) The <x_i> may be integers from 1 up to the value of the variable 'dimension' [default value: 4]. This will cause the differentiation to be carried out with respect to the <x_i>'th member of the list 'coordinates' which should be set to a list of the names of the coordinates, e.g., '[x, y, z, t]'. If 'coordinates' is bound to an atomic variable, then that variable subscripted by <x_i> will be used for the variable of differentiation. This permits an array of

coordinate names or subscripted names like 'X[1]', 'X[2]', ... to be used. If 'coordinates' has not been assigned a value, then the variables will be treated as in (1) above.

There are also some inexact matches for `diff`.

Try `?? diff` to see them.

(%o3) true

determinant(matrix)   newdet(matrix)

returns the determinant for the matrix.

(%i1)   x: matrix ([j, i^2], [u/i, j*k]);

(x)
$$\begin{bmatrix} j & i^2 \\ \dfrac{u}{i} & j\,k \end{bmatrix}$$

(%i2)   determinant (x);
(%o2) $j^2 k - i\,u$ /* newdet(x) returns $-iu + j^2 k$ */

detout

if detout is set to true, the determinant of a matrix, whose inverse is computed. But **doallmxops** and **doscmxops** are set to false.

(%i1)   x: matrix ([j, i^2], [u/i, j*k]);

(x)
$$\begin{bmatrix} j & i^2 \\ \dfrac{u}{i} & j\,k \end{bmatrix}$$

(%i4)   detout: true$doallmxops: false$doscmxops: false$
(%i5)   invert (x);

$$\begin{bmatrix} j\,k & -i^2 \\ -\dfrac{u}{i} & j \end{bmatrix}$$

(%o5) $j^2 k - i\,u$

diag (x,y,z)

constructs a matrix of block sum of the elements from the matrices of x,y,z. If an element is scalar, it is treated as a 1×1 matrix.

To use this function first call, **load("diag")**.

(%i1)   load("diag")$

(%i2)   x1:matrix([a,b,c],[d1,e2,f3]);

(x1) $\begin{bmatrix} a & b & c \\ d1 & e2 & f3 \end{bmatrix}$

(%i3)   x2:matrix([g,h],[4,5],[i6,j7]);

(x2) $\begin{bmatrix} g & h \\ 4 & 5 \\ i6 & j7 \end{bmatrix}$

(%i4)   x3:matrix([k,8],[l,9]);

(x3) $\begin{bmatrix} k & 8 \\ l & 9 \end{bmatrix}$

(%i5)   diag([x1, x3, x2]);

(%o5) $\begin{bmatrix} a & b & c & 0 & 0 & 0 & 0 \\ d1 & e2 & f3 & 0 & 0 & 0 & 0 \\ 0 & 0 & 0 & k & 8 & 0 & 0 \\ 0 & 0 & 0 & l & 9 & 0 & 0 \\ 0 & 0 & 0 & 0 & 0 & g & h \\ 0 & 0 & 0 & 0 & 0 & 4 & 5 \\ 0 & 0 & 0 & 0 & 0 & i6 & j7 \end{bmatrix}$

diag_matrix(matrix1,matrix2,matrix3…)

returns a diagonal matrix for matrices 1,2,3…

(%i1)   diag_matrix((x,y,z), (a,b,c),(q,w,e));

(%o1) $\begin{bmatrix} z & 0 & 0 \\ 0 & c & 0 \\ 0 & 0 & e \end{bmatrix}$

diagmatrix (n, x)

returns a diagonal matrix 'n × n' with diagonal element is equal to 'x'.

(%i1)   y1:matrix([ui, j, nt], [D3, e2, z3]);

(y1) $\begin{bmatrix} ui & j & nt \\ D3 & e2 & z3 \end{bmatrix}$

(%i2)   diagmatrix (2, y1);   /* 2 × 2 matrix */

(%o2) $\begin{bmatrix} \begin{bmatrix} ui & j & nt \\ D3 & e2 & z3 \end{bmatrix} & 0 \\ 0 & \begin{bmatrix} ui & j & nt \\ D3 & e2 & z3 \end{bmatrix} \end{bmatrix}$

diff (expression, x)

returns 1st derivative of expression with respect to variable 'x'.

(%i1)   diff(y*x^2);

(%o1) $x^2 del(y)+2xydel(x)$

(%i2)   diff(g*x^i);

(%i2) $g\ i\ x^{(i-1)}del(x)+ gx^i log(x)\ del(i) + x^i del(g)$

(%i3)   diff(y*sin(u));

(%o3)   sin(u)del(y)+cos(u)ydel(u)

dimensionless (list)

returns the dimensionless quantities from a list of dimensional quantities. To use this function first call, **load (ezunits)\$** .

(%i1)   load ("ezunits") \$

(%i2)   dimensionless ([a ` m, b ` m/s, c ` s]);

             /* ` for unit; m – meter; s – second; m/s – velocity */

                0 errors, 0 <u>warnings</u>   /* printed message twice */

(%o2) $\begin{bmatrix} b\ c \\ a \end{bmatrix}$

(%i3)   f:dimensionless ([q ` g/mol, r ` g, t ` mol]);

(f) $\begin{bmatrix} \dfrac{qt}{r} \end{bmatrix}$ /* mol – mole; g – gram */

dimensions (x)

returns the base dimensional values for the dimension 'x'. To use this function first call, **load(ezunits)\$**.

(%i1)   load ("ezunits") \$

(%i2)   dimensions (1000` g/ml*(cm/s));

(%o2) $\dfrac{mass}{length^2\ time}$ /*g–mass; ml–length³;cm–length; s–time*/

dimensions_as_list (x)

returns the base dimensional values for the list of dimensions 'x' in which the power (integer values) of corresponding base dimension is returned as integer and if the base dimension is absent, returns 0. To use this function first call, **load (ezunits)** and the function 'fundamental_dimensions'.

(%i1)   load ("ezunits")\$

(%i2)   fundamental_dimensions;

(%o2)   [length,mass,time,current,temperature,quantity,

             luminous_intensity]   /* 7 base dimensions */

(%i3)   dimensions_as_list (1 ` A*s/(mol*cm^2*K));

(%o3)   [–2,0,1,1,–1,–1,0]

             /* length (cm⁻²; 2), mass (absent; 0),time (s¹; 1),current
             (A¹;   1),temperature   (K⁻¹;   –1),quantity(mol⁻¹;   –1),
             luminous_intensity (absent; 0) */

(%i4)   dimensions_as_list (z ` kg/(m^2*s^2));

(%o4)   [–2,1,–2,0,0,0,0]

             /* length (m⁻²; 2), mass (kg¹, 1),time (s⁻²; –2),current
             (absent;   0),temperature   (absent;   0),quantity(absent;0),
             luminous_intensity (absent; 0) */

discrete_freq (list)

returns the frequencies (in numbers) in discrete samples for the given list. To use this function first call, **load (descriptive)\$**.

(%i1)   load (descriptive)\$

(%i2)   discrete_freq ([2*n,x,–1,jz,-i,x,2.0,–3.1,–i,x,-3.1,2.0,4,-i,x]);

(%o2)   [[–3.1,–1,2.0,4,–i,jz,2*n,x],[2,1,2,1,3,1,1,4]]

             /*–3.1 frequency 2 times; –1 frequency 1 time; 2.0 frequency
             2 times ... 2n frequency 1 time; x frequency 4 times */

disjoin (x, {set})

returns the set without 'x'.

(%i1)   disjoin (tu, {ij, lm, op, rs, tu,hyn});
(%o1)   {hyn,ij,lm,op,rs}

disjointp (set1, set2)

returns true if set1 and set2 are disjoint (different).

returns false if set1 and set2 are not disjoint (having same member).

(%i1)   disjointp ({x*i, y*j, z*k}, {x, y, z});
(%o1)   true
(%i2)   disjointp ({i, y*j, z*k}, {i, y, z});
(%o2)   false

disolate (expression, x1, x2... xn)

isolate the given variables x1, x2… from the expression.

(%i1)   a: x^3+3*x^2−3*x+i^3−a*x+a^3−j^x;
(a) $x^3 + 3x^2 - ax - 3x - j^x + i^3 + a^3$
(%i2)   disolate (a, j^x, i^3);
(%t2) $x^3 + 3x^2 - ax - 3x + a^3$ /* %t2 before %o2 */
(%o2) $-j^x + i^3 + \%t2$

disp (values)

displays the specific values and not as the equation.

(%i3)   n[k,i,y]:2*x−j^2/(m^u)$; xz:y^s/(3−a)$;y:xz*n$
(%i4)   disp(y/n);

$$\frac{y^s}{3-a}$$

(%o4)   done

dispfun (f1,f2...fn)

displays the definition of given user-defined functions f1, f2… fn.

(%i1)   i(j, k, l) ::= y/x^−n$
(%i2)   h(j, k, l) := cm^k$
(%i3)   b[x](y) := x^(−2*y)$

(%i4)   dispfun (i, b[a]);

(%t4) $i(j, k, l) :: = \dfrac{y}{x^{-n}}$

(%t5) $b_a(y) : = \dfrac{1}{a^2 y}$

(%o5)   [%t4,%t5]

display (values)

similar to the function 'disp', but displays the specific values as equation, whose left side is unevaluated.

(%i3)   n[k,i,y]:2*x–j^2/(m^u)\$; xz:y^s/(3–a)\$;y:xz*n\$

(%i4)   display(y/n);

$$\dfrac{\dfrac{n\, y^s}{3-a}}{n} = \dfrac{y^s}{3-a}$$

(%o4)   done

display2d

default value is true, but if it is set to false, the output becomes 1-dimensional form, from 2-dimensional display.

(%i1)   display2d:true\$

(%i2)   (n^3*m^2)*(n^–2*m^3);

(%o2) $m^5 n$

(%i3)   %o2/(–n^2*m^–1);

(%o3) $-\dfrac{m^6}{n}$

(%i4)   display2d:false\$

(%i5)   (n^3*m^2)*(n^–2*m^3);

(%o5) $m^5 n$ /* 1 dimensional display form */

(%i6)   %o5/(–n^2*m^–1);

(%o6)   – m^6/n

dispterms (expression)

displays expression in parts one below the other.

(%i1)   dispterms((m^x)+(k^i)−(n^−i));

+

m^x

$$-\frac{1}{n^i}$$

k^i

(%o1)   done

distrib (expression)

distributes the expression in sum over products.

(%i1)   distrib ((n*m+k) * (m*k−n));
(%o1) $-mn^2 + km^2n - kn + k^2m$

distribute_over

default value is true and it controls the mapping of functions in lists, matrices, equations.

(%i1)   distribute_over;
(%o1)   true
(%i3)   cos([x,2.0,3]); log([3,10.0,i]);
(%o2)   [cos(x),-0.4161468365471424,cos(3)]
(%o3)   [log(3),2.302585092994046,log(i)]
                   /* to set false, distribute_over: not distribute_over; */
(%i1)   distribute_over: not distribute_over;
(distribute_over)   false
(%i3)   cos([x,2.0,3]); log([3,10.0,i]);
(%o2)   cos([x,2.0, 3])
(%o3)   log([3,10.0,i])

divide (expression1, expression2)

computes the quotient and remainder for division of expression1, by expression2 and the output is a list,where the first element is the quotient and the second element is the remainder of the division.

(%i1)   divide ((x^2+y^3−(a*x)), x);

(%o1)	[x–a,y³]	/*quotient is (x–a); reminder is y^3 */
(%i2)	divide (17, 6);	
(%o2)	[2,5]	

divisors (n)

returns the divisors (number that divides the another without a remainder.) for the non–zero, positive integer, 'n'.

(%i1)	divisors (16);
(%o1)	{1,2,4,8,16}
(%i2)	divisors (15);
(%o2)	{1, 3, 5, 15}

divsum (integer)   divsum (integer, x)

returns the sum of the divisors for the non–zero, positive integer, 'n' or returns the sum of the divisors for the non–zero, positive integer, 'n' raised to the x power.

(%i1)	divisors (16);	
(%o1)	{1,2,4,8,16}	
(%i2)	divsum (16);	
(%o2)	31	/* 1 + 2 + 4 + 8 + 16 = 31 */
(%i3)	divisors (16);	
(%o3)	{1, 2, 4, 8, 16}	
(%i4)	divsum (16, 2);	
(%o4)	341	/* $1^2 + 2^2 + 4^2 + 8^2 + 16^2$ = 341 */

do

important function in statements for doing iterations. Basic algorithm for using 'do' in iterations are:

for variable: initial_value step increment thru limit do body.

for variable: initial_value step increment while condition do body.

(%i1)	for a:–3 thru 26 step 4 do display(a);

a=–3

a=1   /* step increase by 4 up to a maximum 26 */

a=5

a=9

a=13

```
a=17
a=21
a=25          /* do loop breaks as condition becomes false, (25+4)>26 */
(%o1)         done
(%i2)         i:2; while (i^2-2<=36) do (i: i+1, print(i-1));
(i)           2       /* i = 2+1;3^2-2 < 36 */
2
3
4
5             /* i = 5+1; 6^2-2 < 36 */
6             /* do loop breaks as condition becomes false; 7^2-2 < 36  */
(%o2)  done
```

dodecahedron_graph ()   **tetrahedron_graph ()**

returns the vertices and edges for dodecahedron / tetrahedraon. To use this
function first call, **load ("graphs")$**.

```
(%i1)         load ("graphs")$
(%i2)         tetrahedron_graph ();
(%o2)         GRAPH(4 vertices, 6 edges)
(%i3)         print_graph(%o2);
```
Graph on 4 vertices with 6 edges.

```
              Adjacencies:
               3 : 2 1 0
               2 : 3 1 0
               1 : 3 2 0
               0 : 3 2 1
```

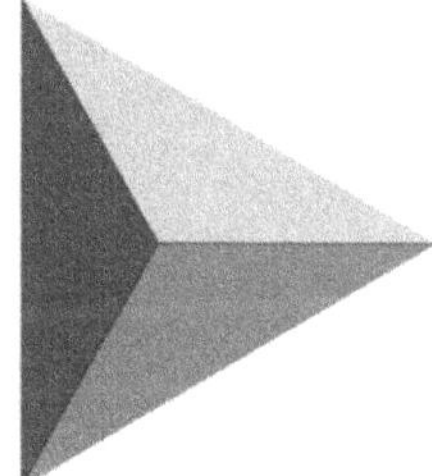

```
(%o3)         done
(%i4)         draw_graph(%o2);
(%o4)         done →
```

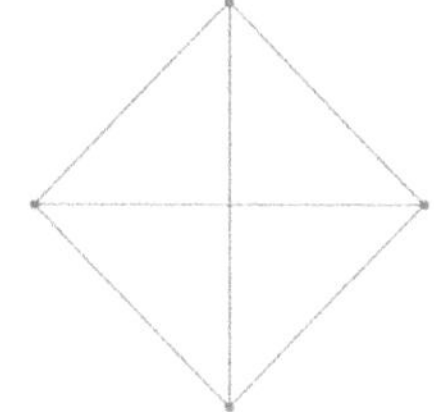

```
(%i1)         load ("graphs")$
(%i2)         dodecahedron_graph ();
(%o2)         GRAPH(20 vertices, 30 edges)
(%i3)         print_graph(%o2);
```

Graph on 20 vertices with 30 edges.   /* 12 pentagonal faces */
20 vertices, 30 edges as shownhere.

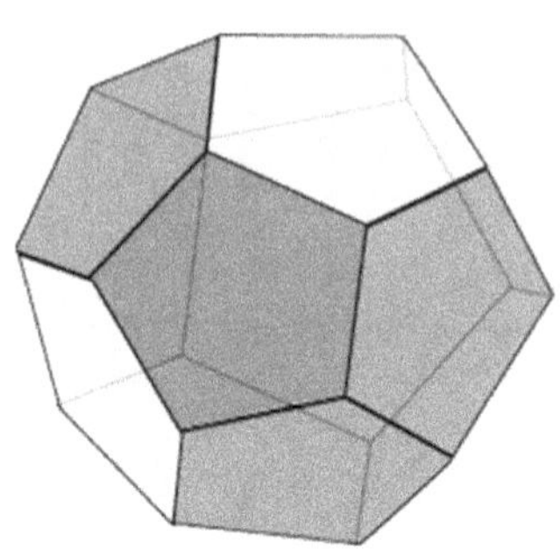

```
Adjacencies:
19 :  14 13 1
18 :  13 12 2
17 :  12 11 3
16 :  11 10 4
15 :  14 10 0
14 :  5 19 15
13 :  7 19 18
12 :  9 18 17
11 :  8 17 16
10 :  6 16 15
 9 :  7 8 12
 8 :  9 6 11
 7 :  5 9 13
 6 :  8 5 10
 5 :  7 6 14
 4 :  16 0 3
 3 :  17 4 2
 2 :  18 3 1
 1 :  19 2 0
 0 :  15 4 1
```

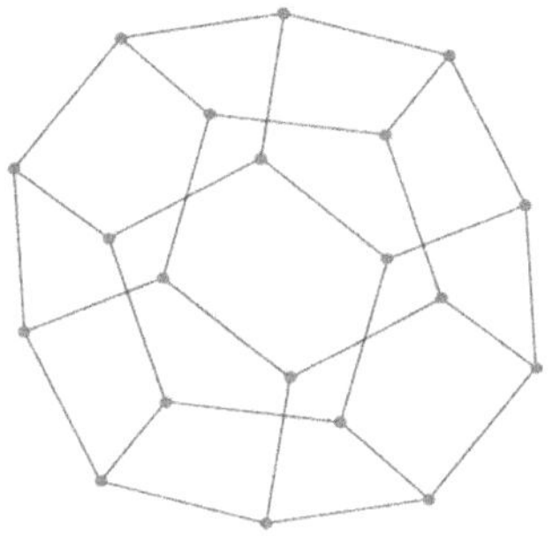

(%o3)   done
(%i4)   draw_graph(%o2);
(%o4)   done

domain

default value: real; if it is set to complex, sqrt (x^2) will remain sqrt (x^2) instead of returning abs(x).

(%i1)   domain:real;
(domain)   real
(%i2)   sqrt(x^2);
(%o2) |x|
(%i3)   domain:complex;
(domain)   complex
(%i4)   sqrt(x^2);

(%o4) $\sqrt{x^2}$

draw (explicit (expression,x, min., max.,y, min., max.))

plots a series of scenes (2 dimensional or 3 dimensional plots) for the given expressions and 'x', 'y' data .   (Refer: 2D, 3D plotting)

(%i1)   draw3d(**explicit**(x^2+y^2,x,–1,1,y,–1,1));

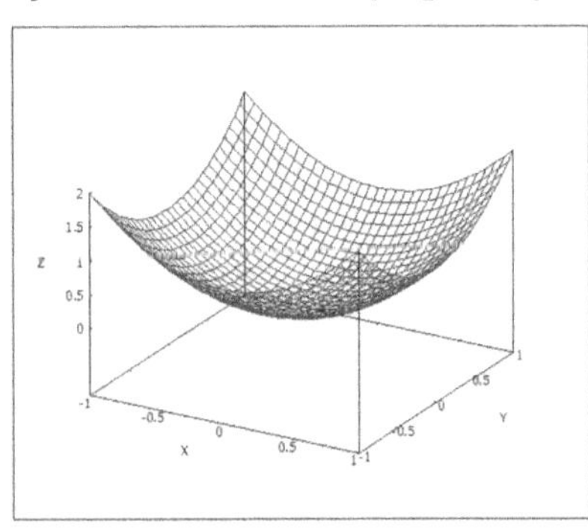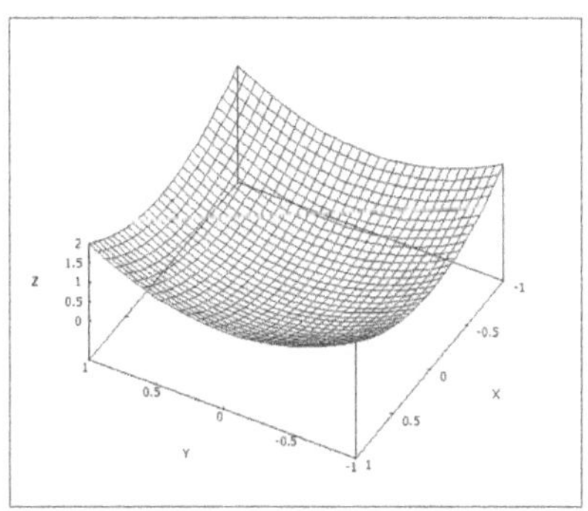

echelon (matrix)

returns the echelon form of the matrix through Gaussian elimination.

(%i1)   matrix ([2,1], [3,0]);

(%o1) $\begin{pmatrix} 2 & 1 \\ 3 & 0 \end{pmatrix}$

(%i2)   echelon(%o1);

(%o2) $\begin{pmatrix} 1 & 0 \\ 0 & 1 \end{pmatrix}$

$/* \begin{pmatrix} 2 & 1 \\ 3 & 0 \end{pmatrix}$ multiply by 1st row by $\frac{1}{2} \rightarrow \begin{pmatrix} 1 & \frac{1}{2} \\ 3 & 0 \end{pmatrix}$

$\begin{pmatrix} 1 & \frac{1}{2} \\ 3 & 0 \end{pmatrix}$ add –3 times the to the 2nd row $\rightarrow \begin{pmatrix} 1 & \frac{1}{2} \\ 0 & \frac{-3}{2} \end{pmatrix}$

$\begin{pmatrix} 1 & \frac{1}{2} \\ 0 & \frac{-3}{2} \end{pmatrix}$ multiply the 2nd row by $\frac{-2}{3} \rightarrow \begin{pmatrix} 1 & \frac{1}{2} \\ 0 & 1 \end{pmatrix}$

$\begin{pmatrix} 1 & \frac{1}{2} \\ 0 & 1 \end{pmatrix}$ add $\frac{-1}{2}$ times the 2nd row to the 1st row $\begin{pmatrix} 1 & 0 \\ 0 & 1 \end{pmatrix}$ $*/$

eivals (matrix)

returns two lists eigen values of the matrix. The first list is eigen values of the matrix, and the second one is the multiplicities of the eigen values in the corresponding order.

(%i1)   M:matrix([1,2],[4,3]);

(M) $\begin{bmatrix} 1 & 2 \\ 4 & 3 \end{bmatrix}$

(%i2)   eivals(M);

(%o2) $[[5, -1],[1,1]]$ $/* \ M = \begin{bmatrix} 1 & 2 \\ 4 & 3 \end{bmatrix}$

$$0 = \det\left(\begin{bmatrix} \lambda & 0 \\ 0 & \lambda \end{bmatrix} - \begin{bmatrix} 1 & 2 \\ 4 & 3 \end{bmatrix}\right) = \det\begin{bmatrix} \lambda - 1 & 0 - 2 \\ 0 - 4 & \lambda - 3 \end{bmatrix}$$

$$= ((\lambda - 1) \times (\lambda - 3)) - 8$$

$$0 = (\lambda^2 - 3\lambda - \lambda + 3 - 8) = (\lambda^2 - 4\lambda - 5) = (\lambda + 5) \times (\lambda - 1) \quad \text{So the}$$

matrix $\begin{bmatrix} 1 & 2 \\ 4 & 3 \end{bmatrix}$ have the eigenvalues 5 and $-1 \ */$

eivects (matrix)

returns eigenv alues and eigen vectors of the matrix as two lists. The first list is eigen values and their multiplicities in the respective order.

The second list is eigen vectors. For each eigen value there is a list.

(%i1)   M:matrix([1,2],[4,3]);

(M) $\begin{bmatrix} 1 & 2 \\ 4 & 3 \end{bmatrix}$

(%i2)   eivects(M);

(%o2) $[[[5,-1],[1,1]],[[[1,2]],[[1,-1]]]]$

$/* \qquad M = \begin{bmatrix} 1 & 2 \\ 4 & 3 \end{bmatrix}$

$\lambda_1 = 5; \ \lambda_2 = -1$ Refer: eigen values

$\text{At} \lambda_1 = 5; \det\left(\begin{bmatrix} 5 & 0 \\ 0 & 5 \end{bmatrix} - \begin{bmatrix} 1 & 2 \\ 4 & 3 \end{bmatrix}\right) = \ker\begin{bmatrix} 4 & -2 \\ -4 & 2 \end{bmatrix} =$

$$\ker\begin{bmatrix} 4 & -2 \\ 0 & 0 \end{bmatrix} = \mathrm{span}\begin{bmatrix} 2 \\ 4 \end{bmatrix} = \mathrm{span}\begin{bmatrix} 1 \\ 2 \end{bmatrix}$$

$$\mathrm{At}\ \lambda_1 = -1;\ \det\left(\begin{bmatrix} -1 & 0 \\ 0 & -1 \end{bmatrix} - \begin{bmatrix} 1 & 2 \\ 4 & 3 \end{bmatrix}\right) = \ker\begin{bmatrix} -2 & -2 \\ -4 & -4 \end{bmatrix} =$$

$$\ker\begin{bmatrix} -2 & -2 \\ 0 & 0 \end{bmatrix} = \mathrm{span}\begin{bmatrix} 2 \\ -2 \end{bmatrix} = \mathrm{span}\begin{bmatrix} 1 \\ -1 \end{bmatrix} \quad */$$

elapsed_real_time ()

returns time in seconds since wxMaxima was started or restart**ed.**

(%i1)   elapsed_real_time ();

(%o1)   6.2241331

elapsed_run_time ()

returns time in seconds for the computation. This is used to compare the computing speed

(%i1)   M:matrix([1,2],[4,3])$

(%i2)   eivects(M);

(%o2)   [[[5,-1],[1,1]],[[[1,2]],[[1,-1]]]]

(%i3)   elapsed_run_time ();

(%o3)   6.4272412

elementp (a, b)

returns true if 'a' is member of the set 'b'.

(%i1)   elementp (i/x^n, {n-i^x, i/x^n, n/x^i, x*n^i, i*n^x, i/n^x});

(%o2)   true

elim (a, b)

returns the variables in the set or list 'b' from the equations in the set or list a.

(%i1)   elim(set(i + j+ k = 1, i – j – k = –1, i–k = –2), set(i,j,k));

(%o1)   elim({i–k=–2, –k–j+i=–1,k+j+i=1},{i,j,k})

elim_allbut (a, x)

Similar to elim function, except that it eliminates all the variables in the list of equations 'a' except for those variables that in in the list 'b'.

To use this function first call, **load(to_poly)**.

(%i1)	load(to_poly)$
(%i2)	elim_allbut (set(i + j+ k = 1, i – j – k = –1, i – k = –2), j);
(%o2)	[[j+1],[2k+j–3,k–i–2]] /* e.g., @ j= –1; i = 0; k = 2 */

eliminate ([expressions], [variables])

eliminates variables from expressions

(%i1)	i:2*x+y^3=10;
(%i2)	j:x^6–7*y=–8;
(%i3)	eliminate ([i, j], [y]);
(%i4)	eliminate ([i, j], [x]);
(i)	$y^3 + 2x = 10$
(j)	$x^6 – 7y = –8$
(%o3)	$[x^{18} + 24\,x^{12} + 192\,x^6 + 686\,x – 2918]$
(%o4)	$[y^{18} – 60\,y^{15} + 1500\,y^{12} – 20000\,y^9 + 150000\,y^6 – 600000\,y^3 – 448\,y + 1000512]$

ematrix (m, n, x, i, j)

returns an 'm×n' matrix, in which all elements are zero, but the [i, j] element is 'x'.

(%i1)	j:ematrix (2, 3, i, 2, 1);
(j)	$\begin{bmatrix} 0 & 0 & 0 \\ i & 0 & 0 \end{bmatrix}$

emptyp ({set} [list])

returns true if the set or list is empty. This function should be combined with map function.

(%i1)	v:map(emptyp, [[(–3*y–1), -4],{i^n,2*x}, []]);
(v)	[false,false,true]

endcons (expression, list)

returns a new list from the elements of list for the expression.

(%i1)   endcons(m*k^y,[2+i,j*x,2*n]);

(%o1)   [i+2,jx,2n,k^y m]

(%i2)   2+e:endcons(m*k^y,[2+i,j*x,2*n]);

(%o2)   [i+4,jx+2,2n+2,k^y m+2]

engineering_format_floats

turns off /on the engineering formats by false / true commands from the default value: true, through **load("engineering-format")** function.

(%i1)   load("engineering-format");

(%o1)   "C:\maxima-5.38.1\share\maxima\5.38.1_5_gdf93b7b_

             dirty\share\contrib\engineering-format.lisp"

(%i2)   float(cos((2.7)/10000));

(%o2)   999.9999635500002 10^{-3}

(%i3)   engineering_format_floats:false$

(%i4)   float(cos((2.7)/10000));

(%o4)   0.9999999635500002

entermatrix (m, n)

interactively prompts for each element and returns 'm×n' matrix.

(%i1)   m: entermatrix (3, 3);

Is the matrix 1. Diagonal 2. Symmetric 3. Antisymmetric 4. General

Answer 1, 2, 3 or 4   4;

Row 1 Column 1:   2+e;

Row 1 Column 2:   n*i;

Row 1 Column 3:   u^t;

Row 2 Column 1:   j−n;

Row 2 Column 2:   x+4;

Row 2 Column 3:   3−z;

Row 3 Column 1:   u*z;

Row 3 Column 2:   e^k;

Row 3 Column 3:   n/r*x;

Matrix entered.

$$(\%o1) \qquad \begin{bmatrix} e+2 & in & u^t \\ j-n & x+4 & 3-z \\ uz & e^k & \dfrac{nx}{r} \end{bmatrix}$$

(%i2)   m: entermatrix (3, 3);

Is the matrix 1. Diagonal 2. Symmetric 3. Antisymmetric 4. General

Answer 1, 2, 3 or 4   2;

Row 1 Column 1:   2+e;

Row 1 Column 2:   n*i;

Row 1 Column 3:   u^t;

Row 2 Column 2:   j–n;

Row 2 Column 3:   x+4;

Row 3 Column 3:   3–z;

Matrix entered.

$$(\%o2) \qquad \begin{bmatrix} e+2 & in & u^t \\ in & j-n & x+4 \\ u^t & x+4 & 3-z \end{bmatrix}$$

entier (number)

returns the integer less than or equal to the given number.

(%i1)   entier(22.9999999999);

(%o1)   22

epsilon_lp

default value: 10_{-8} for linear program, numerical computations.

equal (expression1, expression2)

evaluates whether two expressions (1 & 2) are equal or not. It should be combined with the function 'is'.

(%i1)   is (equal (i^2 – n^2, (i + n) * (i – n)));

(%o1)   true

equiv_classes ({set}, equal)

returns a set of the equivalence classes for the given set.

(%i1)   equiv_classes ({7.0, 3.0, (2/5), 0.4, –3.0,7}, equal);

(%o1) $\{\{-3.0\}, \{\frac{2}{5}, 0.4\}, \{3.0\}, \{7,7.0\}\}$

euler (n)

returns the nth Euler number for non-negative integer and zerobern is set to true.

(%i1)   zerobern: true$

(%i2)   euler(20);

(%o2)   370371188237525

ev (expressions, arguments)

evaluates the expression specified by the arguments

(%i1)   2*i+diff(i^3,i)–integrate(i^3,i);

(%o1) $-\frac{i^4}{4} + 3i^2 + 2i$ /* I term integrate, II term differentiate */

(%i2)   ev (%, i=4);

(%o2)   –8

even odd

by declare function, the given variable is declared as even or odd.

(%i1)   declare(n, even);

(%o1)   done

(%i2)   askinteger(n, odd);

(%o2)   no

every (predicate, arguments)

returns true if the predicate is true for the list or set of arguments.

(%i1)   every ("=", [2+i, x^–1], [i+(2*x/x),1/x]);

(%o1)   true

(%i2)   b:y$c:b/a$

(%i3)   every ("=", [a, b, c], [a, y, y/a]);

(%o3)   true

example ("topic")

displays example for recognized topic, which is a symbol or a string.

(%i1)	example("do");
(%i2)	for a from -3 step 7 thru 26 do ldisplay(a)
(%t2)	a=−3
(%t3)	a=4
(%t4)	a=11
(%t5)	a=18
(%t6)	a=25
(%o8)	done
(%o9)	55
(%i7)	s:0
(%i8)	for i while i <= 10 do s:s+i
(%i9)	s
(%i10)	series:1
(%i11)	term:exp(sin(x))
(%i12)	for p unless p > 7 do
	(term:diff(term,x)/p,series:series+subst(x= 0,term)*x^p)
(%i13)	series

$$(\%o13) \qquad \frac{x^7}{90} - \frac{x^6}{240} - \frac{x^5}{15} - \frac{x^4}{8} + \frac{x^2}{2} + x + 1$$

(%o16)	$5x^5 + 9x^4 + 12x^3 + 14x^2 + 15x$
(%o18)	−3.162280701754386
(%i14)	poly:0
(%i15)	for i thru 5 do (for j from i step −1 thru 1 do poly:poly+i*x^j)
(%i16)	poly
(%i17)	guess:−3.0
(%i18)	for i thru 10 do
	(guess:subst(guess,x,0.5*(x+10/x)),
	if abs(guess^2−10) < 5.0E−5 then return(guess))
(%i19)	for count from 2 next 3*count thru 20 do ldisplay(count)
(%t19)	count=2
(%t20)	count=6
(%t21)	count=18
(%o22)	1000
(%o24)	2.282429035887867

(%o25)   [x]
(%o28)   2.236068027062195
(%t29)   0.0
(%t30) $\rho(1.0)$
(%i22)   x:1000
(%i23)   thru 10 while x # 0 do x:0.5*(x+5/x)
(%i24)   x
(%i25)   remvalue(x)
(%i26)   newton(f,guess):=block([numer,y],local(f,df,x,guess),
              numer:true,define(df(x),diff(f(x),x)),
              do (y:df(guess),
              if y = 0 then error("derivative at",guess,"is zero"),
              guess:guess-f(guess)/y,
              if abs(f(guess)) < 5.0E-6 then return(guess)))
(%i27)   sqr(x):=x^2–5.0
(%i28)   newton(sqr,1000)
(%i29)   for f in [log,rho,atan] do ldisp(f(1.0))
(%t31)   0.7853981633974483
(%o32)   e31
(%o32)   done
(%i32)   ev(concat(e,linenum–1),numer)

exp (value)

returns the exponential function for the given value.

(%i1)   exp(2.303);
(%o1)   10.00414993091771
(%i2)   exp(2);
(%o2)   %e^2
(%i3)   %,numer;
(%o3)   7.38905609893065

expand (expression)

expands the expression.

(%i1)   expand((i–j+n)^3);

(%o1) $n^3 - 3jn^2 + 3in^2 + 3j^2n - 6ijn + 3i^2n - j^3 +$

$3ij^2 - 3i^2j + i^3$

explose (expression, [variables])

returns symmetric polynomial associated with the expression for the list of variables.

(%i1)   explose (n*j+i+2, [i,j,k]);

resolvante

generale

NOTE: To compile the system do

load("sym/compile");

0 errors, 0 warnings

(%o1)   kn+jn+in+k+j+i+2

express (expression)

expands differential operator for expression in terms of partial derivatives. To use this function first call, **load ("vect")\$**.

(%i1)   load ("vect");

(%o1)   "C:\maxima-5.38.1\share\maxima\5.38.1_5_gdf93b7

b_dirty\share\vector\vect.mac"

(%i2)   express (grad(x^n+h));

(%o2) $[\frac{d}{dx}(x^n + h), \frac{d}{dy}(x^n + h), \frac{d}{dz}(x^n + h)]$

exsec (value) returns exsecant. To use this function first call, **load(functs)\$** .

(%i1)   load(functs);

(%o1)   "C:\maxima-5.38.1\share\maxima\5.38.1_5_gdf93b7

b_dirty\share\simplification\functs.mac"

(%i3)   exsec (0.5);

(%o3)   0.139493927324549

extremal_subset (set, function, max)

returns a subset for set, for which the function takes maximum or minimum values.

(%i1)   extremal_subset ({–6, –8, –4, 0, 1, 8, 2}, min, max);

(%o1)   {8}

(%i1)   extremal_subset ({–6, –8, –4, 0, 1, 8, 2}, abs, min);

(%o1)   {0}

ezgcd (expression_1, expression_2, ...)

returns a list in which the first element is the greatest common divisor of the polynomial expressions or for the other elements.

(%i3)   a:x^3+4*x^2+4*x;

      b:2*x^3+5*x^2+2*x;

      c:x^4–x^2+2*x^3–2*x;

(a) x^3+4x^2+4x

(b) $(2x^3+5x^2+2x)$

(c) $x^4+2x^3-x^2-2x$

(%i4)   ezgcd(a, b, c);

(%o4) $[x^2+2x,x+2,2x+1,x^2-1]$

f90 (expression)

returns output as Fortran 90 program. To use this, **load ("f90")**. Long lines are fragmented with &.

(%i1)   load ("f90");

(%o1)   "C:\maxima-5.38.1\share\maxima\5.38.1_5_gdf93b7

      b_dirty\share\contrib\f90.lisp"

(%i2)   expand((i–j+n)^3);

(%o2) $n^3-3jn^2+3in^2+3j^2\,n-6ijn+3i^2\,n-j^3+$

      $3ij^2-3i^2\,j+i^3$

(%i3)   f90 (expand((i–j+n)^3));

      n**3–3*j*n**2+3*i*n**2+3*j**2*n-6*i*j*n+3*i**&

      &2*n–j**3+3*i*j**2–3*i**2*j+i**3

(%o3)   false

factcomb (expression)

combines the coefficients of factorials in expression.

(%i1)   n!*(n +1)*(n +1)*n!;

(%o1) $(n+1)^2 n!^2$

factor (expression)   or   factor (expression, polynomial)

returns the factors for expression, with the minimum polynomial.

(%i1)   factor(99);

(%o1) $3^2 11$

(%i2)   factor (1 + s^4, a^2 – 2);

(%o2) $(s^2 - as+1)\ (s^2 + as+1)$

(%i3)   factor (n + s^4, n^2 – 2);

(%o3) $s^4 + n$

(%i4)   factor(x^3–9*x^2+27*x –27);

(%o4) $(x–3)^3$

factorial(number)

represents the factorial function, !. returns factorial for the number.

(%i1)   factorial(5);

(%o1)   120

factorial_expand

controls the expansion or the simplification of factorial function.

(%i1)   (x+2)!/x!,factorial_expand:true;

WARNING: DEFUN/DEFMACRO: redefining function SIMP-UNIT-

STEP inC:\maxima-.38.1\share\maxima\5.38.1_5_gdf93b7b_dirty

\share\orthopoly\orthopoly.lisp,was defined in top-level

WARNING: DEFUN/DEFMACRO: redefining function SIMP-POCHHAMMER

inC:\maxima-5.38.1\share\maxima\5.38.1_5_gdf93

b7b_dirty\share\orthopoly\orthopoly.lisp,was defined in top-level

(%o1)   (x+1) (x+2)

factorout (expression)

rearranges the expression into a sum of terms.

(%i1)   x:i*j^2*k^2-i*j*k^2-2*i*k^2+2*i*j^2*k-2*i*j*k-4*i*k+i*j^
               2-i*j-2*i$

(%i2)   factorout(x,j);

(%o2)   i(j-2)(j+1) k²+2i(j-2)(j+1)k+i(j-2)(j+1)

factorsum (expression)

rearranges the expression in factors, which are sums into groups of terms such that their sum is factorable.

(%i1)   x:i*j^2*k^2-i*j*k^2-2*i*k^2+2*i*j^2*k-2*i*j*k-4*i*k+i*j^
               2-i*j-2*i;

(x)   ij² k²-ijk²-2ik²+2ij² k-2ijk-4ik+ij²-ij-2i

(%i2)   factorsum (x);

(%o2)   i(j-2)(j+1) (k+1)²

fast_linsolve ([expressions], [variables])

solves the simultaneous linear equations for the list of variables from the list of expressions. To use this function, first call **load(affine)\$**.

(%i1)   load(affine)\$

0 errors, 0 warnings

(%i2)   fast_linsolve([x+y=−1, 3*x−y=−11], [x,y]);

Assuming entries of type RATIONAL

Starting to solve. There are 2 equations with 2 unknowns occurring.

The value of (SP-TYPE-OF-ENTRIES SP-MAT) is RATIONAL

The dimension of the solution space is 0

(%o2)   [x=−3,y=2]

features

These are some mathematical properties of functions and variables, recognized by wxMaxima. /* featurep function explained */

(%i1)   declare (k, even);

(%o1)   done

(%i2)   featurep (k, odd);

(%o2)   false

(%i3)   featurep (k, even);

(%o3)   true

fft([data list])

computes the complex fast Fourier transform for the list, the data to transform. To use this function first call, **load ("fft")$**.

(%i1)	load ("fft")$	
(%i2)	fpprintprec : 4 $	/* for 4 digit precision */
(%i3)	fft ([2, 4, 3, 1, 0, –1, –3, –4]);	
(%o3)	[0.25,1.634%i+0.25,0.75%i+0.25,0.1339%i+0.25,	
	0.25,0.25–0.1339%i,0.25–0.75%i,0.25–1.634%i]	

fib (n)

returns 'nth' Fibonacci number in the sequence.

n	0	1	2	3	4	5	6	7	8
fib(n)	0	1	0+1	1+1	1+2	2+3	3+5	5+8	8+13

(%i1)	fib(8);
(%o1)	21
(%i1)	fib(18);
(%o1)	2584

fibtophi (fib(number));

returns Fibonacci number in terms of Golden ratio,φ (%phi), $(\dfrac{1+\sqrt{5}}{2}) \approx$ 1.61803399.

(%i1)	fibtophi (fib (x));
(%o1)	$\dfrac{\varphi^{n}-(1-\varphi)^{n}}{2\varphi-1}$

file_search (filename)   file_search (filename, pathlist)

file_search searches the file from the given filename and returns the path of that file if it is available but returns false if it is not available.file_search (filename, pathlist) searches the file from the given filename only in the directories as specified by pathlist.

(%i1)	file_search ("D:/Maxima/wxMaxima.pdf");
(%o1)	"D:/Maxima/wxMaxima.pdf"
(%i2)	file_search ("wxMaxima.pdf");
(%o2)	false

fillarray (name, List)array(name, dimension)   arrayinfo(array)

fills array from the list.   (Array dimension must be defined.)

(%i1)   array (k,5);   /* array named 'k' for 5 elements */

(%o1)   k

(%i2)   fillarray (k, [j/i, x*i, i/j,(x+i),j*y]);

(%o2)   k

(%i3)   listarray(k);

(%o3) $[\frac{j}{i}, ix, \frac{i}{j}, x+i, jy, jy]$

(%i4)   arrayinfo (k);

(%o4)   [declared,1,[5]]

find_root (expression, variable, i, j)

returns the root of the expression for the varaible between 'i' and 'j'.

(%i1)   find_root(x^2+x–6,x,–1,3);

(%o1)   2.0

(%i2)   find_root(i^3–5.8=0, i, 0 , 2);   /* $\sqrt[3]{5.8}$ */

(%o2)   1.796701779143053

(%i3)   find_root(log(x)–sin(x)=1,x,1,4);

(%o3)   3.032114018492144

(%i4)   [log(%),sin(%)];

(%o4)   [1.109260072116656,0.1092600721166566]

first (expression)

returns the first part of the expression which may be an element of a list, first row of a matrix or first term of a sum etc. Similarly, second(expression) returns the second part of expression and so on...

(%i1)   k:2*b+(c–i*e/x);

(k) $-\frac{ei}{x} + c + 2b$

(%i2)   [first(%), second(%)];

(%o2) $[-\frac{ei}{x}, c]$

(%i1)   b:matrix([j,n*i,n^2],[–4*x, –3/u, –3*z]);

(b)
$$\begin{bmatrix} j & in & n^2 \\ -4x & -\dfrac{3}{u} & -3z \end{bmatrix}$$

(%i2)   second(%);

(%o2) $\left[-4x, -\dfrac{3}{u}, -3z\right]$

firstn (list, count)

returns the expression according to count number from the given list.

(%i1)   b:[sin(d), cos(f)+k, (1/n-2), c^(-4*x),u*i^e,log(x),x];

(b) $\left[\sin(d), k + \cos(f), \dfrac{1}{n} - 2, \dfrac{1}{c^{4x}}, i^e u, \log(x), x\right]$

(%i2)   firstn (b, 6);

(%o2) $\left[\sin(d), k + \cos(f), \dfrac{1}{n} - 2, \dfrac{1}{c^{4x}}, i^e u, \log(x)\right];$

fix (number)

returns the integer less than or equal to the number as like the function 'entire'.

(%i1)   fix(22.9999999999);
(%o1)   22

flatten (expression, subexpression)

returns a complete list of elements from the expression and also from sub-expression.

(%i1)   flatten ([x,y,z, [x,a,b,d],[n,c,i,d,b]]);
(%o1)   [x,y,z,x,a,b,d,n,c,i,d,b]

float(number)   bfloat(number)

float returns floating point number for the integer, rational number, whereas bfloat returns bigfloat numbers.The number of digits to be displayed is specified by **fpprint**prec precision function.

(%i1)   fpprintprec : 6$
(%i2)   float(%pi);

(%o2)	3.14159
(%i3)	bfloat(%pi);
(%o3)	3.14159b0

floatnump (number)

returns true if the number is a floating point number.

(%i1)	%pi;
(%o1)	π
(%i2)	floatnump (%);
(%o2)	false
(%i3)	float(%o1);
(%o3)	3.141592653589793
(%i4)	floatnump (%);
(%o4)	true

floor (number)

returns the largest integer less than or equal to the given number.

(%i1)	float(%pi^3);
(%o1)	31.00627668029982
(%i2)	floor(%);
(%o2)	31

for   also refer: **do**

important function in statements for doing iterations.

for variable: initial_value   step increment   thru   limit   do   body.

for variable: initial_value   step increment   while condition   do   body.

(%i1)	for x: 0 step 2 thru 11 do(y:x+x+i, print(x, y));

0 i

2i+4

4i+8

6i+12

8i+16

10i+20

(%o1)	done

forget (expression)

removes predicates established by the function **assume**.

(%i1)	assume (a <=0, b >9, c < a);
(%o1)	[a<=0,b>9,a>c]
(%i2)	is (b>6);
(%o2)	true
(%i3)	is (a< 6);
(%o3)	true
(%i4)	is (c< 1);
(%o4)	true
(%i5)	forget(b>9);
(%o5)	[b>9]
(%i6)	is (b>6);
(%o6)	unknown

fortran (expression)

returns expression as a Fortran statement.

(%i1)   f:i^−n+cos(x)*%pi+(x-i)^-3;

(f) $\pi \cos(x) + \dfrac{1}{(x-i)^3} + \dfrac{1}{i^n}$

(%i2)   fortran(f);
             %pi*cos(x)+1/(x-i)**3+1/i**n
(%o2)   done

fourier (f, x, p)

returns Fourier coefficients of, f(x) defined at the intervals [-p, p]. To use this function first call, **load(fourie)**.

(%i1)   load(fourie);
(%o1)   "C:\maxima-5.38.1\share\maxima\5.38.1_5_gdf93b
             7b_dirty\share\calculus\fourie.mac"
(%i2)   f(x):=b*x^2;
(%o2) $f(x):=bx^2$
(%i3)   f(2);
(%o3)   4b

(%i4)   fourier (f, x, 2);

(%t4) $a_0 = f$

(%t5) $a_n = \dfrac{2f \sin(\pi n)}{\pi n}$

(%t5) $b_n = 0$

(%o6)   [%t4,%t5,%t6]

fourier_elim ([linear inequations], [variables])

Fourier elimination compares variables for linear inequations. To use this function first call, **load(fourier_elim)**.

(%i1)   load(fourier_elim);
(%o1)   "C:\maxima-5.38.1\share\maxima\5.38.1_5_gdf93b
               7b_dirty\share\fourier_elim\fourier_elim.lisp"
(%i2)   fourier_elim([b−a>0,b+c>0,c−a<0], [a,b,c]);
(%i2)   [c<a,a<b,max(−c,c)<b]   /* a=−1; b=2; c=−3 */

fourth (expression)

returns the fourth part of the expression which may be an element of a list, fourth row of a matrix or fourth term of a sum etc. Similarly, fifth(expression) returns the fifth part of expression and so on.

(%i1)   k:2*b+(c−i*e/x)−a^−4+c^b;

(k) $-\dfrac{ei}{x} + c^b + c + 2b - \dfrac{1}{a^4}$

(%i2)   [fourth(%), fifth(%)];

(%o2) $[2b, -\dfrac{1}{a^4}]$

fpprintprec

number of digits to be displayed is specified by this.fpprintprec cannot be 1. Default value is 0.

(%i1)   fpprintprec : 8 $
(%i2)   float(%pi);
(%o2)   3.1415927

freeof (x, y, expression)

returns true if no part of expression is equal to 'x' or 'y' or else it returns false.

(%i1)   k:−((1/x^n)+sin(x^(1/n)))−e^(b+n);

(k) $-\sin\left(x^{\frac{1}{n}}\right) - \frac{1}{x^n} - e^{n+b}$

(%i2)   freeof (−x^−n, k); $*/ -\frac{1}{x^n} = -x^{-n} */$

(%o2)   false

(%i3)   freeof (sin(x^(n^−1)), k);

(%o3)   false

(%i4)   freeof (−e^b, k);

(%o4)   true

full_listify (x)

replaces allsets by the list operator with 'x'.

(%i1)   full_listify ({b, {v, {n, −j, i}, {k, s}−g}});

(%o1)   [b,[[i,−j,n],[k,s]−g,v]]

fullmap (function, expression_1, …)

mapping down all subexpressions until the main operators are no longer the same.

(%i1)   2*x^2−3*z;

(%o1) $2x^2x3z$

(%i2)   fullmap (i*y, %);

(%o2) $(iy)(2)\ (iy)(x)^{(iy)(2)} - (iy)(3)\ (iy)(z)$

fullmapl (function, list)

similar to fullmap function, but this maps lists and matrices.

(%i1)   fullmapl ("*", [i, x],[i,j], [[x, −3], [i, f]]);

(%o1) $[[i^2x, -3i^2], [ijx, fjx]]$

fullratsimp (expression)

This simplifies the expression further into, non-rational simplification after simplification by the function ratsimp.

(%i1)   k: (i^(0.5 *x) + 1)^2*(i^(x/2) – 1)^2/(i^x – 1);

(k)
$$\frac{\left(i^{\frac{x}{2}}-1\right)^2 \left(i^{0.5x}+1\right)^2}{i^x-1}$$

(%i2)   ratsimp (k);
     rat: replaced 0.5 by 1/2 = 0.5

(%o2)
$$\frac{i^{2x}-2i^x+1}{i^x-1}$$

     rat: replaced 0.5 by 1/2 = 0.5

(%i3)   fullratsimp (k);

     rat: replaced 0.5 by 1/2 = 0.5

(%o3) i^x-1

fullratsubst ([substitution_condition], expression,)

It is similar to ratsubst function but it further simplifies the substitution condition. To use this function first call, **load ("lrats")\$** .

Instead of **fullratsubst**, the function **lratsubst** also used.

(%i1)   load ("lrats")\$
(%i2)   fullratsubst ([x^2 = –z, x*z = z^2], x^3*z);
(%o2) $-z^3$

fullsetify ([list])

replaces the list with a set operator.

(%i1)   fullsetify ([x, i, [–x*i]]);
(%o1)   {i,x,{–i*x}}

fundamental_dimensions

returns the list of fundamental dimensions. To use this function first call, **load ("ezunits")\$**.

(%i1)   load ("ezunits")\$
(%i2)   fundamental_dimensions;

(%o2)	[length, mass, time, current, temperature, quantity]

/* it can be declared by **declare_fundamental_dimensions** function*/

fundamental_units(x)

returns fundamental_units(x) units associated with the fundamental dimensions of x. To use this function first call, **load ("ezunits")**.

(%i1)	load ("ezunits")$
(%i2)	fundamental_units;
(%o2)	[m, kg, s, A, K, mol]

/* it can be declared by **declare_fundamental_units** function*/

(%i3)	fundamental_units (1` N);	/* N = Newton */

$$(\%o3) \qquad \frac{kgm}{s^2}$$

(%i4)	fundamental_units (1 `C);	/* C = Coulomb */
(%o4)	As	/* Ampere second */

funmake (F, [arguments])

funmake evaluates its list of arguments.

(%i1)	u (k, r) := k^3 – r*2;
(%o1)	u (k, r) := $k^3 - r2$
(%i2)	funmake (u, [b + 2, a – 1]);
(%o2)	u(b + 2, a – 1)
(%i3)	''%;
(%o3)	$(b + 2)^3\ (a - 1)$

fv (intrest_rate, current_value, period)

estimates future value of the money returned, from the current value for the given interest rate (not in percent) and number of periods in months. To use this function first call, load(finance).

(%i1)	load(finance)$
(%i2)	fv(0.010,100000,1);　　Refer: pv
(%o2)	101000.0

gamma([z])

evaluates gamma function numerically.

(%i1)	map('gamma,[4,sqrt(-1),3*x]);
(%o1)	$[6,\Gamma(\%i),\Gamma(3x)]$

gaussprob (x)

returns the Gaussian probability function for 'x' as $\dfrac{\%e^{-\frac{x^2}{2}}}{\sqrt{2}\sqrt{\%pi}}$. To use this function first call, **load(functs)**.

(%i1)	load(functs)$
(%i2)	gaussprob (3*i);
(%o2)	$\dfrac{\%e^{-\frac{9i^2}{2}}}{\sqrt{2}\sqrt{\%pi}}$

gcd (expression_1, expression_2, ...)

returns the greatest common divisor for the given expressions.
Refer **ezgcd** function.

(%i3)	a:x^3+4*x^2+4*x;
	b:2*x^3+5*x^2+2*x;
	c:x^4−x^2+2*x^3−2*x;
(a)	x^3+4x^2+4x
(b)	$2x^3+5x^2+2x$
(c)	$x^4+2x^3−x^2−2x$
(%i4)	gcd(a, b, c);
(%o4)	$x^2 + 2x$
(%i5)	gcd(2/8, 16,1/16);
(%o5)	$\dfrac{1}{4}$
(%i6)	ezgcd(2/8, 16,1/16);
(%o6)	$[\dfrac{1}{16}, 1, 64, 1]$

gcdex (f, x)

returns a list [a, b, u] where u is the greatest common divisor of f and x and u is equal to (a f + b x).

(%i1) gcdex (j^2, j^–2);

(%o1)/R/ $[0,1,\frac{1}{j^2}]$

genmatrix (a,m,n)

returns a 'm×n' matrix generated from 'a'.

(%i1) genmatrix (a,3,2);

(%o1) $\begin{bmatrix} a_{1,1} & a_{1,2} \\ a_{2,1} & a_{2,2} \\ a_{3,1} & a_{3,2} \end{bmatrix}$

(%i2) genmatrix (a/a^2,3);

(%o2) $\begin{bmatrix} \left(\frac{1}{a}\right)(1,1) & \left(\frac{1}{a}\right)(1,2) & \left(\frac{1}{a}\right)(1,3) \\ \left(\frac{1}{a}\right)(2,1) & \left(\frac{1}{a}\right)(2,2) & \left(\frac{1}{a}\right)(2,3) \\ \left(\frac{1}{a}\right)(3,1) & \left(\frac{1}{a}\right)(3,2) & \left(\frac{1}{a}\right)(3,3) \end{bmatrix}$

gensym ()

returns a fresh symbol which is an integer with an internal counter.

(%i1) gensym ();
(%o1) g20104
(%i2) gensym("i");
(%o2) i20105
(%i3) gensym("i*j")
(%o3) i*j20106

geo_amortization (rate, growing_rate, amount,number_of_periods)

returns amortization table from rate, growing rate, amount and number of periods. To use this function first call, **load(finance)** .

```
(%i1)          load(finance)$
(%i2)          geo_amortization(0.05,0.03,50000,12);
               /* executed data are printed in table format */
```

"n"	"Balance"	"Interest"	"Amortization"	"Payment"
0.000	50000.000	0.000	0.000	0.000
1.000	47647.586	2500.000	2352.414	4852.414
2.000	45031.979	2382.379	2615.607	4997.987
3.000	42135.651	2251.599	2896.327	5147.926
4.000	38940.070	2106.783	3195.581	5302.364
5.000	35425.639	1947.004	3514.431	5461.435
6.000	31571.643	1771.282	3853.996	5625.278
7.000	27356.189	1578.582	4215.454	5794.036
8.000	22756.141	1367.809	4600.048	5967.857
9.000	17747.055	1137.807	5009.086	6146.893
10.000	12303.108	887.353	5443.947	6331.300
11.000	6397.025	615.155	5906.083	6521.239
12.000	0.000	319.851	6397.025	6716.876

```
(%o2)          false
```

geo_annuity_fv (rate,growing_rate, future_value, number_of_periods)

returns annuity from future value, interest rate, growing_rate, future value and number of periods. To use this first call, **load(finance)**.

```
(%i1)          load(finance)$
(%i2)          geo_annuity_fv (0.05,0.03,50000,12);
(%o2)          2702.005737294646
```

geo_annuity_pv(rate,growing_rate,current_value, number_of_periods)

returns annuity from present (current) value, interest rate, growing_rate, future value and number of periods.

To use this function first call, **load(finance)**.

```
(%i1)          load(finance)$
(%i2)          geo_annuity_pv (0.05,0.03,50000,12);
(%o2)          4852.414096268679
```

geomap ([list])

draws cartographic maps of countries with gnuplot graph. To use this first, **load(worldmap)$**. This function is out of scope for this book and so further details are not covered.

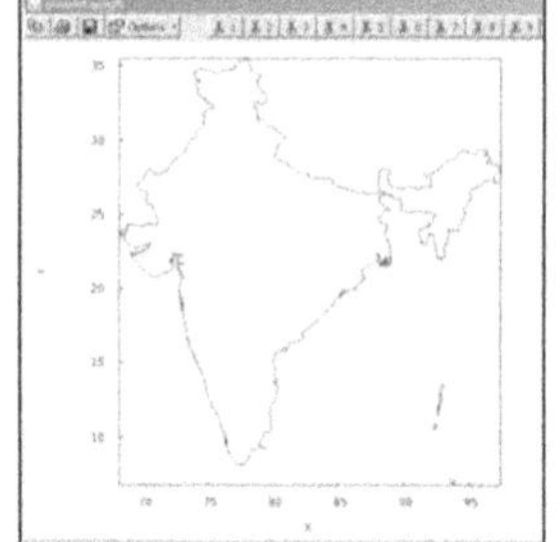

(%i1)	load(worldmap)$
(%i2)	a: gr2d(geomap([India]))$
(%i3)	draw(columns = 2, a)$
	/*Coordinates can be changed*/
	/* displayed in gnuplot */

geometric (x, y, n)

returns the nth term of the geometric series x, xy, xy_2, ... $asxy^{(n-1)}$
To use this function first call, **load(functs)$**.

(%i1)	load(functs)$
(%i2)	geometric (r^-n, u^2, 4);
(%o2)	$\dfrac{u^6}{r^n}$

geometric_mean ([list])

returns geometric mean for the given list. To use this function first call, **load(descriptive)$**.

(%i1)	load (descriptive)$
(%i2)	geometric_mean ([1,2,3,4,5]);
(%o2)	$120^{\frac{1}{5}}$
(%i3)	geometric_mean ([n,(n+1),(n+2),(n+3),(n+4)]);
(%o3)	$n^{\frac{1}{5}}(n+1)^{\frac{1}{5}}(n+2)^{\frac{1}{5}}(n+3)^{\frac{1}{5}}(n+4)^{\frac{1}{5}}$

geosum (y, c, n)

returns the sum of the geometric series from 1 to n. To use this function first call, **load(functs)$**.

(%i1)	load(functs)$
(%i2)	geosum (y, c, n);
(%o2)	$\dfrac{(1-c^n)y}{1-c}$

(%i3)	geosum (1, 3, 2);
(%o3)	4

getcurrentdirectory ()

returns the current working directory. To use this function first call, **load("operatingsystem")\$**.

(%i1)	load("operatingsystem")\$
(%i2)	getcurrentdirectory ();
(%o2)	"C:\maxima-5.38.1\wxMaxima\"

getenv (env)

returns the value of the environment variable such as "PATH". To use this function first call, **load("operatingsystem")\$**.

(%i1)	load("operatingsystem")\$
(%i2)	getenv("PATH");
(%o2)	C:/maxima-5.38.1\lib\maxima\5.38.1_5_gdf93b7b_
	dirty\binary-clisp;C:/maxima-5.38.1\clisp-2.49\base;
	C:/maxima-5.38.1\gnuplot;C:/maxima-5.38.1\gnuplot\
	bin;C:/maxima-5.38.1\bin;C:\ProgramData\Oracle
	\Java\javapath;C:\Windows\system32;C:\Windows;C:\
	Windows\System32\Wbem;C:\Windows\System32\
	WindowsPowerShell\v1.0\;C:\ProgramFiles (x86)\Intel\
	OpenCLSDK\2.0\bin\x86;C:\ProgramFiles (x86)\Intel\
	OpenCL SDK\2.0\bin\x64"

gfactor (expression)

returns the factors for the expression over the Gaussian integers with the imaginary unit %i adjoined, if needed.

(%i1)	gfactor (x^3 – 1);
(%o1)	(x – 1)(x²+x+1)
(%i2)	gfactor (x^4 – 1);
(%o2)	(x – 1) (x + 1) (x – %i) (x + %i)
(%i3)	gfactor (18);
(%i3)	2 3²

girth (graph)

returns the length of the shortest cycle in graph. To use this function first call, **load ("graphs")**.

(%i1)   load ("graphs")$

(%i2)   cube_graph (2);/*number can be changed */

(%o2)   GRAPH(4 vertices, 4 edges)

(%i3)   print_graph(%o2);

Graph on 4 vertices with 4 edges.

```
Adjacencies:
   3 : 1 2
   2 : 0 3
   1 : 3 0
   0 : 2 1
```

(%o3)   done

(%i4)   draw_graph(%o2);

(%t4)   /* display → */

(%o4)   done

(%i5)   girth(%o2);

(%o5)   3

global_variances (matrix)

returns a list of global variance. To use this function first call, **load ("descriptive")$**.

(%i1) load ("descriptive")$

(%i2) x: matrix ([1,–3], [2, 6], [3,–1],[–4,–3]);

$$(\%o2)\quad \begin{bmatrix} 1 & -3 \\ 2 & 6 \\ 3 & -1 \\ -4 & -3 \end{bmatrix}$$

(%i3) global_variances (x);

$$(\%o3)\quad \left[\frac{335}{12}, \frac{335}{24}, \frac{2491}{18}, \frac{\sqrt{2491}}{3\sqrt{2}}, \frac{\sqrt{2491}}{3\sqrt{2}}, \frac{2491^{\frac{1}{4}}}{2^{\frac{1}{4}}\sqrt{3}}\right]$$

go (loop)

It is used within a block to transfer control to the statement of the block which is tagged in the loop with the argument to go.

(%i1)   f(n) := block([j:2], loop, j:j+1, for i:1 thru 6 do (print(i+2), if i>=n then return(false)), if j<=n then go(loop), print(done))$

(%i2)   f(2);

3

4

done

(%o2)   done

gramschmidt (matrix)

returns the Gram-Schmidt orthogonalization algorithm for a matrix or a list. To use this function first call, **load ("eigen")$**.

(%i1)   load ("eigen")$

(%i2)   i: matrix ([a, 2], [x,1]);

(i) $\begin{bmatrix} a & 2 \\ x & 1 \end{bmatrix}$

(%i3)   gramschmidt (i);

(%o3) $[[a, 2], [\frac{2(2x-a)}{a^2+4}, -\frac{a(2x-a)}{a^2+4}]]$

graph_flow ([list])

returns a xy plot (displays in gnuplot) for the flow (particularly for money flow) with arbitrary units of time. Positive data are in blue and upside and the negative data are in red and downside. To use this function first call, load(finance)$.

(%i1)   load(finance)$

(%i2)   graph_flow([−100,−3000,2000,2200,−1300,2220])$

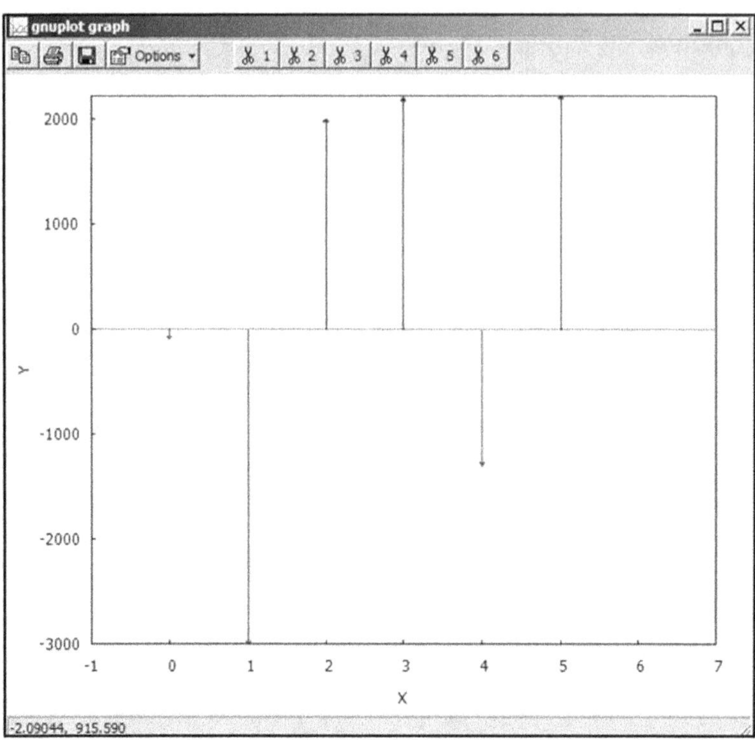

grid_graph (n, m)

returns the 'n × m' grid graph. To use this function first call, **load(graphs)$**.

(%i1)   load(graphs)$

(%o1)   "C:\maxima-5.38.1\share\maxima\5.38.1_5_gdf93b7
         b_dirty\share\graphs\graphs.mac"

(%i2)   grid_graph (2, 3);

(%o2)   GRAPH(6 vertices, 7 edges)

(%i3)   draw_graph(%)$

(%t3)

grind (expression or data)

converts and prints the expression or data to suitable input format.

(%i1)   matrix([-1.0,3/-i],[2.2,y^j],[-3.0,x^-3]);

$$(\%o1) \qquad \begin{bmatrix} -1.0 & -\dfrac{3}{i} \\ 2.2 & y^j \\ -3.0 & \dfrac{1}{x^3} \end{bmatrix}$$

(%i2)   y*%;

$$(\%o2) \qquad \begin{bmatrix} -1.0y & -\dfrac{3y}{i} \\ 2.2y & y^{j+1} \\ -3.0y & \dfrac{y}{x^3} \end{bmatrix}$$

(%i3)   grind(%);

matrix([−1.0*y,−(3*y)/i],[2.2*y,y^(j+1)],[−3.0*y,y/x^3])$
(%o3)   done

halfangles

when halfangles is set to true, trigonometric functions are simplified.

(%i1)   halfangles : true$
(%i2)   sin(x/2);

WARNING: DEFUN/DEFMACRO: redefining function SIMP-UNIT-STEP in C:\maxima-5.38.1\share\maxima\5.38.1_5_gdf93b7b_
dirty\share\orthopoly\orthopoly.lisp,was defined in top-level

WARNING: DEFUN/DEFMACRO: redefining function SIMP-POCHHAMMER inC:\maxima-5.38.1\share\maxima\5.38.1_5_gdf93 b7b_dirty \share\orthopoly\orthopoly.lisp,was defined in top-level

$$(\%o2) \qquad \frac{(-1)^{\text{floor}\left(\frac{x}{2\%pi}\right)}\sqrt{1-\cos(x)}}{\sqrt{2}}$$

harmonic (a, b, c, n)

returns the n   term of the harmonic series a/b, a/(b + c), a/(b + 2*c), … a/(b + (n − 1)*c). To use this function first call, **load(functs)**.

(%i1)	load(functs)$
(%i2)	harmonic (a, b, c, 6);
(%o2)	$\dfrac{a}{5c+b}$

harmonic_mean ([list])

returns the harmonic mean for the given list. To use this function first call **load (descriptive)$**.

(%i1)	load (descriptive)$
(%i2)	harmonic_mean ([n,m]);
(%o2)	$\dfrac{2}{\frac{1}{n}+\frac{1}{m}}$
(%i3)	harmonic_mean ([i, y, z]);
(%o3)	$\dfrac{3}{\frac{1}{z}+\frac{1}{y}+\frac{1}{i}}$

hav (x)

returns the haversine value for 'x'. To use this function first call, **load(functs)$**.

(%i1)	load(functs)$
(%i2)	hav (x);
(%o2)	$\dfrac{1-\cos(x)}{2}$

height [height, pixels]

controls the graphics window properties. Default value is 500. Alters the height, in pixels and it must be a positive integer.

hermite (n, x)

returns Hermite polynomial of degree 'n'.

(%i1)	hermite (i, y);
(%o1)	$H_i(y)$
(%i2)	hermite (2, j);
(%o2)	$-2(1-2j^2)$

(%i3)   hermite (j, 2);
(%o3)   H$_j$(2)
(%i4)   hermite (3, 2);
(%o4)   40

hessian (f, [x, y])

returns Hessian matrix of 'f' with respect to variables list 'x' and 'y'.

(%i1)   hessian (n^3-m^6, [n,m]);

0 errors, 0 warnings

(%o1) $\begin{bmatrix} 6n & 0 \\ 0 & -30m^4 \end{bmatrix}$

hgfred (x, y, t)

simplifies hypergeometric function into simpler forms. 'x'and 'y' are the list of numerator and denominator parameters respectively.

(%i1)   hgfred([1,2],[3],z);

(%o1) $-2 \left(\frac{\log(1-z)}{z} + \frac{1}{z} + \frac{\log(1-z)(1-z)}{z^2} \right)$

hilbert_matrix (n)

returns the 'n×n' Hilbert matrix where 'n' is positive integer.

(%i1)   hilbert_matrix (3);

(%o1) $\begin{bmatrix} 1 & \frac{1}{2} & \frac{1}{3} \\ \frac{1}{2} & \frac{1}{3} & \frac{1}{4} \\ \frac{1}{3} & \frac{1}{4} & \frac{1}{5} \end{bmatrix}$

hipow (expression, x)

returns the highest explicit exponent of 'x' in the expression.

(%i1)   hipow (i*j^k * r^-g, j);
(%o1)   k

horner (expression, variable)

returns a rearranged representation for the expression as in orner's rule with variable.

(%i1)   horner (a*x^3 +b*x^6 –c*x,x);

(%o1)   x (x²(bx³+ a)–c)

hypergeometric ([expression], x)

returns hypergeometric simplifying function for polynomial expression by setting expand_hypergeometric is true.

(%i1)   hypergeometric([–3],[2], x),

               expand_hypergeometric : true;

WARNING: DEFUN/DEFMACRO: redefining function FLOAT-OR-RATIONAL-P in C:\maxima-5.38.1\share\maxima\5.38.1_5_gdf93b7b_dirty \share\hypergeometric\hypergeometric.lisp, was defined in Z:\home\dauti \Software \maxima-code\crosscompile-windows\ build\maxima-prefix\src \maxima\src \inary-clisp\trigi.fas

(%o1) $\dfrac{x^3}{24} + \dfrac{x^2}{2} \quad \dfrac{3x}{2} + 1$

hypergeometric_simp ([expression], x)

simplifies hypergeometric functions by applying hgfred. To use this function first call, **load ("hypergeometric")$**.

(%i1)   load ("hypergeometric")$

(%i2)   hypergeometric([1,2],[3],z)

(%o2)   hypergeometric([1,2],[3],z)

(%i3)   hypergeometric_simp(%);

(%o3) $-2 \left(\dfrac{\log(1-z)}{z} + \dfrac{1}{z} + \dfrac{\log(1-z)(1-z)}{z^2} \right)$ /* Refer: hgfred */

(%i4)   hypergeometric([–3],[2], x)

(%o4)   hypergeometric([–3],[2],x)

(%i5)   hypergeometric_simp(%);/* Refer: **hypergeometric** */

(%o5) $-\dfrac{x^3}{24} + \dfrac{x^2}{2} - \dfrac{3x}{2} + 1$

ibase

Default value: 10. It is the base for integers. For binary digits ibase:2. ibase can be assigned any integer between 2 to 36 (decimal). When it is greater than 10, the numerals include the decimal numerals 0 to 9 and alphabets A, B, C...

(%i1)	ibase : 2 $	/* binary */
(%i2)	obase;	
(%o2)	10	
(%i3)	111	
(%o3)	7	

Restart

(%i1)	ibase : 3 $	/* base: 3 */
(%i2)	obase;	
(%o2)	10	
(%i3)	11	
(%o3)	4	

ident (n)

returns an 'n × n' identity matrix.

(%i1)   ident (6);

$$
(\%o1) \quad
\begin{bmatrix}
1 & 0 & 0 & 0 & 0 & 0 \\
0 & 1 & 0 & 0 & 0 & 0 \\
0 & 0 & 1 & 0 & 0 & 0 \\
0 & 0 & 0 & 1 & 0 & 0 \\
0 & 0 & 0 & 0 & 1 & 0 \\
0 & 0 & 0 & 0 & 0 & 1
\end{bmatrix}
$$

identfor (matrix)

returns an identity matrix that has the same shape as the matrix.

(%i1)   matrix ([2^n, i,4], [−a, uy,r]);

$$
(\%o1) \quad
\begin{bmatrix}
2^n & i & 4 \\
-a & uy & r
\end{bmatrix}
$$

(%i2)   identfor (%);

0 errors, 0 warnings

$$
(\%o2) \quad
\begin{bmatrix}
0 & 1 & 0 \\
0 & 0 & 1
\end{bmatrix}
$$

if (condition)

conditional operator in programming.

/* The following program asks for the user input and compares the numerical data. */

(%i3) a:read("Enter a"),numer$ b:read("Enter b"), numer$

if(b>a) then print("b is greater") else print("a is greater")$

Enter a 3;   /* use Shift + Enter after the input */

Enter b 8;   /* use Shift + Enter after the input */

b is greater

(%o3) b is greater

ifactors (integer)

returns factorization of the given positive integer.

(%i1) ifactors (1000);

(%o1) [[2,3],[5,3]]   /* $2^3 \times 5^3$ */

igcdex (n, i)

returns a list [x, y, z] where 'z' is the greatest common divisor of 'n' and 'i','z' is equal to x n + yi where 'n' and 'i' must be integers.

To use this function first call, **load(gcdex)$**.

(%i1) load(gcdex)$

(%i2) igcdex (24, 40);

(%o2) [2,–1,8]

inchar: "input"

default value: %i and this changes the prefix for the input.

(%i1) inchar: "en";

(inchar) en

(en2) ifactors (1000);

(%o2) [[2,3],[5,3]]

(en3) hermite (3, 2);

(%o3) 40

(en4) hgfred([1,2],[3],z);

(%o4) $-2\left(\dfrac{\log(1-z)}{z} + \dfrac{1}{z} + \dfrac{\log(1-z)(1-z)}{z^2}\right)$

infinity

refers complex infinity. Similarly 'ind' refers, indefinite result. 'inf' refers real positive infinity.

(%i1)	limit(log(1/x), x, 0);
(%o1)	infinity
(%i2)	limit(log(1/x), x, 0);
(%o2)	ind

inference_result ("title", ['value1, 'value2…], [number for display])

constructs an inference result for the given object with its title along with its values and numbers as list. Numbers for order of the display.

To use this function first call, **load(inference_result)\$**.

(%i1)	load(inference_result)\$
(%i3)	b: 3\$ h: 2\$ /* b = base; h = height */
(%i4)	inference_result("Rectangle", ['base=b, 'height=h, 'area=b*h,'perimeter=2*(b+h)],[1,2,4,3]);

$$
(\%o4) \quad \begin{bmatrix} \text{Rectangle} \\ \text{base} = 3 \\ \text{height} = 2 \\ \text{perimeter} = 10 \\ \text{area} = 6 \end{bmatrix} \quad \text{/* [1,2,4,3] refers display order */}
$$

/* perimeter displayed at 3rd */

inprod ([x],[y])   **innerproduct ([x],[y])**

returns the inner product (scalar or dot product) of list of x and y, of equal length. To use this function first call, **load("eigen")\$**.

(%i1)	load("eigen");
(%o1)	"C:\maxima-5.38.1\share\maxima\5.38.1_5_gdf93b7 b_dirty\share\matrix\eigen.mac"
(%i2)	inprod ([i*x, u^2,–3/r], [e/n,e^j,0.5*x]);

rat: replaced –1.5 by –3/2 = –1.5

$$
(\%o2) \quad \frac{(2eir-3n)x+2e^{j}nru^{2}}{2nr}
$$

inrt (x, n)

returns the integer of nth root of the absolute value of 'x'.

(%i1)	inrt ((625, 5),2);	
(%o1)	2	$/* \ 5^2 \times 5^2 \ */$
(%i2)	inrt ((625, 5),4);	
(%o2)	1	$/* \ 5^1 \times 5^1 \times 5^1 \times 5^1 \ */$

integer

declares integer or non-integer.   (Refer: declare function)

(%i1)	declare(a, integer, b, integer);
(%o1)	done
(%i3)	a:–2*1.75$ b:–2*a$
(%i5)	askinteger(a); askinteger(b);

rat: replaced –3.5 by –7/2 = –3.5

(%o4)	no

rat: replaced 7.0 by 7/1 = 7.0

(%o5)	yes

integer_partitions (n)   **integer_partitions (n, length)**

returns set of integers which is the sum of 'n'and if needed length of integers can be specified. By using the function 'cardinality' total number of possibilities can be counted.

(%i1)	integer_partitions (6);
(%o1)	{[1,1,1,1,1,1],[2,1,1,1,1],[2,2,1,1],[2,2,2],[3,1,1,1],[3,2,1], [3,3], [4,1,1],[4,2],[5,1],[6]}
(%i2)	integer_partitions (6,2);
(%o2)	{[3,3],[4,2],[5,1],[6,0]}
(%i3)	integer_partitions (6);
(%o3)	{[1,1,1,1,1,1],[2,1,1,1,1],[2,2,1,1],[2,2,2],[3,1,1,1],[3,2,1], [3,3], [4,1,1],[4,2],[5,1],[6]}
(%i4)	cardinality (%); /* Refer: cardinality */
(%o4)	11

integerp (n)

returns true if 'n' is a numeric integer, if not it returns false.

(%i1)   integerp (n);
(%o1)   false
(%i2)   integerp (2);
(%o2)   true
(%i3)   integerp (–31);
(%o3)   true
(%i4)   integerp (0.0);
(%o4)   false
(%i5)   integerp (%pi);
(%o5)   false

integervalued(function)

declares the given function as an integervalued function.

integrate (expression, x)

integrate (expression, x, a, b)

returns the integral of expression with respect to 'x'. In a definite integral, limits of integration 'a' (lower limit) and 'b' (upper limit) are given. In indefinite integration, **integrate (expression=n, x)** integration constant and integration constant counter are also given.

(%i1)   integrate (x^3, x);

(%o1) $\dfrac{x^4}{4}$

(%i2)   integrate (x^3, x,a,b);

(%o2) $\dfrac{b^4}{4} - \dfrac{a^4}{4}$

(%i3)   integrate (x^3, x,1,2);

(%o3) $\dfrac{15}{4}$ $/* \dfrac{2^4}{4} - \dfrac{1^4}{4} */$

(%i4)   integrate (x^3=2, x);

(%o4) $\dfrac{x^4}{4} = 2x + \%c1$ /%c integration constant */

(%i5)   integrate (x^3=3, x);

(%o5) $\dfrac{x^4}{4} = 3x + \%c2$

(%i6)   integrate (x^3=b, x);

(%o6) $\dfrac{x^4}{4} = bx + \%c3$

(%i7)   integration_constant : 'k; /* constant can be changed */

               (integration_constant) k

(%i8)   integrate (x^3=b, x);

(%o8) $\dfrac{x^4}{4} = bx + k4$

(%i9)   reset (integration_constant_counter);

               /* counting number can also be reset */

(%o9)   [integration_constant_counter]

(%i10)   integrate (x^3=b, x);

(%o10) $\dfrac{x^4}{4} = bx + k1$

intersection ({a},{b},{c}…)   intersect ({a},{b},{c}…)

returns a set with common elements to the sets **({a},{b},{c}…)**

(%i1)   i_1: {−n, k, s, l, r};i_2: {-g, −r, −s, k};i_3: {k, i, −r};

(i_1)   {k,l,−n,r,s}

(i_2)   {−g,k,−r,−s}

(i_3)   {i,k,−l,−r}

(%i4)   intersection (i_1,i_2,i_3);

(%o4)   {k}

inv_mod (n, m)

returns the inverse of 'n' modulo (remainder after division)'m'.

(%i1)   inv_mod(2, 9);

(%o1)   5

(%i2)   inv_mod(9, 2);

(%o3)   1

inverse_fft ([L])

returns the inverse complex fast Fourier transform. To use this function first call, **load ("fft")$**.

(%i1)   load ("fft")$

(%i2)   inverse_fft ([1, 2, 3, 4, –1, –2, –3, –4]);

(%o2)   [0.0,–14.48528137423857*%i–0.82842712474461894,0.0,4.828
           42712474619–2.48528137423857*%i,0.0,

           2.485281374238571*%i+4.82842712474619,0.0,

           14.48528137423857*%i–0.82842712474461907]

invert (matrix)   **invert_by_adjoint (matrix)**

returns the inverse of the matrix.

(%i1)   x: matrix ([j, i^2], [u/i, j*k]);

(%i1) $\begin{bmatrix} j & i^2 \\ \dfrac{u}{i} & jk \end{bmatrix}$

(%i2)   invert (x);

(%o2) $\begin{bmatrix} \dfrac{jk}{j^2k-iu} & -\dfrac{i^2}{j^2k-iu} \\ -\dfrac{u}{i(j^2k-iu)} & \dfrac{j}{j^2k-iu} \end{bmatrix}$

(%i3)   y: matrix ([2, 1], [3, 4]);

(y) $\begin{bmatrix} 2 & 1 \\ 3 & 4 \end{bmatrix}$

(%i4)   invert (y); $/* \dfrac{1}{(2\times4)-(1\times3)}\begin{bmatrix} 4 & -1 \\ -3 & 2 \end{bmatrix} */$

(%o4) $\begin{bmatrix} \dfrac{4}{5} & -\dfrac{1}{5} \\ -\dfrac{3}{5} & \dfrac{2}{5} \end{bmatrix}$ $/* \dfrac{1}{5}\begin{bmatrix} 4 & -1 \\ -3 & 2 \end{bmatrix} = \begin{bmatrix} \dfrac{4}{5} & \dfrac{-1}{5} \\ \dfrac{-3}{5} & \dfrac{2}{5} \end{bmatrix} */$

is (expression)

returns true or false or unknown from the expression by comparison.

(%i2)	a:−1/4\$b:2.85\$
(%i3)	is(a>b);
(%o3)	false
(%i4)	is(a>d);
(%o4)	unknown
(%i5)	is(b>2.8499999999);
(%o5)	true

isolate (expression, x)

returns the isolated expression which contain 'x' and remaining terms are replaced by atomic symbols like %t1, %t2…

(%i1)	expand((i−j+n)^3);
(%o1)	$n^3 - 3jn^2 + 3in^2 + 3j^2n - 6ijn + 3i^2n - j^3 + 3ij^2 - 3i^2j + i^3$
(%i2)	isolate (expand((i−j+n)^3), n);
(%t2)	$-j^3 + 3ij^2 - 3i^2j + i^3$
(%o2)	$n^3 - 3jn^2 + 3in^2 + 3j^2n - 6ijn + 3i^2n + \%t2$

isolate_wrt_times

if it is set to true, the function, 'isolate' will isolate with respect to products, but default value is false. /* refer isolate */

(%i1)	isolate_wrt_times: true\$
(%i2)	isolate (expand((i−j+n)^3), n);
(%t2)	$3i^2$
(%t3)	$-6ij$
(%t4)	$3j^2$
(%t5)	$3i$
(%t6)	$-3j$
(%t7)	$-j^3 + 3ij^2 - 3i^2j + i^3$
(%o7)	$n^3 + \%t6n^2 + \%t5n^2 + \%t4n + \%t3n + \%t2n + \%t7$
(%i8)	isolate_wrt_times: false\$

(%i9)   isolate (expand(((i–j+n)^3), n);

(%o9) $n^3 - 3jn^2 + 3in^2 + 3j^2n - 6ijn + 3i^2n + \%t7$

isqrt (integer)

returns the integer square root of the <u>absolute</u> value of the integer.

(%i1)   isqrt (–11);

(%o1)   3   /* $\sqrt{11}$ = 3.31662 */

items_inference (stored)

returns a list with the names of the items stored. To use this function first call, load(inference_result)$.

(%i1)   load(inference_result)$

(%i2)   inference_result(“x”,   ['a=–1*%i,b=j^k*s,s=–3*g/4],[2]);

$$(\%o2) \quad \left[b = \overset{x}{j^k s} \right.$$

iteration can be done by combination of different functions, which is important aspect in logical programing.

(%i2)   x:2; while (x^2–2<=36) do (x: x+1, display(x–1));

(x)   2

3+–1=2

4+–1=3

5+–1=4

6+–1=5

7+–1=6

(%o2)   done

On iteration (repetition by step up or step down with desired increment or decrement) from the given value until the desired result is obtained.

/* Caution: The following iteration will run for several hours. */

(%i2)   x:0; while (x^2–5<=0) do (x:x+0.000000001, print(x));

(x)   0   /* iteration to determine: x= $\sqrt{5}$ (or) $x^2–5 =0$ */

x = 0.00001   /* iterations are done by incremented 'x'values */

...   /* 'x' value is displayed in each increment till the

...   condition is satisfied($x^2–5 =0$) */

x =2.236068   /* execution stopped, as condition was satisfied */

(%o2)   done

JF (lambda,n)

returns the Jordan cell of order 'n' with eigenvalue lambda. To use this function first call, **load("diag")\$**.

(%i1)   load("diag")\$

(%i2)   JF(k,7);

(%o2)
$$\begin{bmatrix} k & 1 & 0 & 0 & 0 & 0 & 0 \\ 0 & k & 1 & 0 & 0 & 0 & 0 \\ 0 & 0 & k & 1 & 0 & 0 & 0 \\ 0 & 0 & 0 & k & 1 & 0 & 0 \\ 0 & 0 & 0 & 0 & k & 1 & 0 \\ 0 & 0 & 0 & 0 & 0 & k & 1 \\ 0 & 0 & 0 & 0 & 0 & 0 & k \end{bmatrix}$$

join (list1, list2)

returns a new list containing the elements of listl and list2, interspersed.

(%i1)   b:[2*y, j];

(b)   [2y, j]

(%i2)   join (b,[−u,−g,t]);

(%o2)   [2*y,−u,j,−g]

jordan (matrix)

returns Jordan form of matrix. To use this function first call, **load("diag")\$.**

(%i1)   load("diag")\$

(%i2)   x: matrix ([j, i^2], [u/i, j*k]);

(x)
$$\begin{bmatrix} j & i^2 \\ \dfrac{u}{i} & jk \end{bmatrix}$$

(%i3)   jordan (x);

(%o3) $\left[\left[-\dfrac{\sqrt{4iu+j^2k^2-2j^2k+j^2}-jk-j}{2}, 1\right], \left[\dfrac{\sqrt{4iu+j^2k^2-2j^2k+j^2}+jk+j}{2}, 1\right]\right]$

(%i4)   dispJordan(%);

(%o4)
$$\begin{bmatrix} -\dfrac{\sqrt{4iu+j^2k^2-2j^2k+j^2}-jk-j}{2} & 0 \\ 0 & \dfrac{\sqrt{4iu+j^2k^2-2j^2k+j^2}+jk+j}{2} \end{bmatrix}$$

keepfloat

prevents floating point numbers into rational when keep float is set to true. Default value: false

(%i1)   rat(5*x/2.0);

rat: replaced 2.5 by 5/2 = 2.5

(%o1)/R/ $\dfrac{5x}{2}$

(%i2)   rat(5*x/2.0), keepfloat;
(%o2)/R/   2.5x

kill (values)   **kill (all)**

removes /clears all bindings, values, functions, rules etc.

(%i2)   x:9; while (x^2–16>0) do (x: x–1, display(x));

(x)   9   /* iteration to find $\sqrt{16}$ */

x=8

x=7

x=6

x=5

x=4

(%i2)   done
(%i3)   v:x*i
(v)   4i
(%i4)   kill(x);
(%o4)   done
(%i5)   z:x*i
(z)   ix

kron_delta (x,y...)

refers the Kronecker delta function.

(%i2)   kron_delta(x,x,x);kron_delta(x,x,y);
(%o1)   1
(%o2)   kron_delta(x,y)
(%i4)   kron_delta(x,y,y);kron_delta(y,y,y);
(%o3)   kron_delta(x,y)
(%o4)   1

kronecker_product (x, y)

return the Kronecker products of matrices 'x' and 'y'.

(%i1)   x: matrix ([a, b], [c, d]);

(%i2)   y: matrix ([1, 2], [3, 4]);

(x)
$$\begin{bmatrix} a & b \\ c & d \end{bmatrix}$$

(y)
$$\begin{bmatrix} 1 & 2 \\ 3 & 4 \end{bmatrix}$$

(%i3)   kronecker_product (x, y);

(%o3)
$$\begin{bmatrix} a & 2a & b & 2b \\ 3a & 4a & 3b & 4b \\ c & 2c & d & 2d \\ 3c & 4c & 3d & 4d \end{bmatrix}$$

(%i4)   kronecker_product (y, x);

(%o4)
$$\begin{bmatrix} a & b & 2a & 2b \\ c & d & 2c & 2d \\ 3a & 3b & 4a & 4b \\ 3c & 3d & 4c & 4d \end{bmatrix}$$

kurtosis ([list])

returns kurtosis coefficient, for the list of data (for x and y set). To use this function first call, **load (descriptive)$**. It measures the sharpness of the peak of a frequency-distribution curve.

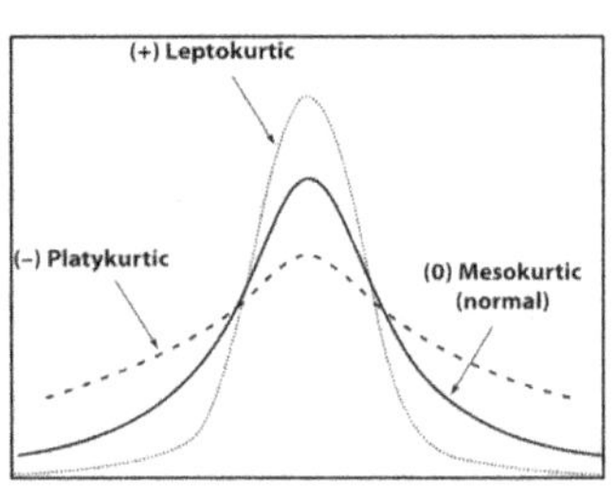

$$k = \frac{\sum_{i=1}^{n} \frac{(x_i - \bar{x})}{n}}{n\,s^4} - 3; \quad s - \text{standard deviation}; \ \bar{x} - \text{mean}; \ n - \text{data number}$$

(%i1)   load (descriptive)$

(%i2)   k:[0.021705365,0.040225261],

       [2.175768116,1.26307321],

       [3.448723255,3.032984714],

       [3.898781151,5.913113435],

       [4.320785997,9.967819791],

```
                    [4.924920596,6.090104586],
                    [5.601855942,2.968624296],
                    [6.540301992,1.777956557],
                    [7.941326922,0.796460177],
                    [9.97836439,0.056315366]])$
(%i3)           kurtosis (k), numer;
(%o3)           –2.0
```

lagrange (list, option)

returns the polynomial interpolation by the Lagrange method. To use this function first call, load(interpol)$.

The following example is the interpolation at irregular (unequally spaced) intervals for: y=f(x)=sin(x).

x	21	25	26	31	22
y=sin(x)	0.3584	0.4226	0.4384	0.5150	?

```
(%i1)           load(interpol)$
(%i2)           a:[[21, 0.3584], [25, 0.4226], [26, 0.4384], [31, 0.5150]]$
(%i3)           lagrange(a);
(%o3)           0.001716666666666667*(x–26)*(x–25)*(x–21)–
                0.017536*(x–31)*(x-25)*(x–1)+
                0.01760833333333333*(x–31)*(x–26)*(x–21)–
                0.001792*(x–31)*(x–26)*(x–25)
(%i4)           f(x):="%;
(%o4)           f(x):=0.001716666666666667*(x–26)*(x–25)*(x–21)–
                0.017536*(x–31)*(x–25)*(x-1)+0.01760833333333333
                *(x–31)*(x–26)*(x–21)–0.001792*(x–31)*(x-26)*(x–25)
(%i5)           f(22);              /* interpolation for sin(22) */
(%o5)           0.374564
```

lambda([i], function(i))

returns a lambda expression for the given defined function.

(%i1)	f: lambda ([x], x^3+2);
(f)	lambda ([x], x^3 +2)
(%i2)	f(2*i);
(%o2)	$8i^3$+2
(%i3)	f(3);
(%o2)	29

laplace (expression, t, s)

returns the Laplace transform of expression with respect to the variable 't' and transform parameter 's'.

(%i1)	laplace (cos(a*t),t,s);
(%o1)	$\dfrac{s}{s^2+a^2}$
(%i2)	laplace (sin(a*t),t,s);
(%o2)	$\dfrac{s}{s^2+a^2}$
(%i3)	laplace (exp(a*t),t,s);
(%o3)	$\dfrac{1}{s-a}$
(%i4)	laplace (diff(f(t),t),t,s);
(%o4)	slaplace(f(t),t,s)−f(0)

last (expression)   lastn (expression, count)

returns the last expression or the count from the list.

(%i1)	u:[−i/n, 2*j^k, 3*s^−g, exp(−u/n), z^k*y]$
(u)	$[-\dfrac{i}{n}, 2j^k, \dfrac{3}{s^g}, \%e^{-\frac{u}{n}}, yz^k]$
(%i2)	m:last (u)*i;
(m)	iyz^k

lcm (expression)

returns the least common multiple for expression(s) ornumbers. To use this function first call, **load ("functs")$**.

(%i1)	load ("functs")$
(%i2)	lcm(-n/r,-r/n,-3*g/(4*u));
(%o2)	-3gnr
(%i3)	lcm(3,21);
(%o3)	21
(%i6)	a:x^3+4*x^2+4*x;
	b:2*x^3+5*x^2+2*x;
	c:x^4-x^2+2*x^3-2*x;
(a)	x^3+4x^2+4x
(b)	$2x^3+5x^2+2x$
(c)	$x^4+2x^3-x^2-2x$
(%i7)	lcm(a, b, c);
(%o8)	$(x-1)x\,(x+1)\,(x+2)^2\,(2x+1)$

ldefint (expression, x, lower_limit, upper_limit)

returns the definite integral of expression with respect to 'x' between the upper limit 'b' and the lower limit 'a'.

(%i1)	ldefint (2*x^4, x, a, b);
(%o1)	$\dfrac{2b^5}{5} - \dfrac{2a^5}{5}$
(%i2)	ldefint ((2*x)^4, x, a, b);
(%o3)	$\dfrac{16b^5}{5} - \dfrac{16a^5}{5}$

ldisp (expression)   ldisplay (expression)

returns expression into intermediate expressions and returns the list of labels.

(%i1)	a:((n-r)^3);
(a)	$(n-r)^3$
(%i2)	b:expand(a);
(b)	$-r^3+3nr^2-3n^2r+n^3$
(%i3)	ldisp (a,b);

(%t3) $\qquad (n-r)^3$

(%t4) $\qquad -r^3+3nr^2-3n^2r+n^3$

(%o4) $\qquad [\%t3,\%t4]$

legendre_p (n, x);

returns Legendre polynomial of first kind of degree 'n'. To use this function first call, **load ("orthopoly")$**.

(%i1) $\qquad$ load ("orthopoly")$

(%i2) $\qquad$ legendre_p (2, x); $\qquad\qquad$ /* for II order polynomial */

(%o2) $\qquad -3(1-x) + \dfrac{3(1-x)^2}{2} + 1$

(%i3) $\qquad$ legendre_p (4, x); $\qquad\qquad$ /* for IV order polynomial */

(%o4) $\qquad -10(1-x) + \dfrac{35(1-x)^4}{8} - \dfrac{35(1-x)^3}{2} + \dfrac{45(1-x)^2}{2} + 1$

legendre_q (n, x);

returns Legendre polynomial of second kind of degree 'n'. To use this function first call, **load ("orthopoly")$**.

(%i1) $\qquad$ load ("orthopoly")$

(%i2) $\qquad$ legendre_q (2, x); $\qquad\qquad$ /* for II order polynomial */

(%o2)/R/ $\qquad \dfrac{3\log\left(-\frac{x+1}{x-1}\right)x^2 - 6x - \log\left(-\frac{x+1}{x-1}\right)}{4}$

length (expression)

returns the number of parts in the expression.

(%i1) $\qquad$ u:[-i/n, 2*j^k, 3*s^-g, exp(-u/n), z^k*y]$

(u) $\qquad \left[-\dfrac{i}{n}, 2j^k, \dfrac{3}{s^g}, \%e^{-\frac{u}{n}}, yz^k\right]$

(%i2) $\qquad$ v:length(u)+i;

(v) $\qquad$ i+5

let (x, r) $\qquad\qquad$ letrat $\qquad\qquad$ letsimp(expression(x))

defines a substitution rule for the function 'letsimp' such that 'x' is 'r' and 'x' is a product of powers. And the function 'matchdeclare' for 'x' is set to true. Expression at letsimp can be executed by setting the function 'letrat' to true.

(%i1) $\qquad$ matchdeclare (a, true)$

(%i2)	let (a/(a^2), b);	
(%o2)	$\dfrac{1}{a} \rightarrow b$	$/* \ \dfrac{1}{a} = b \ */$
(%i3)	letrat: true\$	
(%i4)	letsimp (a/(a^4));	$/* \ \dfrac{a}{a^4} = \dfrac{1}{a^3} \ */$
(%o4)	b^3	

lfreeof ([list], expression)
returns false, if any call to freeof function does. Refer 'freeof' function.

(%i1)	lfreeof ([i, o], x^(a));
(%o2)	true
(%i2)	lfreeof ([i, o], i^b);
(%o2)	false
(%i3)	lfreeof ([i, o], b^i);
(%o3)	false

lgtreillis (integer, length)   Refer: ltreillis
returns the list of partitions for the integer with the given length.

(%i1)	lgtreillis (8, 5);
resolvante	
generale	
NOTE: To compile the system do	
load("sym/compile");	
0 errors, 0 warnings	
(%o1)	[[4,1,1,1,1],[3,2,1,1,1],[2,2,2,1,1]]
(%i2)	lgtreillis (8, 6);
(%o2)	[[3,1,1,1,1,1],[2,2,1,1,1,1]]

lhs (expression)
returns the left-hand side of the expression.

(%i1)	(j+k)^3= (r^g)*(s^n);
(%o1)	$(k+j)^3 = r^g s^n$
(%i2)	expand(lhs(%));
(%o2)	$k^3+3jk^2+3j^2k+j^3$

li [order] (arguement)

returns the polylogarithm function of order and argument, defined by the infinite series.

(%i1)	li [b] (a);
(%o1)	$li_b(a)$
(%i2)	li [2] (8);
(%o2)	$li_2(8)$
(%i3)	%,numer;
(%o3)	0.99868897109545936-6.532758270910805*%i

limit (expression, variable, value)

returns limit of expression for the variable approaches the value.

(%i1)	limit(log(x), x, 1);
(%o1)	0
(%i2)	limit(sin(x), x, 0);
(%o2)	0
(%i3)	limit(log(x), x, %e); /* %e = 2.718281828459045 */
(%o3)	1

linear (expression, variable)

returns a list of three equations for the variable, if expression of the linear form a*x + b where a ≠ 0 and a and b are independent of x. To use this function first call, **load (antid)**.

(%i1)	load (antid");
(%o1)	"C:\maxima-5.38.1\share\maxima\5.38.1_5_gdf93b7
	b_dirty\share\integration\antid.mac"
(%i2)	linear ((((1– a)*(1+b))*(x)*c, x);
(%o2)	[bargumentb=0,aargumenta=((1–a)*b–a+1)*c,xargumentx=x]

linear_regression(x)

estimates the linear regression for 'x' with confident level 95%. To use this function first call, **load("stats")$**.

(%i1)	load("stats");
(%o1)	"C:\maxima-5.38.1\share\maxima\5.38.1_5_gdf93b7
	b_dirty\share\stats\stats.mac"

(%i2)   a:matrix([1.00,1.00],[2.00,2.00],[3.00,1.30],[4.00,3.75],
           [5.00,2.25]);

(a)
$$\begin{bmatrix} 1.0 & 1.0 \\ 2.0 & 2.0 \\ 3.0 & 1.3 \\ 4.0 & 3.75 \\ 5.0 & 2.25 \end{bmatrix}$$

(%i3)   linear_regression(a);

(%o3)
$$\text{LINEAR REGRESSION MODEL}$$
$$b_{\text{estimation}} = [0.7850000000000019, 0.4249999999999998]$$
$$b_{\text{statistics}} = [0.7760210016181804, 1.393442622950819]$$
$$b\_p\_values = [0.4942986846956039, 0.2577773028538888]$$
$$b_{\text{distribution}} = [\text{student}_t, 3]$$
$$v_{\text{estimation}} = 0.9302499999999999$$
$$v\_conf\_int = [0.2985269055625475, 12.93239576911373]$$
$$v_{\text{distribution}} = [\text{chi2}, 3]$$
$$adc = 0.1905590602566893$$

linearinterpol ([matrix])

computes linear polynomial interpolation. To use this function first call,
load(interpol)$.

(%i1)   load(interpol)$
(%i2)   x:matrix([2.1,6.5], [3.1,8.5], [3.4,9.1], [5.2,12.7],
           [6.5,15.3], [8.2,18.7], [8.5,19.3]);

(x)
$$\begin{bmatrix} 2.1 & 6.5 \\ 3.1 & 8.5 \\ 3.4 & 9.1 \\ 5.2 & 12.7 \\ 6.5 & 15.3 \\ 8.2 & 18.7 \\ 8.5 & 19.3 \end{bmatrix}$$

(%i3)   linearinterpol(x);
(%o3)   (2.0*x+2.3)*charfun2(x,−inf,3.1)+(2.0*x+
           2.300000000000001)*charfun2(x,8.2,inf)+(2.0*x+2.300000
           000000001)*charfun2(x,6.5,8.2)+(2.000000000000001*x+2.
           299999999999992)*charfun2(x,5.2,6.5)+ (2.0*x
           +2.300000000000001)*charfun2(x,3.4,5.2)+(2.0*x+2.
           3)*charfun2(x,3.1,3.4)

(%i4)   f(x):="%;

(%o4)   f(x):=(2.0*x+2.3)*charfun2(x,–inf,3.1)+(2.0*x+
               2.300000000000001)*charfun2(x,8.2,inf)+(2.0*x+2.300000
               000000001)*charfun2(x,6.5,8.2)+(2.000000000000001*x+2
               .299999999999992)*charfun2(x,5.2,6.5)+(2.0*x+2.3000000
               00000001)*charfun2(x,3.4,5.2)+(2.0*x+2.3)*charfun2(x,3.1,
               3.4)

(%i5)   f(2.8);   /* interpolate at x = 2.8 */

(%o5)   7.9   f(x) = 2.0x+2.3 = (2.0×2.8)+2.3

linsolve ([equations], [variables])

solves simultaneous linear equations for the list of variables.

(%i1)   linsolve([x+y=–1, 3*x–y=–11], [x,y]);

(%o1)   [x=–3,y=2]

linechar

it is the prefix for the labels of intermediate expressions. Default value is'%t'. It can be changed with this function.

(%i1)   a:((n–r)^3);

(a) $(n–r)^3$

(%i2)   b:expand(a);

(b) $–r^3+3nr^2–3n^2r+n^3$

(%i3)   ldisp (a,b);   /* Refer **ldisp** function */

(%t3) $(n–r)^3$ /* default linecahr: 't' */

(%t4) $–r^3+3nr^2–3n^2r+n^3$

(%o4)   [%t3,%t4]

/* Restart wxMaxima with line character as %u */

(%i1)   linechar:%u;

(linechar)   %u

(%i2)   a:((n–r)^3);

(a) $(n–r)^3$

(%i3)   b:expand(a);

(b) $–r^3+3nr^2–3n^2r+n^3$

(%i4)   ldisp (a,b);

(%u4) $(n-r)^3$ /*linechar is changed to 'u' from 't' */
(%u5) $-r^3+3nr^2-3n^2r+n^3$
(%o5)   [%u4,%u5]

list_correlations(matrix)

returns a list of correlations for the matrix. To use this function first call, **load ("descriptive")$**.

(%i1)   load ("descriptive")$.
(%i2)   x:matrix([2.1,6.5], [3.1,8.5], [3.4,9.1], [5.2,12.7],
               [6.5,15.3], [8.2,18.7], [8.5,19.3]);

$$(x) \quad \begin{bmatrix} 2.1 & 6.5 \\ 3.1 & 8.5 \\ 3.4 & 9.1 \\ 5.2 & 12.7 \\ 6.5 & 15.3 \\ 8.2 & 18.7 \\ 8.5 & 19.3 \end{bmatrix}$$

(%i3)   fpprintprec : 4$ /* to restrict number of digits */
(%i4)   list_correlations (x);

$$(\%o4) \quad [\begin{bmatrix} 6.066 \ 10^{13} & -3.033 \ 10^{13} \\ -3.033 \ 10^{13} & 1.516 \ 10^{13} \end{bmatrix}, [1.0,1.0], \begin{bmatrix} -1.0 & 1.0 \\ 1.0 & -1.0 \end{bmatrix}]$$

(%i5)   y:list_correlations (x)$

(%i6)   y[2];   /* y may have 1 or 2 or 3 index only */

$$(\%o6) \quad \begin{bmatrix} -1.0 & 1.0 \\ 1.0 & -1.0 \end{bmatrix}$$

linsolvewarn

if linsolvewarn is set to true, the function 'linsolve' prints a message "Dependent equations eliminated".

list_matrix_entries (matrix)

returns a list containing the elements of the matrix.

(%i1)   x: matrix ([j, i^2], [u/i, j*k]);

(x)
$$\begin{bmatrix} j & i^2 \\ \frac{u}{i} & jk \end{bmatrix}$$

(%i2)   list_matrix_entries(x);

(%o2) $[j, i^2, \frac{u}{i}, jk]$

list_nc_monomials (polynomial)

returns a list of the non-commutative monomials in a polynomial. To use this function first call, **load(affine)$**.

(%i1)   load(affine)$

(%i2)   list_nc_monomials ((a*x^–i)+((2*b)^3)+(–3*c*x^-u)

                       +(–4*x*d));

(%o2)   [1,d,a,c]

listarray (array)

returns a list of the elements in the array.

(%i1)   array (k, 5);   /* array named 'k' for 5 elements */
(%o1)   k
(%i2)   fillarray (k, [j/i, x*i, i/j,(x+i),j*y]);
(%o2)   k
(%i3)   listarray(k);

(%o3) $[\frac{j}{i}, ix, \frac{i}{j}, x + i, jy, jy]$

(%i4)   arrayinfo (k);
(%o4)   [declared,1,[5]]

listconstvars   listofvars

if listconstvars is set to true, the list by listofvars contains constant variables, like %e, %pi (or any variables declared as constant) and their values are returned. Default value: false

(%i1)   listconstvars:true;
(listconstvars)true
(%i2)   listofvars([%pi]);

(%o2)   π
(%i3)   %,numer;
(%o3)   [3.141592653589793]
(%i4)   listconstvars:false;
(listconstvars)true
(%i5)   listofvars([%pi]);
(%o5)   []
(%i6)   %,numer;
(%o6)   []

listdummyvars   listofvars

if listdummyvars is false, then dummy variables will not be included in the list returned by listofvars. Default value: true

(%i1)   listdummyvars: false;
(listdummyvars)false
(%i2)   listofvars ('sum(f(i), i, 2, k));
(%o2)   [k]   /* Note: 2 is constant */
(%i3)   listdummyvars: true;
(listdummyvars)true
(%i4)   listofvars ('sum(f(i), i, 2, k));
(%o4)   [i,k]   /* 'i' and 'k' are variables*/

listify (set)

returns a list for the given set.   Refer: full_listify

(%i1)   listify ({b, v, n, –j, i, k, s –g});
(%o1)   [b,i,–j,k,n,s,–g,v]

listofvars (expression)   Refer: **listconstvars**, **listdummyvars**

returns a list of the variables in the given expression.

(%i1)   listofvars ('sum(f(i), i, 2, k));
(%o1)   [i,k]   /* 'i' and 'k' are variables*/

listp (expression)

returns true, if expression is a list or else it returns false.

(%i2)	a:{b, v, n, –j, i, k, s –g}$ b:listify (a)$
(%i4)	listp (a);listp (b); /* Refer: listify */
(%o3)	false
(%o4)	true

lmxchar

changes the character displayed as the left delimiter for a matrix from the default '['.

(%i1)	x: matrix ([j, i^2], [u/i, j*k]);

$$(x) \qquad \begin{bmatrix} j & i^2 \\ \dfrac{u}{i} & jk \end{bmatrix}$$

(%i2)	lmxchar: "|"$
(%i3)	x: matrix ([j, i^2], [u/i, j*k]);

$$(x) \qquad \begin{bmatrix} j & i^2 \\ \dfrac{u}{i} & jk \end{bmatrix}$$

load (package)

loads the required package.

(%i1)	load(interpol); /* interpolation package */
(%o1)	"C:\maxima-5.38.1\share\maxima\5.38.1_5_gdf93b 7b_dirty\share\numeric\interpol.mac"

log (x)

returns the natural (base exp) logarithm of 'x'.

(%i1)	log(2),numer;
(%o1)	0.6931471805599453
(%i2)	diff(log(x),x);
(%o2)	$\dfrac{1}{x}$

log_gamma (x)

returns the natural logarithm of the gamma function for 'x'.

(%i1)   log_gamma (3),numer;

(%o1)   0.6931471805599454

logcontract (expression)

returns the subexpressions by transformation and simplification.

(%i1)   a*log(g)–a*log(r);

(%o1)   alog(g)–alog(r)

(%i2)   logcontract(%);

(%o2) $a \log\left(\frac{g}{r}\right)$

logexpand

if it is set to true, then expressions like log(a^b) will simplified to b*log(a) and if it is set to 'all', then log(a*b) will simplified to log(a)+log(b). If it is set to 'super', then log(a/b) will simplified to log(a)–log(b). Default value: true

(%i1)   log(a^2), logexpand=false;

(%o1) $\log(a^2)$

(%i2)   log(a^2), logexpand=true;

(%o2)   2log(a)

(%i3)   log(a^2), logexpand=all;

(%o3)   2log(a)

(%i4)   log(a*2), logexpand=all;

(%o4)   log(a)+log(2)

(%i5)   log(a/2);

(%o5) $\log\left(\frac{a}{2}\right)$

(%i6)   log(a/2), logexpand=super;

(%o6)   log(a)–log(2)

lognegint

if it is set to true then it follows, $\log(-n) \rightarrow \log(n)+\%i*\%pi$; and its default value is false.

(%i1)	log(–2);
(%o1)	log(–2)
(%i2)	%,lognegint=true;
(%o2)	log(2)+%i%pi

logsimp

If it is set to true then power of %e for 'log' values will be simplified. Default value: true

(%i1)	exp(log(a+b)), logsimp:false;
(%o1)	$\%_0^{\log(b+a)}$
(%i2)	exp(log(a+b)), logsimp:true;
(%o2)	b+a

lopow (expression, x)

returns the lowest exponent of 'x' in the expression.

(%i1)	lopow ((a^–3)+(a^2),a);
(%o1)	–3

lowercasep (character)

returns true if character is lowercase.

(%i1)	lowercasep ("w");
(%o1)	true
(%i2)	lowercasep ("W");
(%o2)	false

lratsubst ([substitution], expression)

returns the expression after substitution. To use this function first call, **load ("lrats")$**.

(%i1)	load ("lrats");
(%o1)	"C:\maxima-5.38.1\share\maxima\5.38.1_5_gdf93b7 b_dirty\share\simplification\lrats.mac"
(%i2)	lratsubst ([a^n = b, g/n = b, 1/r=i], a^n + g/n–1/r);
(%o2)	2b–i

lreduce (f, [List])

extends the binary function 'f' to the list.

(%i1)   lreduce (f, [n,j]);

(%o1)   f(n,j)

lsquares_estimates ([List], [Variables], Equation, [Coefficients])

returns the least square best fit coefficients from the given list or matrix for the proposed polynomial equation containing variables, which are given as list. To use this function first call, **load(lsquares)$**.

(%i1)   load(lsquares)$

(%i2)   k:matrix([1.0,15.6],[2.0,17.5],[3.0,36.6],[4.0,43.8],
               [5.0,58.2],[6.0,61.6],[7.0,65.2],[8.0,72.6],[9.0,98.9]);

(k)
$$\begin{bmatrix} 1.0 & 15.6 \\ 2.0 & 17.5 \\ 3.0 & 36.6 \\ 4.0 & 43.8 \\ 5.0 & 58.2 \\ 6.0 & 61.6 \\ 7.0 & 65.2 \\ 8.0 & 72.6 \\ 9.0 & 98.9 \end{bmatrix}$$

/* List of independent and its dependent values are given as matrix*/

(%i3)   lsquares_estimates(k, [x, y], y = a*x^3 + b*x^2+c*x+d,
               [a,b,c,d]);   /* 3rd order polynomial curve fit */

(%o3) $[[a = \frac{497}{2376}, b = -\frac{607}{198}, c = \frac{52411}{2376}, d = -\frac{145}{18}]]$

(%i4)   %,numer;

(%o4)   [[a=0.2091750841750842,b=−3.065656565656566,
               c=22.05850168350169,d=−8.055555555555555]]

Based on the above data, the 3rd polynomial curve fit (trendline option) using spread sheet is sketched below:

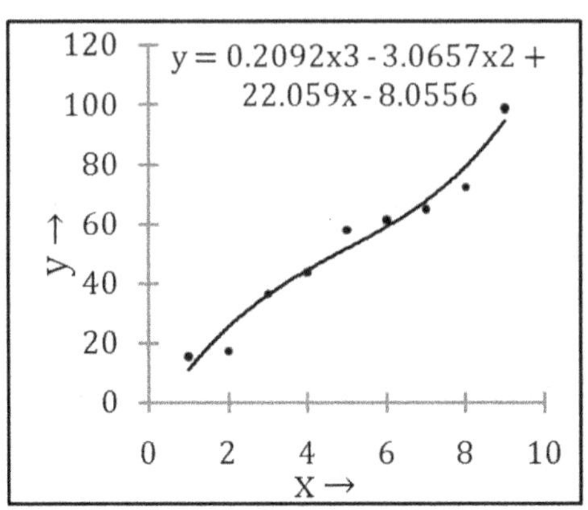

lsquares_mse ([list], [variables], equation)

returns the mean square error, for the equation with the variables for the list. To use this function first call, **load(lsquares)$** .

(%i1)   load(lsquares)$

(%i2)   k:matrix([1.0,15.6],[2.0,17.5],[3.0,36.6],[4.0,43.8],

     [5.0,58.2],[6.0,61.6],[7.0,65.2],[8.0,72.6],[9.0,98.9]);

(k)
$$\begin{bmatrix} 1.0 & 15.6 \\ 2.0 & 17.5 \\ 3.0 & 36.6 \\ 4.0 & 43.8 \\ 5.0 & 58.2 \\ 6.0 & 61.6 \\ 7.0 & 65.2 \\ 8.0 & 72.6 \\ 9.0 & 98.9 \end{bmatrix}$$

(%i3)   lsquares_mse (k, [x, y], x+y = a*x^3 + b*x^2+c*x+d);

(%o3) $\displaystyle\sum_{i=1}^{9} \frac{\left(k_{i,2}-ak_3^{i,1}-bk_2^{i,1}-ck_{i,1}+k_{i,1}-d\right)^2}{9}$

lsquares_estimates_exact (mean square error, coefficient)

returns the coefficients for the given data from mean square error. To use this function first call, **load(lsquares)$**.

Refer:	lsquares_mse (List, [Variables], Equation)
(%i1)	load(lsquares);
(%o1)	"C:\maxima-5.38.1\share\maxima\5.38.1_5_gdf93b7
	b_dirty\share\lsquares\lsquares.mac"
(%i2)	k:matrix([1.0,15.6],[2.0,17.5],[3.0,36.6],[4.0,43.8],
	[5.0,58.2],[6.0,61.6],[7.0,65.2],[8.0,72.6],[9.0,98.9])$
	/ * Refer: 'lsquares_mse' for this data matrix output */
(%i3)	lsquares_mse (k, [x, y], x+y = a*x^3 + b*x^2+c*x+d);
(%i4)	lsquares_estimates_exact (k, [a, b, c, d]);

$$(\%o3) \qquad \sum_{i=1}^{9} \frac{\left(k_{i,2}-ak_3^{i,1}-bk_2^{i,1}-ck_{i,1}+k_{i,1}-d\right)^2}{9}$$

lsum (expression, variable, List)

returns the sum of expression for the list from the variable.

(%i1)	lsum (x*j, j, [−n, k, m]);
(%o1)	−nx+mx+kx
(%i2)	lsum (2*j, j, [8,7]);
(%o2)	30 /* (2×8) + (2×7) */

ltreillis (integer, length)

returns the list of partitions for integer, with the specified length.

(%i1)	ltreillis (8, 2);
resolvante	generale

NOTE: To compile the system doload("sym/compile");

0 errors, 0 warnings

(%o1)	[[8,0],[7,1],[6,2],[5,3],[4,4]]
(%i2)	ltreillis (4, 5);
(%o2)	[[4,0,0,0,0],[3,1,0,0,0],[2,2,0,0,0],[2,1,1,0,0],[1,1,1,1,0]]
(%i3)	ltreillis (3, 4);
(%o3)	[[3,0,0,0],[2,1,0,0],[1,1,1,0]]

lu_factor (square matrix, field)

return LU factorization for the square matrix for the specified field Different fields are available. Some of the important fields are:

i) generalring:for Maxima expressions

ii) floatfield:for floating point numbers

iii) complexfield: for complex floating point numbers

iv) rationalfield: for rational numbers

(%i1)   k:matrix([x,y],[2,z]);

(%o1) $\begin{bmatrix} x & y \\ 2 & z \end{bmatrix}$

(%i2)   lu_factor (k, generalring);

(%o2) $[\begin{bmatrix} x & y \\ \frac{2}{x} & z-\frac{2y}{x} \end{bmatrix}, [1,2], generalring]$

(%i3)   j:matrix([1,2],[−4,−3]);

(%o3) $\begin{bmatrix} 1 & 2 \\ -4 & -3 \end{bmatrix}$

(%i4)   lu_factor (j, floatfield);

(%o4) $[\begin{bmatrix} -0.25 & 1.25 \\ -4.0 & -3.0 \end{bmatrix}, [2,1],$

floatfield,5.6,7.437500000000002]

lucas (n)

returns the nth Lucas number.

$$L_n = L_{n-1}+L_{n-2}\ \text{if}\ n>1;\ L_n = 2\ \text{if}\ n = 0;\ L_n = 1\ \text{if}\ n = 1$$

n	0	1	2	3	4	5	6	7	8	9	10	11
L_n	2	1	3	4	7	11	18	29	47	76	123	199

(%i1)   lucas (21)

(%o1)   24476

::=   macro function definition operator

defines a macro function

(%i1)	x:k;
(x)	k
(%i2)	x::2;
(%o2)	2
(%i3)	k;
(%o3)	2
(%i4)	x(k)::=x^k;
(%o4)	$x(k)::=x^k$
(%i5)	x(3);
(%o5)	8
(%i6)	x(k):=x^k; /* Refer functional operator */
(%o6)	$x(k):=x^k$
(%i7)	x(3);
(%o7)	k^3

make_array (type, n)

returns a Lisp array with 'n' indices with type as: 'any', 'flonum', 'fixnum', 'hashed', ' functional'.

(%i1)	k : make_array (fixnum, 5);
(%o1)	{Array: #(0 0 0 0 0)}
(%i2)	k[3]:2;
(%o2)	2
(%i3)	k;
(%o3)	{Array: #(0 0 0 2 0)}
(%i1)	k : make_array (flonum, 5);
(%o1)	{Array: #(0.0 0.0 0.0 0.0 0.0)}
(%i2)	k[3]:2.0;
(%o2)	2.0
(%i3)	k;
(%o3)	{Array: #(0.0 0.0 0.02.0 0.0)}

make_random_state (n)

it represents state of the random number generator and comprises 67, 32 bit words. make_random_state (n) returns a new random state object from an integer 'n' modulo ^. make_random_state (true) returns a new random state object, using computer clock time. make_random_state (false) returns a cop of the current state of the random number generator.

```
(%i1)        make_random_state (2);
(%o1)        "#S(MT19937:RANDOM-STATE:STATE
             #(0  2567483615  624  2  3624866507  846688490  2733819477
             1447939927         2751582963523383323         3998955438
             1552125001         4687709293174827423          721042428
             3535242872393824706024221981 77               2908759646
             3086638684 3470362919 4130561862
             1461945164 1969357429 3290893273 2478135064
             2883471193 442423807... ...))    /* continued*/
```

make_string_input_stream ("string", start, end)

returns parts of string from start to end.

```
(%i1)        make_string_input_stream("wxMaxima", 2);
(%o1)        Stream [CHARACTER]
(%i2)        readchar(%o1);
(%o2)        x
```

make_string_output_stream ()

returns an output stream that accepts characters and returned by the function get_output_stream_string.

```
(%i1)        make_string_output_stream();
(%o1)        Stream [CHARACTER]
(%i3)        printf(%o1, "wx")$printf(%o1, "Maxima")$
(%i4)        get_output_stream_string(%o1);
(%o4)        wxMaxima
```

makefact (expression)

transforms binomial, gamma and beta functions in the expression into factorials.

```
(%i1)        gamma(3*x);
(%o1)        Γ(3x)
```

(%i2)   makefact (%); /* Refer: makegamma (expression) */
(%o2)   (3x–1)!

makegamma (expression)   Refer: **makefact (expression)**

transforms binomial, factorial, beta functions in the expression into gamma functions.

(%i1)   factorial(3*x–1);
(%o1)   (3x–1)!
(%i2)   makegamma(%);
(%o2) $\Gamma(3x)$

makelist (expression, x, x_minimum, x_maximum, step)

returns a list for expression from x_minimum to x_maximum.

(%i1)   makelist (x^2, x, 2, 6);
(%o1)   [4,9,16,25,36]
(%i2)   makelist (n=–r/2, r, [a, –2*b, c/2]);
(%o2) $[n = -\frac{a}{2}, n = b, n = -\frac{c}{4}]$
(%i3)   makelist (n=–r/2, n, [a, –2*b, c/2]);
(%o3) $[a = -\frac{r}{2}, -2b = -\frac{r}{2}, \frac{c}{2} = -\frac{r}{2}]$

makeOrders ([x,y], [order])

returns a list of all powers for 'x' and 'y' from the order list. To use this function first call, **load("makeOrders")$**.

(%i1)   load("makeOrders")$
(%i2)   makeOrders([x,y],[1,2]);
(%o2)   [[0,0],[0,1],[0,2],[1,0],[1,1],[1,2]]
                /* $[x^0,y^0]$, $[x^0,y^1]$,$[x^0,y^2]$,$[x^1,y^0]$,$[x^1,y^1]$,$[x^1,y^2]$ */

makeset (expression, [variable], [sets])

returns a set from the expression for a list of variables and sets.

(%i1)   makeset (k*j, [k], [[–a/j*n], [n*j*b], [–c/n*3]]);
(%o1) $\{-\frac{3cj}{n}, -an, bj^2 n\}$
(%i2)   makeset (k*j, [k], [[–a*c], [b]]);
(%o2)   {bj,–acj}

map ("function", [expression_1], ..., [expression_n])

returns an expression for the function whose operator is same as that of expression_1, ..., expression_n.

(%i1)	map("*",[a,b],[c^-n,j]);
(%o1)	$[\frac{a}{c^n}, bj]$
(%i2)	map(f,a*c^-n+b*j);
(%o2)	$f(bj) + f\left(\frac{a}{c^n}\right)$
(%i3)	map("=",[a,b],[c^-n,j]);
(%o3)	$[a = \frac{1}{c^n}, b = j]$

maplist (function, expression_1, ..., expression_n)

returns a list of the applications for the function whose operator is same as that of expression_1, ..., expression_n.

(%i1)	maplist("*",[a,b],[c^-n,j]);
(%o1)	$[\frac{a}{c^n}, bj]$
(%i2)	maplist (f,a*c^-n+b*j);
(%o2)	$f(bj) + f\left(\frac{a}{c^n}\right)$
	/* Refer: map (function, expression_1, ..., expression_n) */
(%i3)	maplist("=",[a,b],[c^-n,j]);
(%o3)	$[a = \frac{1}{c^n}, b = j]$

mapprint

if it is set to true, information messages from map, maplist, as well as fullmap functions are shown. If it is set to false, these messages are suppressed. Default value: true

(%i1)	mapprint:true;
	(mapprint)true;
(%i2)	maplist("*",[a,b,d],[c^-n,j]);

map: arguments must be the same length.

-- an error. To debug this try: debugmode(true);

mat_cond (matrix, 1 or inf)   mat_norm (matrix, frobenius)

returnsp-norm of the matrix. The allowed values for p are 1, inf, and frobenius (Frobenius matrix norm). Refer: mat_norm.

(%i1)	matrix ([1,2], [0,3]);

$$(\%o1) \quad \begin{bmatrix} 1 & 2 \\ 0 & 3 \end{bmatrix}$$

(%i2)	mat_cond (%, 1);
(%o2)	5
(%i5)	matrix ([x,b], [a,c]);

$$(\%o5) \quad \begin{bmatrix} x & b \\ a & c \end{bmatrix}$$

(%i6)	mat_cond (%, 1);

0 errors, 0 warnings

$$(\%o6) \quad \max[|c| + |b|, |x| + |a|]$$

$$\max\left[\frac{|b|}{\left|\frac{ab}{x}-c\right||x|} + \frac{1}{\left|\frac{ab}{x}-c\right|}, \frac{\left|\frac{ab}{\left|c-\frac{ab}{x}\right|x}+1\right|}{|x|} + \frac{|a|}{\left|\frac{ab}{x}-c\right||x|} \right]$$

(%i3)	matrix ([2,1], [0,3]);

$$(\%o3) \quad \begin{bmatrix} 2 & 1 \\ 0 & 3 \end{bmatrix}$$

(%i4)	mat_cond (%, 1);
(%o4)	2

mat_fullunblocker (matrix)   mat_unblocker (matrix)

unblock the matrix for the block matrices in one level or all levels.

(%i1)	x:matrix ([b, a], [d, c]);

$$(x) \quad \begin{bmatrix} b & a \\ d & c \end{bmatrix}$$

(%i2)	y:matrix ([i, 2], [-3, -1]);

$$(y) \quad \begin{bmatrix} i & 2 \\ -3 & -1 \end{bmatrix}$$

(%i3)	matrix ([x,y]);

$$(\%o3) \quad \begin{bmatrix} \begin{bmatrix} b & a \\ d & c \end{bmatrix} \begin{bmatrix} i & 2 \\ -3 & -1 \end{bmatrix} \end{bmatrix}$$

(%i4)   mat_fullunblocker (%);

(%o4) $\begin{bmatrix} b & a & i & 2 \\ d & c & -3 & -1 \end{bmatrix}$

mat_function (function, matrix)

returns an analytic function for the matrix. To use this function first call, load("diag")$.

(%i1)   load("diag");

(%o1)   "C:\maxima-5.38.1\share\maxima\5.38.1_5_gdf93b7

                b_dirty\share\contrib\diag.mac"

(%i2)   x: matrix ([2,1],[0,-1]);

(x) $\begin{bmatrix} 2 & 1 \\ 0 & -1 \end{bmatrix}$

(%i3)   ratsimp (mat_function (exp, v*x)[1]);

(%o3) $[\%e^{2v}, \frac{\%e^{-v}[\%e^{3v}-1]}{3}]$

mat_norm (matrix, 1 or inf)   mat_norm (matrix, frobenius)

return p-norm of the matrix. The allowed values for p are 1, inf, and frobenius (Frobenius matrix norm).

(%i1)   matrix ([x,b], [a,c]);

(%o1) $\begin{bmatrix} x & b \\ a & c \end{bmatrix}$

(%i2)   mat_norm (%, 1);   /* Refer: mat_cond */
0 errors, 0 warnings

(%o2) $\max[|c|+|b|,|x|+|a|\,]$

(%i3)   mat_norm (%o1, frobenius);

(%o3) $\sqrt{x^2 + c^2 + b^2 + a^2}$

mat_trace (matrix)

return the trace of the square matrix.

(%i1)   matrix ([x,b,j], [a,c,d],[f,e,i]);

(%o1) $\begin{bmatrix} x & b & j \\ a & c & d \\ f & e & i \end{bmatrix}$

(%i2)   mat_trace (%);

(%o2)   x+i+c
(%i3)   matrix ([2,-1,-3], [4,5,3],[6,9,8]);

(%o3)
$$\begin{bmatrix} 2 & -1 & -3 \\ 4 & 5 & 3 \\ 6 & 9 & 8 \end{bmatrix}$$

(%i4)   mat_trace (%);
(%o4)   15

matchdeclare (variable_1, predicate_1, ..., variable_n, predicate_n)
defrule(function, predicate expression, ["name" = predicate _variable]

connects a predicates with variables and used with **defrule** function.

(%i1)   matchdeclare (a, integerp, c, atom);
(%o1)   done
(%i2)   defrule (x, c^a, ["num" = a, "string" = c]);/*definerule*/
(%o2)   x:c^a →[num =a, string=c]
(%i3)   x (b^2);
(%o3)   [num=2,string=b]

matchfix (left_delimiter, right_delimiter)

declares left and right delimiters.

(%i1)   matchfix ("a", "9");
(%o1)   a
(%i2)   a 1,2,3,4,5,6 9;
(%o2)   a1,2,3,4,5,69

matrix ([row_1], ..., [row_n])

constructs a matrix from list of rows row_1, ..., row_n.

(%i1)   matrix ([x,b,j], [a,c,d],[f,e,i]);

(%o1)
$$\begin{bmatrix} x & b & j \\ a & c & d \\ f & e & i \end{bmatrix}$$

Arithmetic operations can be done with matrix.

(%i1)   matrix ([x,b,j], [2,-c,i],[-3,e,-i])$

(%i2)   %/(3*i)+%;

$$(\%o2) \quad \begin{bmatrix} \dfrac{x}{3i}+x & \dfrac{b}{3i}+b & \dfrac{j}{3i}+j \\[2mm] \dfrac{2}{3i}+2 & -\dfrac{c}{3i}-c & i+\dfrac{1}{3} \\[2mm] -\dfrac{1}{i}-3 & \dfrac{e}{3i}+e & -i-\dfrac{1}{3} \end{bmatrix}$$

matrix_size (matrix)

returns a list of number for rows and columns in the matrix.

(%i1)   x: matrix ([2*m, 6^k, j^2], [−u/g, j*k, −g*r]);

$$(x) \quad \begin{bmatrix} 2m & 6^k & j^2 \\[2mm] -\dfrac{u}{g} & jk & -gr \end{bmatrix}$$

(%i2)   matrix_size (%)

0 errors, 0 warnings

(%o2)   [2,3]

matrixexp (matrix)

returns the matrix exponential for square matrix.

(%i1)   x: matrix ([0, 1], [1, 0]);

$$(x) \quad \begin{bmatrix} 0 & 1 \\ 1 & 0 \end{bmatrix}$$

(%i2)   matrixexp(x)

0 errors, 0 warnings

$$(\%o2) \quad \begin{bmatrix} \dfrac{\%e^{-1}\left(\%e^2+1\right)}{2} & \dfrac{\%e^{-1}\left(\%e^2-1\right)}{2} \\[3mm] \dfrac{\%e^{-1}\left(\%e^2-1\right)}{2} & \dfrac{\%e^{-1}\left(\%e^2+1\right)}{2} \end{bmatrix}$$

matrixmap ("function", matrix)

returns a matrix with function.

(%i1)   matrix([a,b],[c^−n,j]);

$$(\%o1) \quad \begin{bmatrix} a & b \\ \dfrac{1}{c^n} & j \end{bmatrix}$$

(%i2)   matrixmap("*",[a,b],[c^−n,j]);

$$(\%o2) \quad \left[\dfrac{a}{c^n}, bj\right]$$

matrixp (matrix)

returns true for matrix form.

(%i1)	matrixmap("*",[a,b],[c^–n,j]); /* Refer: matrixmap */

$$(\%o1) \qquad [\tfrac{a}{c^n}, bj]$$

(%i2)	matrix (%o1);

$$(\%o2) \qquad \begin{bmatrix} \frac{a}{c^n} & bj \end{bmatrix}$$

(%i3)	matrixp (%);
(%o4)	true

mattrace (matrix)

return the trace of the square matrix. To use this function first call, **load ("nchrpl")$**.

(%i1)	load ("nchrpl")$
(%i2)	matrix ([x,b,j], [a,c,d],[f,e,i]);

$$(\%o2) \qquad \begin{bmatrix} x & b & j \\ a & c & d \\ f & e & i \end{bmatrix}$$

(%i3)	mat_trace (%);

0 errors, 0 warnings

(%o3)	x+i+c
(%i4)	matrix ([2,–1,–3], [4,5,3],[6,9,8]);

$$(\%o4) \qquad \begin{bmatrix} 2 & -1 & -3 \\ 4 & 5 & 3 \\ 6 & 9 & 8 \end{bmatrix}$$

(%i5)	mat_trace (%);
(%o5)	15

max (expression)   lmax ([list] or {set}])

function 'max' returns the maximum from the expression whereas the function 'lmax' returns the maximum for a list or set.

(%i1)	max(1,21,–12,2,3,4,13);
(%o1)	21
(%i2)	lmax([1,22,–12,2,3,4,13]);
(%o2)	22

maxima_tempdir

returns the directory for temporary files.

(%i1)   maxima_tempdir

(%o1)   C:/Users/"directory_name"

maxima_userdir

returns the directory for Maxima and Lisp files.

(%i1)   maxima_tempdir

(%o1)   C:/Users/"directory_name"/maxima

maximize_lp(function, [equation])

minimize_lp (function, [equation])

returns minimized or maximized linear objective function for a list of linear equations. If the problem is not bounded, it returns "Problem not bounded!". To use this function first call, **load(simplex)$**.

(%i1)   load(simplex)$

(%i2)   minimize_lp(x+y, [x+y=−1, 3*x−y=−11]);

(%o2)   [−1,[y=2,x=−3]]

(%i2)   maximize_lp(x+y, [x+y=−1, 3*x−y<−11]);

(%o2) $[-1, [y = -\frac{7}{2}, x = \frac{5}{2}]]$

maybe (expression)

returns true or falsefor the predicated expression.

(%i1)   k:2$n:−1$

(%i2)   maybe (k > n);

(%o2)   true

(%i3)   maybe (k = n);

(%o3)   false

(%i4)   maybe (k < n);

(%o4)   false

mean ([list])

returns mean value for the list. To use this function first call, **load (descriptive)$**.

(%i1)   load (descriptive)$

(%i2)   a:[x+2,x−1,x−3,x*4]$

(%i3)   mean(a);

(%o3) $\dfrac{7x-2}{4}$

(%i4)   [x^2,x–1,x–3,x/4]$
(%i5)   mean(%);

(%o5) $\dfrac{x^2+\frac{9x}{4}-4}{4}$

(%i6)   mean([2.5,–3.1,–1.3,6.2,2.8,9.2]);
(%o6)   2.716666666666666

mean_deviation ([list]or [matrix])

returns the statistical mean deviation for the list. To use this function first call,
load (descriptive)$.

(%i1)   load (descriptive);
(%o1)   "C:\maxima-5.38.1\share\maxima\5.38.1_5_gdf93b7
               b_dirty\share\descriptive\descriptive.mac"
(%i2)   matrix([1.0,15.6],[2.0,17.5],[3.0,36.6],[4.0,43.8],
               [5.0,58.2],[6.0,61.6],[7.0,65.2],[8.0,72.6],[9.0,98.9]);

(%o2) $\begin{bmatrix} 1.0 & 15.6 \\ 2.0 & 17.5 \\ 3.0 & 36.6 \\ 4.0 & 43.8 \\ 5.0 & 58.2 \\ 6.0 & 61.6 \\ 7.0 & 65.2 \\ 8.0 & 72.6 \\ 9.0 & 98.9 \end{bmatrix}$

(%i3)   mean_deviation (%);
(%o3)   [2.222222222222222,21.19753086419753]
(%i4)   [x+2,x–1,x–3]$
(%i5)   mean_deviation (%o4);

(%o5) $\dfrac{\frac{3x-2}{3}-x+6}{3}$

mean_discrete_uniform (integer)

returns the mean discrete uniform for a positive integer. To use this function first call, **load(distrib)$**.

(%i1)   load(distrib)$

(%i2)   mean_discrete_uniform (8);

(%o2) $\frac{9}{2}$ /* $\frac{9}{2}$ (8+1) */

mean_exp (n)

returns the mean exponential form>0. To use this function first call,

load(distrib)$.

(%i1)   load(distrib)$

(%i2)   mean_exp(8);

(%o2) $\frac{1}{8}$ /*mean_exp($\frac{1}{8}$) returns 8 */

mean_f (m,n)

returns the mean for 'F' random variable with m>0, n>2. To use this function first call, **load(distrib)$**.

(%i1)   load(distrib)$

(%i2)   mean_f (1,10);

(%o2) $\frac{5}{4}$

mean_gamma (m,n)

Returns the mean of a Gamma with m,n>0. To use this function first call, **load(distrib)$**.

(%i1)   load(distrib)$

(%i2)   mean_gamma (2,1);

(%o2)   2

mean_hypergeometric (n1,n2,n)

returns the mean of a discrete for non-negative integers with the condition n<=n1+n2. To use this function first call, **load(distrib)$**.

(%i1)   load(distrib)$

(%i2)   mean_hypergeometric (1,2,1);

(%o2) $\frac{1}{3}$

median ([list] or [matrix])

returns the statistical median (sample is ordered and if the sample size is odd, the median is the central value, otherwise it is the mean of the two central values) for list or matrix. To use this function first call, **load (descriptive)\$**.

(%i1)   load (descriptive)\$

(%i2)   matrix([1.0,15.6],[2.0,17.5],[3.0,36.6],[4.0,43.8],

      [5.0,58.2],[6.0,61.6],[7.0,65.2],[8.0,72.6]);

$$
(\%o2) \quad \begin{bmatrix} 1.0 & 15.6 \\ 2.0 & 17.5 \\ 3.0 & 36.6 \\ 4.0 & 43.8 \\ 5.0 & 58.2 \\ 6.0 & 61.6 \\ 7.0 & 65.2 \\ 8.0 & 72.6 \end{bmatrix}
$$

(%i3)   median (%);

(%o3)   [4.5,51.0] $/* [\frac{4.0+5.0}{2},\frac{43.8+58.2}{2}] */$

(%i4)   [x+2,x+1,x+3,x+6]\$

(%i5)   median (%o4);

(%o5) $\dfrac{2x+5}{2}$

median_deviation([list] or [matrix])

returns the statistical median deviation for list or matrix. To use this function first call, **load (descriptive)\$**.

(%i1)   load (descriptive)\$

(%i2)   matrix([1.0,15.6],[2.0,17.5],[3.0,36.6],[4.0,43.8],

      [5.0,58.2],[6.0,61.6],[7.0,65.2],[8.0,72.6]);

$$
(\%o2) \quad \begin{bmatrix} 1.0 & 15.6 \\ 2.0 & 17.5 \\ 3.0 & 36.6 \\ 4.0 & 43.8 \\ 5.0 & 58.2 \\ 6.0 & 61.6 \\ 7.0 & 65.2 \\ 8.0 & 72.6 \end{bmatrix}
$$

(%i3)   median_deviation (%);

(%o3)   [2.0,14.3]

(%i4)   [a,b,c,d]\$

(%i5)	median (%o4);
(%o5)	$\dfrac{c+b}{2}$
(%i6)	median_deviation (%o4);
(%o6)	$\dfrac{\left|\frac{c+b}{2}-c\right|+\left|\frac{c+b}{2}-b\right|}{2}$

member (member, [list] or {set})

returns true, if member is in the list or set or else it returns false.

(%i1)	member (a, [b, c, 2]);
(%o1)	false
(%i2)	member (b, {b, c, 2});
(%o2)	true

min (expression)   lmin ([list] or {set}])

function 'min' returns the minimum from the expression whereas the function 'lmin' returns the minimum for a list or set.

(%i1)	min(1,21,–13,2,3,4,13);
(%o1)	–13
(%i2)	lmin([1,22,–1,2,3,4,13]);
(%o2)	–1

minf

minf represents real negative infinity$(-\infty)$.

minimalPoly (list)

returns the minimal polynomial of the Jordan matrix list. To use this function first call, **load("diag")$.**

(%i1)	load("diag")$
(%i2)	x: matrix ([2, 4], [3, 8]);
(x)	$\begin{bmatrix} 2 & 4 \\ 3 & 8 \end{bmatrix}$
(%i3)	jordan (x); /* Refer jordan(matrix) */
(%o3)	$[[5 - \sqrt{21}, 1], [\sqrt{21} + 5,1]]$
(%i4)	minimalPoly(%);
(%o4)	$\left(x - \sqrt{21} - 5\right)\left(x + \sqrt{21} - 5\right)$

(%i1)   load("diag")$

(%i2)   x: matrix ([a, b], [c, d]);

(x) $\begin{bmatrix} a & b \\ c & d \end{bmatrix}$

(%i3)   jordan (x);   /* Refer jordan(matrix) */

(%o3) $\left[\left[-\frac{\sqrt{d^2-2ad+4bc+a^2}-d-a}{2},1\right],\left[\frac{\sqrt{d^2-2ad+4bc+a^2}+d+a}{2},1\right]\right]$

(%i4)   minimalPoly(%);

(%o4) $\left(x+\frac{\sqrt{d^2-2ad+4bc+a^2}-d-a}{2}\right)\left(x-\frac{\sqrt{d^2-2ad+4bc+a^2}+d+a}{2}\right)$

minor (matrix, row, column)

returns the matrix with the specified row and column removed.

(%i1)   x: matrix ([1,2,3,4], [5,6,7,8]);

(x) $\begin{bmatrix} 1 & 2 & 3 & 4 \\ 5 & 6 & 7 & 8 \end{bmatrix}$

(%i2)   minor (x, 1, 3);

(%o2)   [5,6,8]

(%i3)   matrix ([i,j,k], [a,b,c], [n,m,i]);

(%o3) $\begin{bmatrix} i & j & k \\ a & b & c \\ n & m & i \end{bmatrix}$

(%i4)   minor (%, 1, 3);

(%o4) $\begin{bmatrix} a & b \\ n & m \end{bmatrix}$

mkdir (directory)

creates directory

mnewton ([functions], [variables],[initial approximation])

returns solution for the list of non-linear functions using the Newton method for the list of variables from the list of initial approximations. To use this function first call, **load("mnewton")$**.

(%i1)   load("mnewton")$

(%i2)   mnewton([x+y=-1, 3*x-y=-11], [x,y],[-3,-1]);

0 errors, 0 warnings

(%o2)   [[x=-3.0,y=2.0]]   /* Refer solve */

multi_orbit (polynomial, [variables])

returns the orbit of the polynomial by product of the symmetric groups in the sets of variables.

(%i1)   multi_orbit (i*x + j*y^2, [[x, y], [i, j]]);

resolvante

generale

NOTE: To compile the system do   load("sym/compile");

0 errors, 0 warnings

(%o1) $[iy^2 + jx, jy^2 + ix, jy + ix^2, iy + jx^2]$

multinomial_coeff (n1, n2)

returns the multinomial coefficient for n1 and n2.

(%i1)   multinomial_coeff (x,y);

(%o1) $\dfrac{(y+x)!}{x!y!}$

(%i2)   multinomial_coeff (3,4);

(%o2)   35

ncharpoly (matrix, element)   charpoly (matrix, element)

returns the characteristic polynomial of the matrix with respect to the element. To use this function first call, **load ("nchrpl")**.

(%i1)   load ("nchrpl")\$

(%i2)   matrix ([x,y], [a,b])\$ $/*\begin{bmatrix} x & y \\ a & b \end{bmatrix}*/$

(%i3)   ncharpoly (%, y)

0 errors, 0 warnings

(%o3) $y^2+(-x-b-a)y+bx$

(%i1)   matrix ([x,y], [a,b])\$

(%i2)   charpoly (%, y)

(%o2) $(b-y)(x-y)-ay$

newton (expression, variable, minimum, maximum)

returns an approximate solution for expression = 0 by Newton's method, for the variable. To use this function first call, **load ("newton1")\$**.

(%i1)   load ("newton1")\$

(%i2)   newton (x^2+x−6, x,0,5);

(%o2)   2.203013481363997

next

command in programming for the logical sequence flow.

(%i1)   f(a):=a^2+2

(%i2)   for a: 2 next 2*a thru 20 do display (f(a))$

f(2)=6

f(4)=18

f(8)=66

f(16)=258

next_prime (n)

returns the next prime bigger than n.

(%i1)   next_prime (5);

(%o1)   7

noeval

it suppresses the evaluation of the function 'ev'.

(%i1)   2*i+diff(i^3,i)–integrate(i^3,i);

(%o1) $-\dfrac{i^4}{4} + 3i^2 + 2i$ /* I term integrate, II term differentiate */

(%i2)   ev (%, i=4);

(%o2)   –8

(%i1)   2*i+diff(i^3,i)–integrate(i^3,i);

(%o1) $-\dfrac{i^4}{4} + 3i^2 + 2i$ /* I term integrate, II term differentiate */

(%i2)   noeval;ev (%, i=4);

(%o2)   noeval

(%o3)   noeval

(%i4)   ev (%, i=4);

(%o4)   noeval

nolabels

if it is set to true, input (%i) and output (%o) labels are displayed, but the labels are not bound to results. Default value: false

(%i1)   nolabels:false;

(nolabels)   false;

(%i2)   [1,22,–12,2,3,4,13];

(%o2)   [1,22,–12,2,3,4,13]

(%i3)   lmax(%o2);

(%o3)   22

(%i4)   nolabels:true;

(nolabels)   true;

(%i5)   [1,22,–12,2,3,4,13];

(%o5)   [1,22,–12,2,3,4,13]

(%i6)   lmax(%o5);   /*returns error message for the label %o5*/

"$lmax": argument must be a list or a set; found: %o5

-- an error. To debug this try: debugmode(true);

nonarray

declares a non-array.

(%i1)   a:b$

(%i2)   a[x];

(%o2) b_x

(%i3)   declare(a, nonarray);

(%o3)   done

(%i4)   a[x];

(%o4) a_x

noncentral_moment ([list] or [matrix], k)

returns non-central moment of order 'k'. To use this function first call, **load (descriptive)$**.

(%i1)   load (descriptive)$

(%i2)   noncentral_moment([–c,x,2],1);

(%o2) $\dfrac{x-c+2}{3}$

(%i3)   noncentral_moment([–c,x,2],2);

(%o3) $\dfrac{x^2+c^2+4}{3}$

(%i4)   noncentral_moment([n,y,i,–f],2);

(%o4) $\dfrac{y^2+n^2+i^2+f^2}{4}$

noninteger

declares non-integer.   (Refer: declare function)

(%i1)   declare(a, noninteger, b, noninteger);
(%o1)   done
(%i3)   a:-2*1.75$ b:-2*a$
(%i5)   skinteger(a);   askinteger(b);
rat: replaced -3.5 by -7/2 = -3.5
(%o4)   no
rat: replaced 7.0 by 7/1 = 7.0
(%o5)   yes
(%i6)   declare(y, integer, x, noninteger);
(%o6)   done
(%i7)   askinteger(y);
(%o7)   yes
(%i8)   askinteger(x);
(%o8)   no

nonnegintegerp (n)

returns true if 'n' is an integer and n >= 0.

(%i1)   nonnegintegerp (5);
(%o1)   true
(%i2)   nonnegintegerp (-1);
(%o2)   false
(%i3)   nonnegintegerp (1.3);
(%o3)   false

nonzeroandfreeof (x, expression)

returns true if expression is non-zero. To use this function first call, **load(functs)$**.

(%i2)   y:2$z:0$
(%i3)   load(functs)$
(%i4)   nonzeroandfreeof (x, y);
(%o4)   true
(%i5)   nonzeroandfreeof (x, z);
(%o5)   false

not

logical negation operator.

(%i2)   a:-1/4$b:2.85$

(%i3)   not(d>a);

(%o3) $d <= -\dfrac{1}{4}$

(%i4)   is(b>a);

(%o4)   true

(%i5)   not(b>a);

(%o5)   false

notequal (x, y)

represents the negation of equal(x, y).

(%i1)   notequal (a, b)$

(%i2)   is(a=b);

(%o2)   false

noun

it won't allow the function to evaluate automatically, assigned in 'declare' function.

(%i1)   h:x^3$

(%i2)   diff(h, x);

(%o2) $3x^2$

(%i3)   declare (diff, noun);

(%o3)   done

(%i4)   diff(h, x);

(%o4) $\dfrac{d}{dx}x^3$ /* not returned $3x^2$ */

nterms (expression)

returns the number of terms that the expression is fully expanded.

(%i1)   nterms ((x–i)^4);

(%o1)   5

(%i2)   expand((x–i)^4);

(%o2) $x^4 - 4ix^3 + 6i^2x^2 - 4i^3x + i^4$

nthroot (polynomial, power)

returns the power of polynomial.

(%i1)	nthroot((i^4–12*i^3+54*i^2–108*i+81),4);
(%o1)	i–3
(%i2)	expand((i–3)^4);
(%o2)	$i^4 - 12i^3 + 54i^2 - 108i + 81$

nullspace (matrix)

return the dimension of the nullspace of matrix.

(%i1)	nullspace(matrix ([j,k], [b,c], [n,m]));

Proviso:notequal(x,0) and notequal(bx–ay,0)

(%o1)	span()

nullity (matrix)

return the dimension of the nullspace of matrix.

(%i1)	nullity(matrix ([x,y], [a,b],[i,j]));

Proviso:notequal(x,0) and notequal(bx–ay,0)

(%o1)	0

num (ratio)

returns the numerator of a ratio.

(%i1)	b:(j^k*n^–r);
(b)	$\dfrac{j^k}{n^r}$
(%i2)	num(%)
(%o2)	j^k

num_distinct_partitions (non–negative integer, list)

returns the number of distinct integer partitions for a given non-negative integer.

(%i1)	num_distinct_partitions (5);
(%o1)	3 /*Refer: num_partitions */
(%i2)	num_distinct_partitions (5,list);
(%o2)	[1,1,2,2,3]

num_partitions (non-negative integer, list)

returns the number of integer partitions for a non-negative integer.

5				
4	1			
3	2			
3	1	1		
2	2	1		
2	1	1	1	
1	1	1	1	1

```
(%i1)          num_partitions (5);
(%o1)          7
(%i2)          num_partitions (5,list);
(%o2)          [1,2,3,5,7]
/*Refer: num_distinct_partitions */
```

numberp (expression)

returns true if expression is a literal integer, rational number, floating point number, otherwise false.

```
(%i1)          numberp(%e);
(%o1)          false
(%i2)          numberp(-3.14);
(%o2)          true
```

numer

returns number format

```
(%i1)          %pi,numer;
(%o1)          3.141592653589793
```

numerval (variable, wxMeric_value)

declares the variables to numeric values.

```
(%i1)          numerval (a,-1.0,b,2.0,c,3^-1);
(%o1)          [a,b,c]   /* a=-1.0; b=2.0; c=0.333333333333333*/
(%i2)          a+b+c, numer;
(%o2)          1.333333333333333
```

obase

obase is the base for integers assigned any integer between 2 and 36. Default value: 10. Refer 'ibase'.

(%i1)	obase:2;
(%o1)	10
(%i2)	3
(%o2)	11
(%i3)	obase:3;
(%o3)	10
(%i4)	4
(%o4)	11
(%i5)	obase:8;
(%o5)	10
(%i6)	8
(%o6)	10

oddp (integer)   evenp (integer)

returns true or false if the integer is even or odd integer.

(%i1)	oddp (8);
(%o1)	false
(%i2)	evenp(8);
(%o2)	true

ode2 (equation, dependent_variable, independent_variable)

solves an ordinary differential equation of first or second order.

(%i1)   'diff(y,x) + y*'diff(y,x^2)^2 = 0;

$$(\%o1) \qquad y\left(\frac{d}{dx^2}y\right)^2 + \frac{d}{dx}y = 0$$

(%i2)   ode2(%,y,x);

$$(\%o2) \qquad \int\left(\frac{d}{dx^2}y\right)^2 dx + \log(y) = \%c$$

op (expression)

returns the main operator of the expression if 'stringdisp' set to true.

(%i1)	stringdisp: true$
(%i2)	x:cos(x)$
(%i3)	op(%)
(%o3)	cos
(%i4)	op (x/c);
(%o4)	"/"

operatorp (expression, operator)

returns true if operator is equal to expression.

(%i1)	x:cos(x)$
(%i2)	operatorp (x,sin);
(%o2)	false
(%i3)	operatorp (x,cos);
(%o3)	true

opsubst ("operator", "substitute", expression)

makes substitutions for the operator in the expression. To use this function first call, **load ("opsubst")$**.

(%i1)	x:a+c$
(%i2)	load ("opsubst")$
(%i3)	x:opsubst("+","−",a−c);
(x)	a−c
(%i6)	a:1$c:3$x,numer;
(%o6)	−2;

optimize (expression)

returns an expression that produces the same value but by avoiding the recomputation of common subexpressions.

(%i1)	diff((x^2+x)/(2*x),x,2);
(%o1)	$\dfrac{x^2+x}{x^3} - \dfrac{2x+1}{x^2} + \dfrac{1}{x}$
(%i2)	optimize(diff((x^2+x)/(2*x),x,2));
(%o2)	$\text{block}\left([\%1], \%1 : x^2, \dfrac{\%1+x}{x^3} - \dfrac{2x+1}{\%1} + \dfrac{1}{x} \right)$

optimprefix

changes the prefix from default '%' while using 'optimize' function.

(%i1)   optimprefix:y$optimize(diff((x^2+x)/(2*x),x,2));

(%o1) $\text{block}\left([y1], y1{:}x^2, \frac{y1+x}{x^3} - \frac{2x+1}{y1} + \frac{1}{x}\right)$ /* Refer: optimize */

or

logical disjunction operator for Boolean expressions and returns a Boolean value.

(%i1)   b:2$a:−1$c:−3$

(%i2)   b>c or b>a;

(%o2)   true

(%i3)   c>b or a>b;

(%o3)   false

(%i4)   b>c or a>b;

(%o4)   true

(%i5)   (y^2 >= 2*y−1)or(x^2 >= 2*x−1);

(%o5)   true

orbit (polynomial, {variables})

returns the orbit of the polynomial from the list or set of variables.

(%i1)   orbit (x^2+ x/2, [x,y,z]);

resolvante

generale

NOTE: To compile the system doload("sym/compile");

0 errors, 0 warnings

(%o1) $[z^2 + \frac{z}{2}, y^2 + \frac{y}{2}, x^2 + \frac{x}{2}]$

ordergreat (expressions,order)

returns the canonical order given for the expressions.

(%i1)   expand((i−j+n)^3);

(%o1) $n^3 - 3jn^2 + 3in^2 + 3j^2n - 6ijn + 3i^2n - j^3 +$
               $3ij^2 - 3i^2j + i^3$

(%i1)   ordergreat(i,n};

(%o1)   done

(%i2)   expand((i–j+n)^3);
(%o2) $i^3+3ni^2-3ji^2+3n^2i-6jni+3j^2i+n^3-3jn^2+3j^2n-j^3$

(%i1)   ordergreat(j,n);
(%o1)   done
(%i2)   expand((i–j+n)^3);
(%o2) $-j^3+3nj^2-3jj^2+3n^2j-6inj+3i^2j+n^3+3in^2+3i^2n+i^3$

(%i1)   ordergreat(j,i,n);
(%o1)   done
(%i2)   expand((i–j+n)^3);
(%o2) $-j^3+3ij^2+3nj^2+3i^2j-6nij-3n^2j+1^3+3ni^2+3n^2n+n^3$

ordergreatp (order)

returns true whether the given canonical order is followed in the 'ordergreat' function or else it returns false. Refer: ordergreat.

(%i1)   ordergreat(j,n);
(%o1)   done
(%i2)   expand((i–j+n)^3);
(%o2) $-j^3 + 3nj^2 + 3ij^2 - 3n^2j - 6inj - 3i^2j + n^3 + 3in^2 + 3i^2n + i^3$

(%i3)   ordergreatp(i,n);
(%o3)   false
(%i4)   ordergreatp(j,n);
(%o4)   true

orderless (expressions, order)

reverses the canonical order given for the expressions.

(%i1)   orderless(j,i,n);
(%o1)   done
(%i2)   expand((i–j+n)^3);
(%o2) $n^3 + 3in^2 - 3jn^2 + 3i^2n - 6jin + 3j^2n + i^3 - 3ji^2 + 3j^2i - j^3$

(%i1)	ordergreat(j,i,n);	/*Refer: ordergreat */
(%o1)	done	
(%i2)	expand((i–j+n)^3);	

(%o2) $\quad -j^3 + 3ij^2 + 3nj^2 - 3i^2j - 6nij - 3n^2j + i^3 +$

$\qquad 3ni^2 + 3n^2i + n^3$

orderlessp (order)

returns true whether the given canonical order is followed in the 'orderless' function or else it returns false.

(%i1)	ordergreat(i,n);
(%o1)	done
(%i2)	expand((i–j+n)^3);

(%o2) $\quad i^3 + 3ni^2 - 3ji^2 + 3n^2i - 6jni + 3j^2i + n^3 - 3jn^2 + 3j^2n - j^3$

(%i3)	orderlessp(i,n);
(%o3)	false
(%i4)	orderlessp(n,i);
(%o4)	true
(%i1)	orderless(j,i,n);
(%o1)	done
(%i2)	expand((i–j+n)^3);

(%o2) $\quad n^3 + 3in^2 - 3jn^2 + 3i^2n - 6jin + 3j^2n + i^3 - 3ji^2 + 3j^2i - j^3$

(%i3)	orderlessp(j,n);
(%o3)	true
(%i4)	orderlessp(i,n);
(%o4)	true
(%i5)	orderlessp(n,i);
(%o5)	false

origin [origin, [x,y,z]]

represents the coordinates of the object. Default value: 0,0,0.

(%i1)	origin [x,y,z, [–1,2,–3]];
(%o1)	$\text{origin}_{x,y,z,[-1,2,-3]}$

outative

with declare(function, outative) it instructs to simplify that constant factors in the function.

(%i1)   f(2*a);

(%o1)   f(2a)

(%i2)   declare(f,outative);

(%o2)   done

(%i3)   f(2*5);

(%o3)   10f(1)

outchar

changes the prefix of the output label from default value: %o.

(%i1)   outchar: "max_o"$

(%i2)   (2*k+j)^n+(k^n);

(max_o2) $(2k+j)^n+k^n$

outermap (function, [elements])

applies the function to each elements in the given lists.

(%i1)   outermap ("*", [a, b, c], [x, b, −c]);

(%o1) $[[ax, ab, −ac], [bx, b^2, −bc], [cx, bc, −c^2]]$

part (expression, [parts])

returns parts of the expression.

(%i1)   expand((i−j+n)^3);

(%o1) $n^3 - 3jn^2 + 3in^2 + 3j^2n - 6ijn + 3i^2n - j^3 +$

          $3ij^2 - 3i^2j + i^3$

(%i3)   part(%,[2,5,7]);

(%o3) $-3jn^2-6ijn-j^3$

part2cont (partitioned_form, [variables])

goes from the partitioned form to the contracted form.

(%i1)   part2cont ([[i^−3−2*b, 5, 2]], [j, k]);

resolvante

generale

NOTE: To compile the system do load("sym/compile");

0 errors, 0 warnings

(%o1) $\left(\frac{1}{i^3} - 2b\right) j^5 k^2$

partpol (symmetric_form, [variables])

goes from the contracted form to partitioned form.

(%i1)   part2cont ([[i^–3–2*b, 5, 2]], [j, k]);

resolvante

generale

NOTE: To compile the system do load("sym/compile");

0 errors, 0 warnings

(%o1) $\left(\frac{1}{i^3} - 2b\right) j^5 k^2$

(%i2)   partpol(%,[j,k]);

(%o2) $[[\frac{1}{i^3} - 2b, 5, 2]]$

partfrac (expression, variable)

returns the expanded expression in partial fractions with respect to the main variable.

(%i1)   expand((1/(i+2)^3));

(%o1) $\dfrac{1}{i^3+6i^2+12i+8}$

(%i2)   partfrac (%, i);

(%o2) $\dfrac{1}{(i+2)^3}$

partition_set ({set}, predicate)

partitions the set into two with respect to predicate.

(%i1)   partition_set ({2, 7, –1.3, 5, 6,8, 4.13, 3.14}, integerp);

(%o1) $[\{-1.3, 3.14, 4.13\}, \{2,5,6,7,8\}]$

pathname_directory (path_name)

pathname_name (path_name)

pathname_type (path_name)

these functions return the components of pathname.

(%i1)   pathname_directory("/home/dieter/maxima/changelog.txt");

(%o1)	|home|dieter|maxima|
(%i2)	pathname_name("/home/dieter/maxima /changelog.txt");
(%o2)	changelog
(%i3)	pathname_type("/home/dieter/maxima /changelog.txt");
(%o3)	txt

pearson_skewness (list or matrix)

returns Pearson's skewness coefficient for the list or matrix. To use this function first call, **load (descriptive)$**.

$$/* \text{ Pearson's skewness coefficient} = \frac{3\times(\text{average} \quad \text{median})}{\text{standard deviation}} \, */$$

(%i1)	load (descriptive)$
(%i2)	[15.6,17.5,36.6,43.8,58.2,61.6,65.2,72.6,98.9]$
(%i3)	pearson_skewness (%), numer;
(%o3)	−0.6690345687532784

permanent (matrix)

returns the permanent of the matrix.

(%i1)	matrix([a,b,c], [d,e,f], [g,h,i]);
(%o1)	$\begin{bmatrix} a & b & c \\ d & e & f \\ g & h & i \end{bmatrix}$
(%i2)	permanent (%);
(%o2)	(ae+bd)i +(af+cd)h+(bf+ce)g

permut ([list])

returns the list of permutations for the list or set.

(%i1)	permutations ([x,y,z]);
(%o1)	[[x,y,z],[x,z,y],[y,x,z],[y,z,x],[z,x,y],[z,y,x]]

permutations ([list])   Refer: **permutation**

returns the set of permutations for the list or set.

(%i1)	permutations ([x,y,z]);
(%o1)	{[x,y,z],[x,z,y],[y,x,z],[y,z,x],[z,x,y],[z,y,x]}

pfeformat

ratio of integers is displayed with the solidus (/) if it is set to true. Default value: false.

(%i1)   3^7/2^4;

(%o1) $\dfrac{2187}{16}$

(%i2)   pfeformat: true$
(%i1)   3^7/2^4;
(%o1)   2187/16

pickapart (expression, n)

returns an expression in terms of intermediate subexpressions with reference to integer 'n'.

(%i1)   k: ((a–b)/2)+((x+a)/2)+((b–x)/2);

(k) $\dfrac{x+a}{2}+\dfrac{b-x}{2}+\dfrac{a-b}{2}$

(%i2)   pickapart (k, 0);

(%t2) $\dfrac{x+a}{2}+\dfrac{b-x}{2}+\dfrac{a-b}{2}$

(%o2)   %t2
(%i3)   pickapart (k, 1);

(%t3) $\dfrac{x+a}{2}$

(%t4) $\dfrac{b-x}{2}$

(%t5) $\dfrac{a-b}{2}$

(%o5)   %t5+%t4+%t3
(%i6)   pickapart (k, 2);
(%t6)   x+a
(%t7)   b–x
(%t8)   a–b

(%o8) $\dfrac{\%t8}{2}+\dfrac{\%t7}{2}+\dfrac{\%t6}{2}$

related function dpart

dpart (expression, n)

returns the expression with the selected subexpression displayed inside a **box**, which is part of the expression.

(%i1)   k: ((a–b)/2)+((x+a)/2)+((b–x)/2);

(k) $\dfrac{x+a}{2} + \dfrac{b-x}{2} + \dfrac{a-b}{2}$

(%i2)   dpart (k,1,0);

(%o2) $\boxed{\dfrac{x+a}{2}} + \dfrac{b-x}{2} + \dfrac{a-b}{2}$

(%i3)   dpart (k,2,0);

(%o3) $\dfrac{x+a}{2} + \boxed{\dfrac{b-x}{2}} + \dfrac{a-b}{2}$

piece

holds the last expression selected while using the part functions.

(%i1)   expand((i–j+n)^3);

(%o1) $n^3 - 3jn^2 + 3in^2 + 3j^2n - 6ijn + 3i^2n - j^3 +$
                $3ij^2 - 3i^2j + i^3$

(%i2)   part(%,[2,5]);

(%o2) $-3jn^2-6ijn$

(%i3)   (piece/2),numer;

(%o3) $0.5(-3jn^2-6ijn)$

playback ([m, n])

displays all input and output with integer numbers from 'm'to'n'. playback (input) displays all input expressions generated so far. playback (time) displays the computation time for each expression.

(%i1)   expand((x–a)*(x–c));

(%o1) $x^2-cx-ax+ac$

(%i2)   expand(%/(x–b));

(%o2) $\dfrac{x^2}{x-b} - \dfrac{cx}{x-b} - \dfrac{ax}{x-b} + \dfrac{ac}{x-b}$

(%i3)   playback ([2, 3])

(%i2)   expand(%/(x-b));

(%o2) $\dfrac{x^2}{x\ b} \quad \dfrac{cx}{x\ b} - \dfrac{ax}{x-b} + \dfrac{ac}{x-b}$

(%o3)   done

(%i3)   playback([2,3]);

plot2d – Basics of 2d plot functions with Gnuplot are outlined here.

For discrete data, style: line

(%i1)   x:[1,2,3,4,5,6,7,8,9]$y:[7,10,17,28,43,62,85,112,143]$

(%i3)   plot2d([discrete,x,y])$

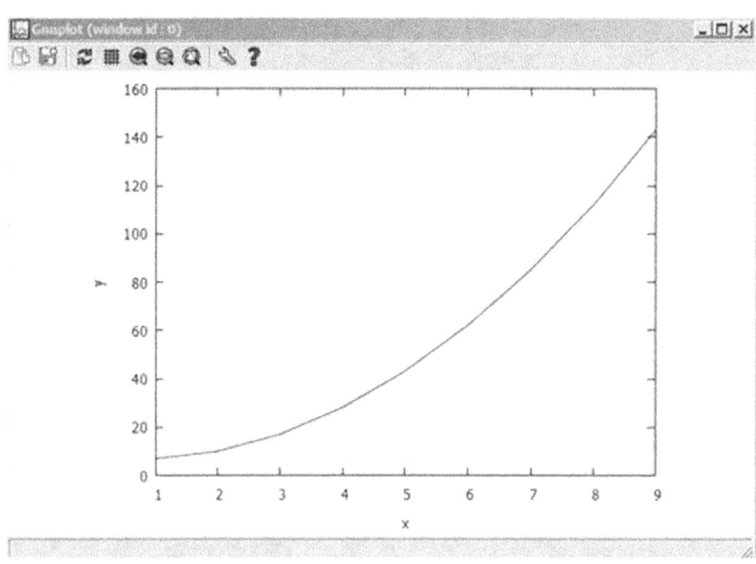

For discrete data, style: points

(%i2)   x:[1,2,3,4,5,6,7,8,9]$y:[7,10,17, 28,43,62,85,112,143]$

(%i3)   plot2d([discrete,x,y], [style, points])$

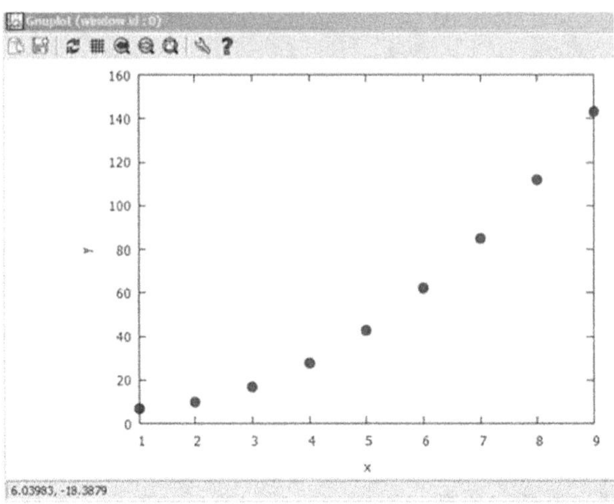

For discrete data, style: points option, color, axis labels, legends.

(%i2)   x:[1,2,3,4,5,6,7,8,9]$y:[7,10,17,28,43,62,85,112,143]$

(%i3)   plot2d([discrete,x,y],   [style,points],   [color,red],   [point_
             type, asterisk], [legend, "Trial 1"], [xlabel, "Time (s)"], [ylabel,
             "Temperature (k)"])$

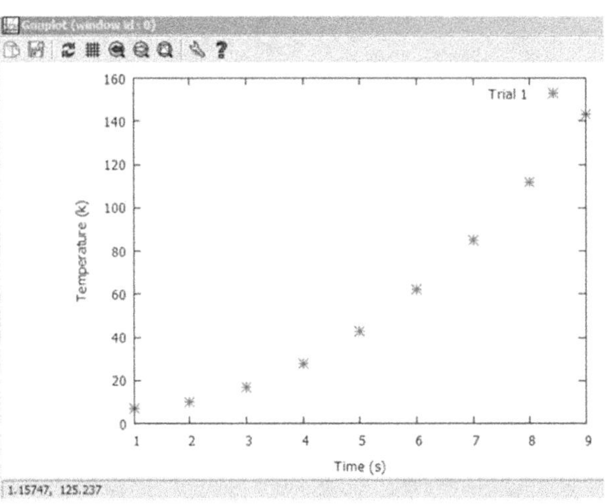

(%i1)   xy:[[1,7],[2,10],[3,17],[4,28],[5,43],[6,62],[7,85],
             [8,112],[9,143]]$

(%i2)   plot2d([discrete,xy],[style, points],[point_type,
             diamond])$

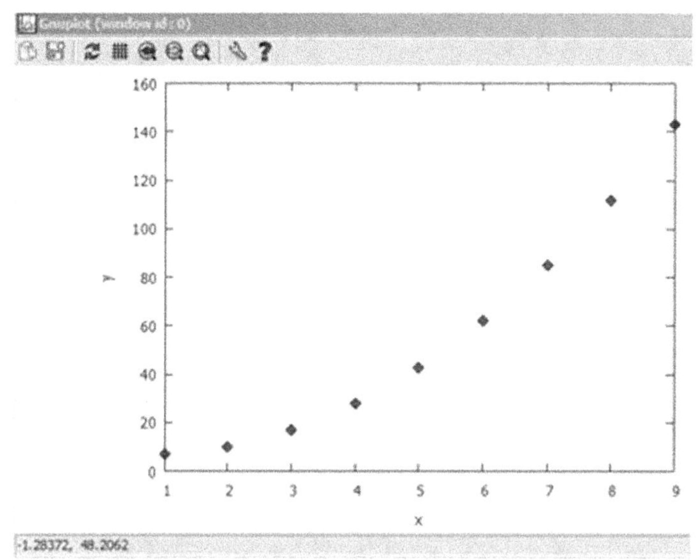

For function based plot

(%i1)   plot2d (2*x^2, [x, –8, 8], [xtics, –7, 1, 7],
             [ytics, 0, 15, 120])$

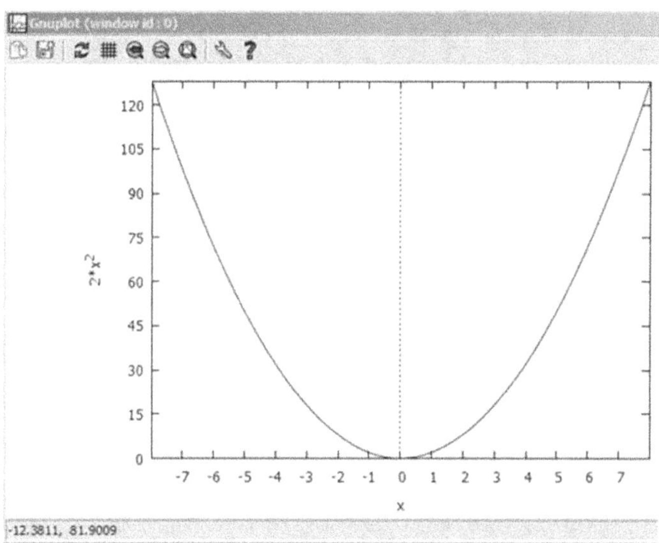

(%i1)   plot2d (2*x^2, [x, –8, 8], [xtics, –7,1,7],[ytics, 0,15, 120],[axes,
             solid], grid2d,[**yx_ratio, 0.5**],[label, ["m", 6, 15]],[xlabel, "Time
             (s)"], [ylabel, "Temperature (k)"])$

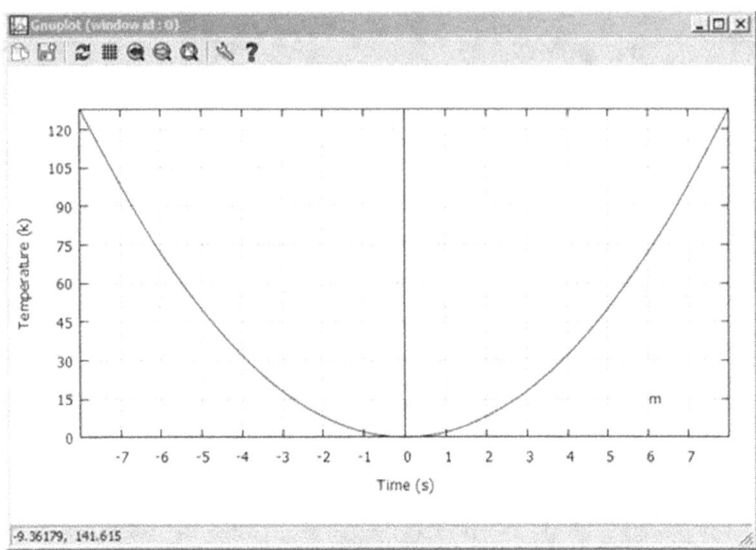

(%i1)   plot2d (2*x^2, [x, –8, 8], [xtics, –7,1,7],[ytics, 0,15,120], [color, red],[axes, solid], grid2d,[**yx_ratio, 2**],[label, ["m", 5,60]],[xlabel, "Time (s)"], [ylabel, "Temperature (k)"])$

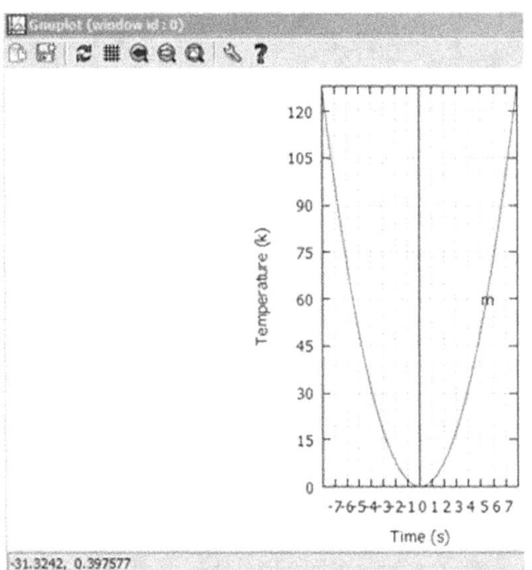

plot3d Few fundamental functions and plotting options related to 3d plot, through Gnuplot are outlined here.

(%i1)   plot3d (2*x^2 , [x,–8,8], [y,–10,10])$

/* all 3D plots can be viewed by rotating at various angles */

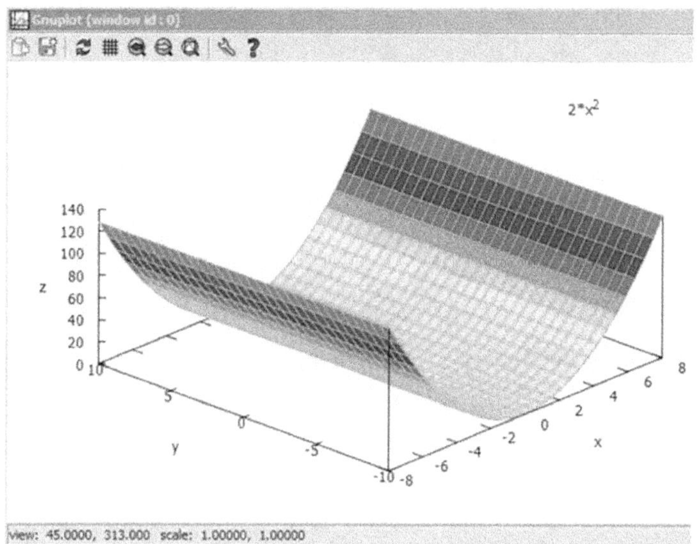

(%i1)   plot3d (2*x^2, [x, –8,8], [y, –10,10], [grid, 4, 4])$

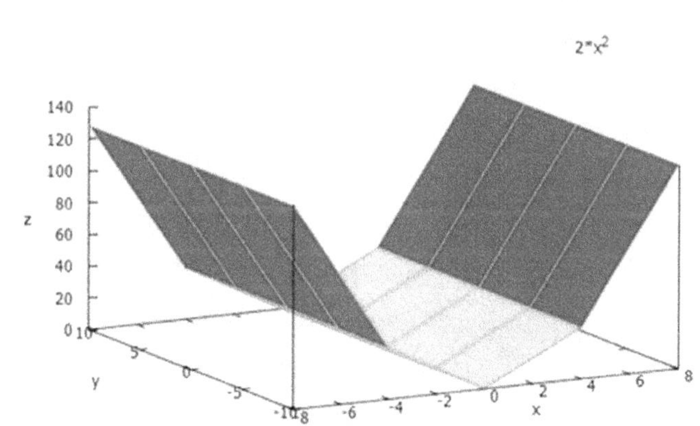

(%i1)   plot3d (2*x^2, [x, –8,8], [y, –10,10], [grid, 20, 20])$

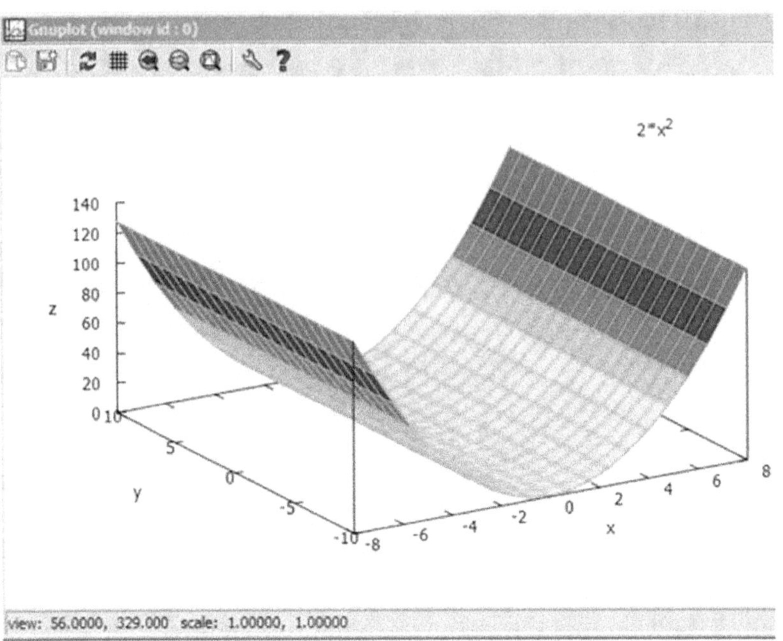

(%i1)   plot3d (2*x^2, [x, −8,8], [y, −10,10], [grid, 10, 10], [palette, [gradient, red, green]])$ /* options */

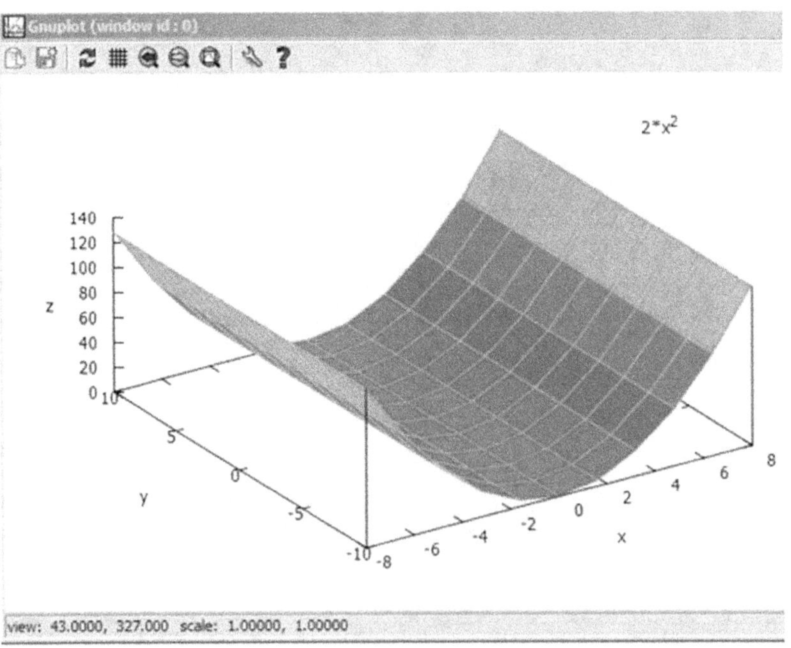

(%i1)   plot3d (2*x^2 , [x, −8,8], [y, −10,10], [grid, 15, 15], [palette, [gradient, red, green]],color_bar, [xtics, 1], [ytics, 2], [ztics, 25],[color_bar_tics, 20])$

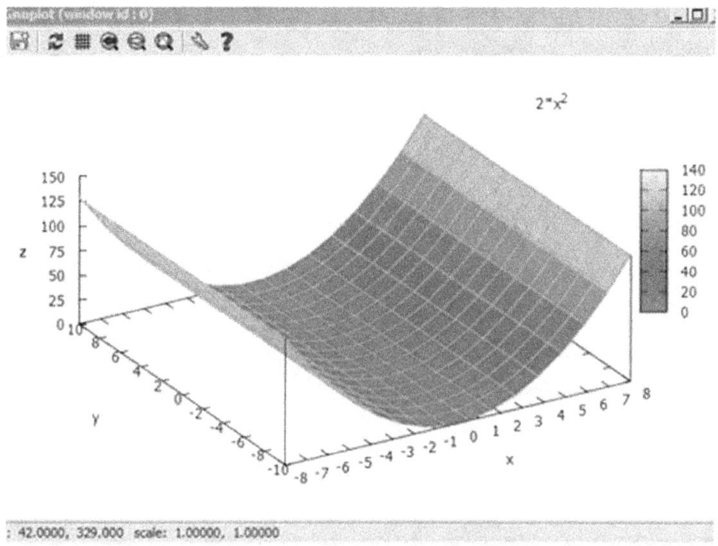

(%i1)   plot3d (2*x^2 , [x, −8,8], [y, −10,10], [grid, 15, 15], [palette, [gradient, red, yellow]], color_bar, [xtics, 1], [ytics, 2], [ztics, 25],[color_bar_tics, 20], [xlabel, "Time (s)"], [ylabel, "Current (A)"],[zlabel, "EMF (V)"], [title, "Electrochemical"])$

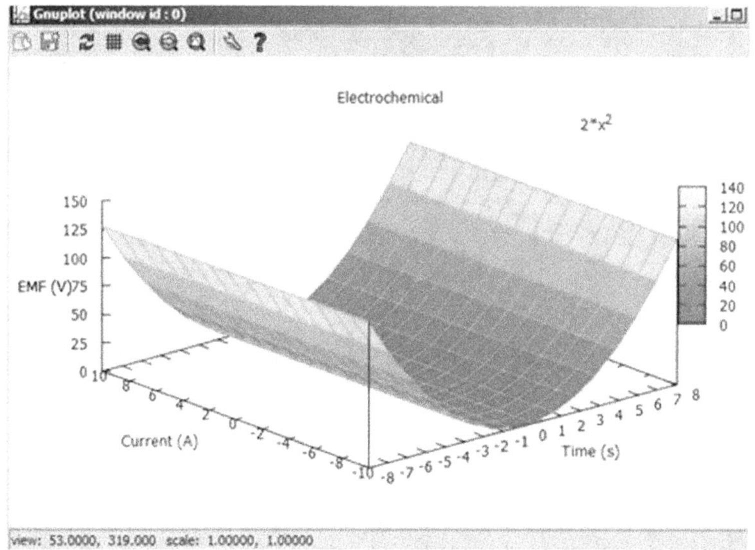

(%i1)   plot3d (2*x^2, [x, −8,8], [y, −10,10], [grid, 15, 15], [mesh_lines_

color,false],[palette, [gradient, red, yellow]],color_bar, [xtics, 1], [ytics, 2], [ztics, 25],[color_bar_tics, 20], [xlabel, "Time (s)"], [ylabel, "Current (A)"],[zlabel, "EMF (V)"], [title, "Electrochemical"])$

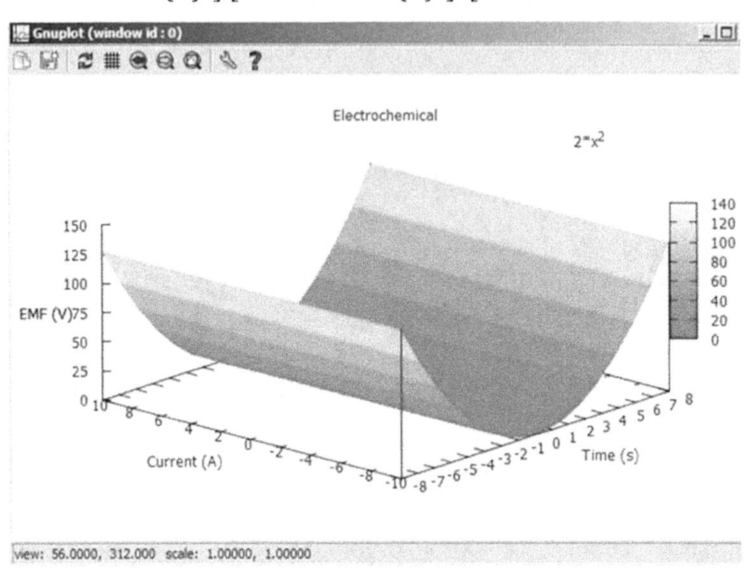

(%i1)   plot3d(1/(1+x^2+y^2),[x,−4,4],[y,−3,3])$

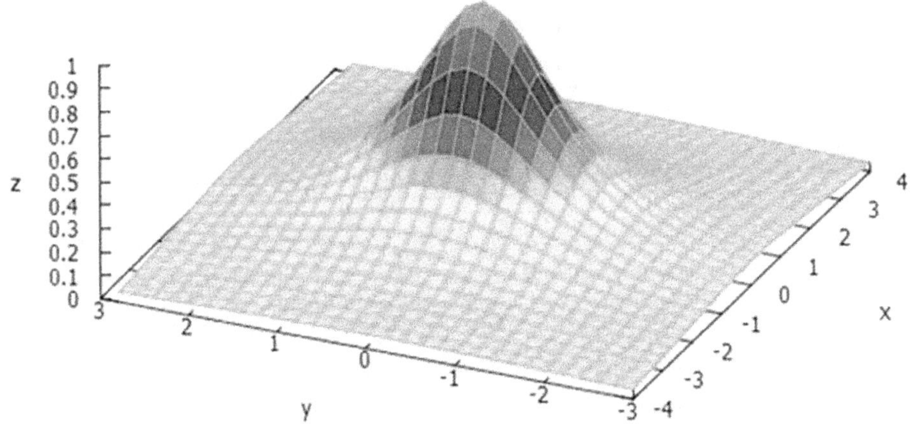

(%i1)   plot3d(1/(1+x^2+y^2),[x,–4,4],[y,–3,3],[elevation, 30],[grid, 10, 10])\$

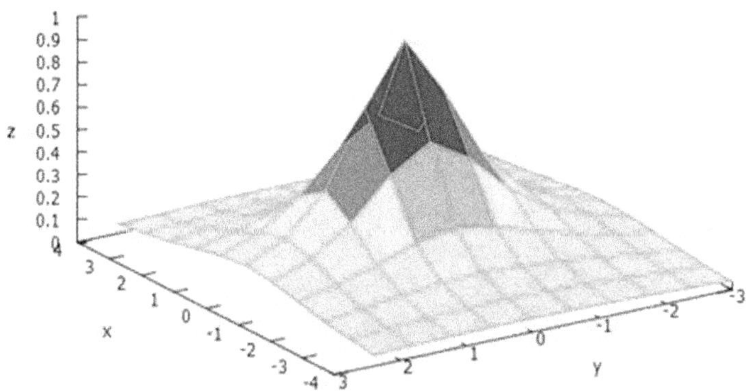

(%i1)   plot3d(1/(1+x^2+y^2),[x,–4,4],[y,–3,3],[elevation, 120],[grid, 60, 60])\$

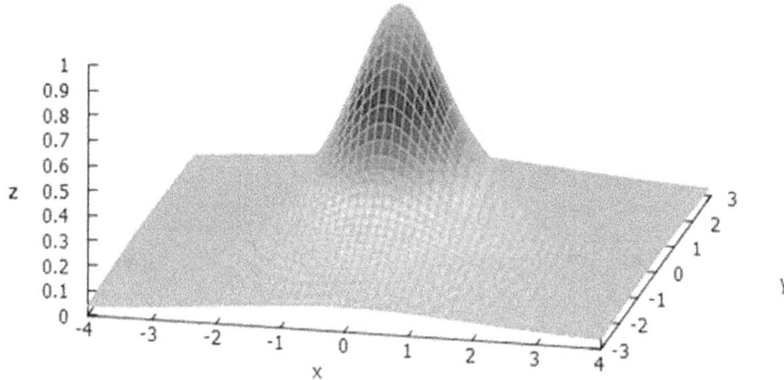

(%i1)   **contour_plot**(1/(1+x^2+y^2),[x,–4,4],[y,–3,3])\$

(%i1)   y:[2,1,–3,–3,2,2]$ piechart(y, title = "This is pie chart")$

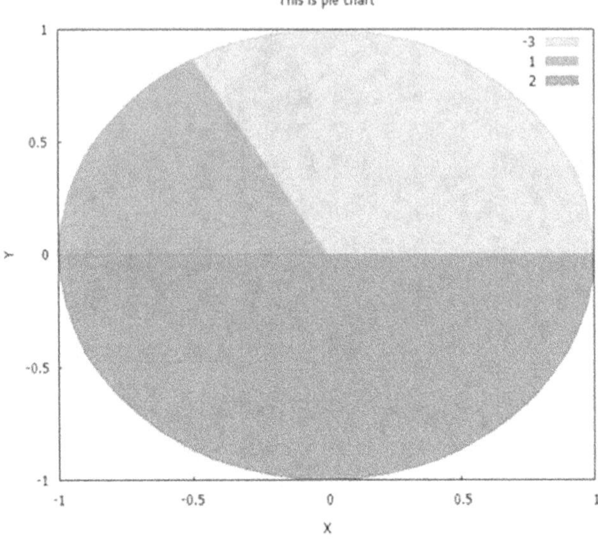

(%i1)   y:[2,1,–3,–3,2,2]$ piechart(y, xrange   = [–1.5, 1.5], yrange   = [–2,2],title = "This is pie chart")$

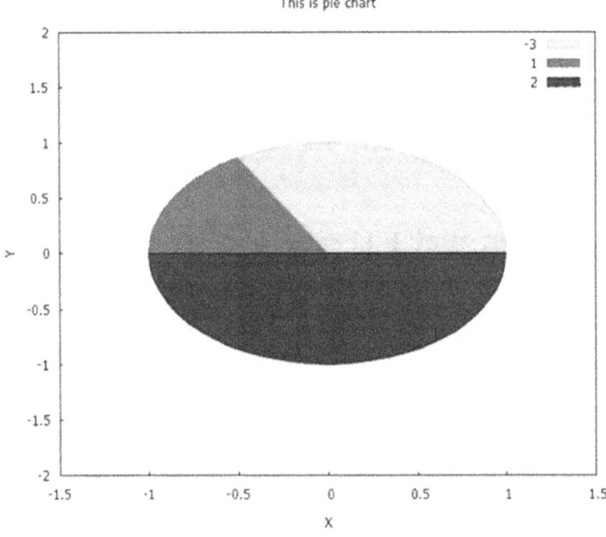

(%i1)   x:[1,2,3,7]$y:[−3,−6,2,4,3,−3,−1]$ barsplot(x,y, box_width =1, fill_density=1, bars_colors=[yellow,red], frequency = relative, sample_keys= ["years", "growth"], title="This is bar plot")$

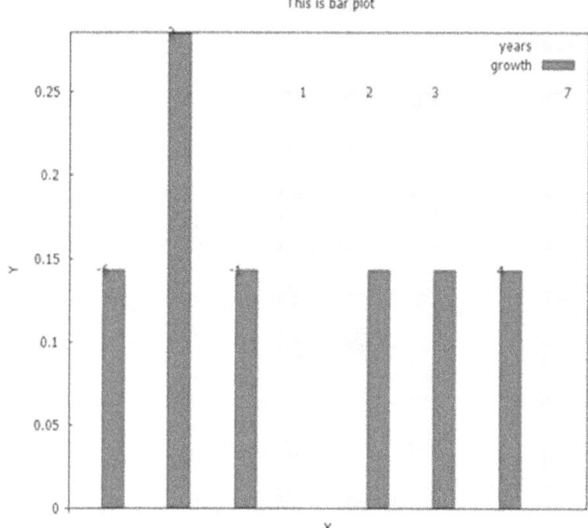

(%i1)   x:[1,2,3,4,5,6,7,8,9]$y:[7,10,17, 28,43,62,85,112,143]$

plot2d([discrete,x,y],[style,points],[box,false],[axes, false], [point_type,delta])$

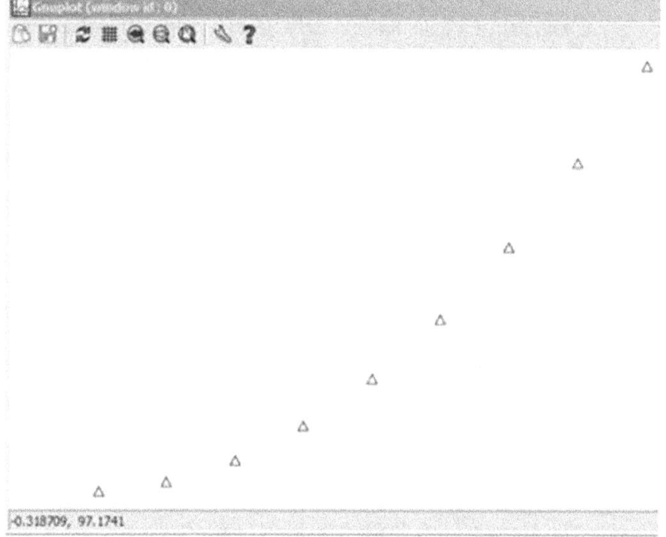

(%i1)   load ("descriptive")$

(%i2)   x:[1,2,3,4,5,6,7,8,9]$y:[7,10,17, 28,43,62,85,112,143]$

(%i3)   **starplot**(x, y,   stars_colors = [red,yellow], sample_keys = ["V","A"], star_center= [2,4], star_radius=10, proportion al_axes = xy, line_width=3)$

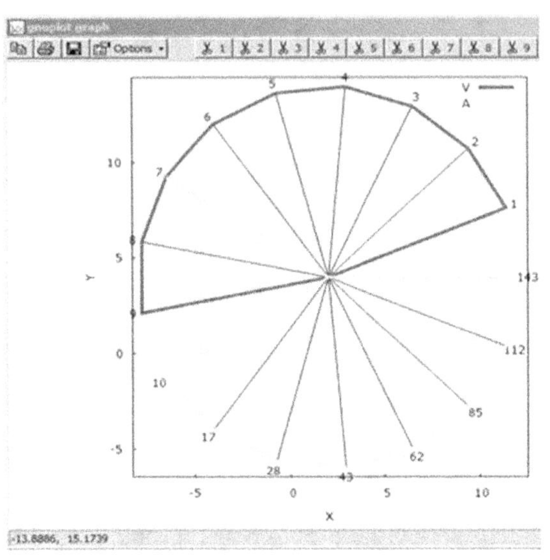

(%i1)   load ("descriptive")$ x:[1,2,4,3,2,1,2,2]$

(%i3)   histogram(x,nclasses=5, title= **"Histogram"**, xlabel= "Numbers", ylabel= "Counts", fill_color = orange, fill_density = 0.3)$

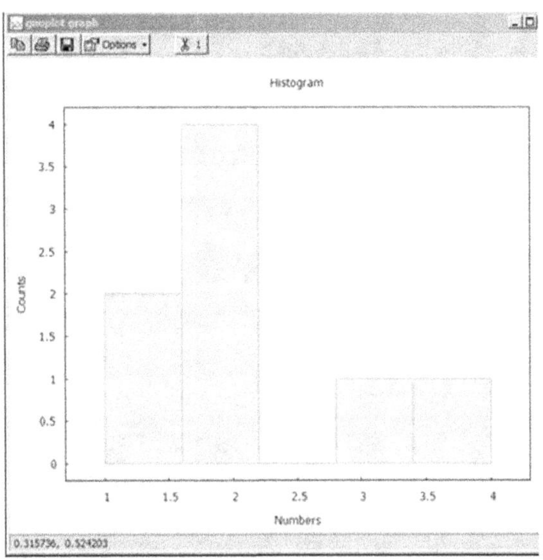

(%i1)   a:matrix([0,1,2],[1,2,3],[2,3,4]);

(a) $\begin{bmatrix} 0 & 1 & 2 \\ 1 & 2 & 3 \\ 2 & 3 & 4 \end{bmatrix}$

(%i2)   b:image(a,0,0,5,5)\$

(%o2)   draw2d(b)\$

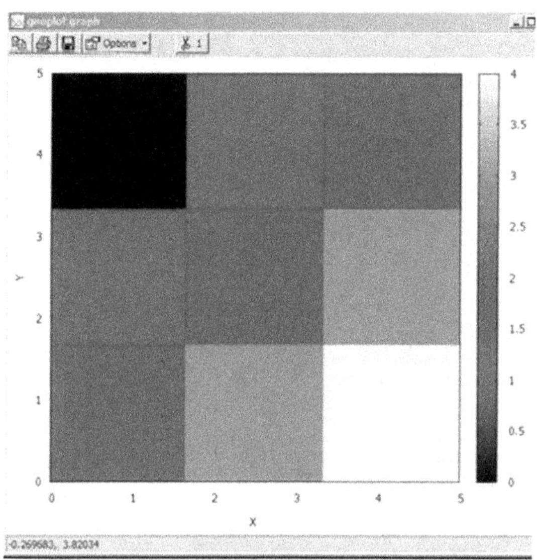

(%i1)   a:implicit(1=x^2+y^2+z^2,x,-1,1,y,-1,1,z,-1,1)\$

(%i2)   b:explicit(sin(2*x)*sin(2*y),x,-2,2,y,-2,2)\$

(%i3)   draw3d(surface_hide=false,color=red,b,color=blue,a)\$

(%i1)   draw3d (color = orange, enhanced3d = false, cbtics = {["High",2],["Medium",0],["Low",-2]},cbrange=[-2, 2],explicit(x^2+y^2, x,-2,2,y,-2,2)) $

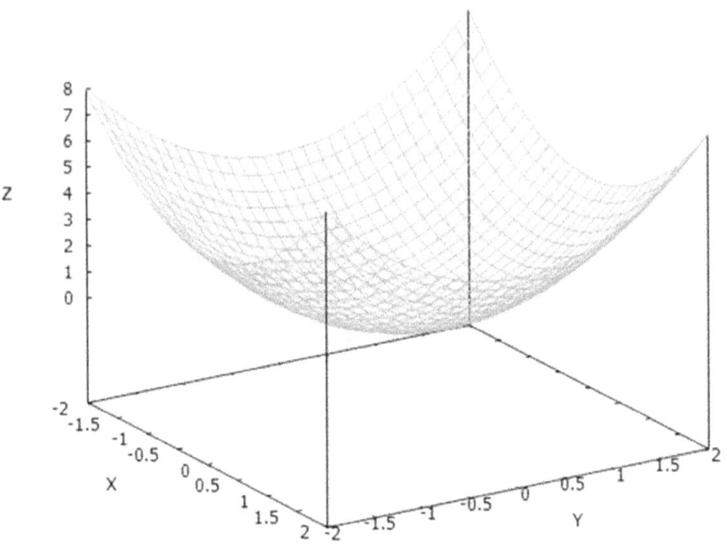

(%i1)   draw3d (color = yellow, enhanced3d = true, cbtics = {["High",2],["Medium",0],["Low",-2]},cbrange=[-2, 2], explicit(x^2+y^2, x,-2,2,y,-2,2)) $

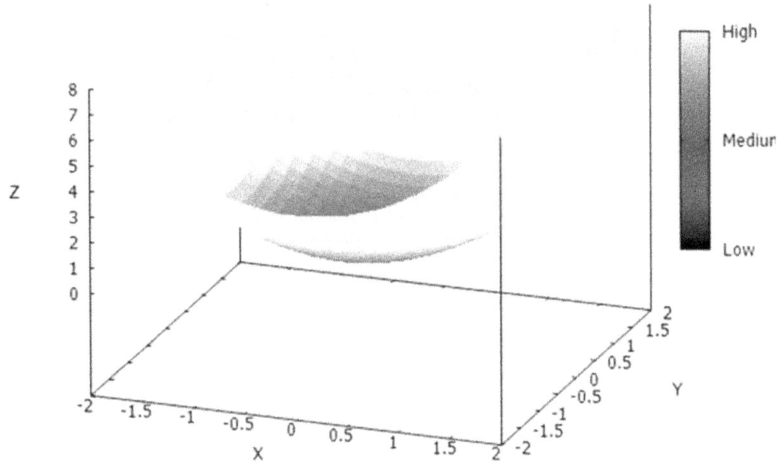

png_file [png_file, file_name]

saves the plot into a .png file with file_name, rather than showing in the screen.

plsquares(matrix,[x,y,z],z);

returns the coefficient for 'z' in 'n×3' matrix. To use this function first call, **load("plsquares")$**.

(%i1)   load("plsquares")$

(%i2)   matrix ([2,–1,–3], [4,5,3],[6,9,8],[0,–1,–6]);

(%o2) $\begin{bmatrix} 2 & -1 & -3 \\ 4 & 5 & 3 \\ 6 & 9 & 8 \\ 0 & -1 & -6 \end{bmatrix}$ /* $\begin{bmatrix} x_1 & y_1 & z_1 \\ x_2 & y_2 & z_2 \\ x_3 & y_3 & z_3 \\ x_4 & y_4 & z_4 \end{bmatrix}$ 4×3 matrix */

(%i3)   plsquares(%,[x,y,z],z);

Determination Coefficient forz=1.0

(%o3) $z = \frac{y+3x-11}{2}$ /* (y + (3x) –11) / 2 = z */

pochhammer (x, number)

returns pochhammer format from the number.

(%i1)   pochhammer (a, –4);

(%o1) $\dfrac{1}{(a-4)(a-3)(a-2)(a-1)}$

(%i2)   pochhammer (b, 7);

(%o2)   b(b+1)(b+2)(b+3)(b+4)(b+5)(b+6)

poly_add(polynomial_1, polynomial_2, [variables_list])

adds polynomial_1 and polynomial_2 with the list of variables. To use this function first call, **load(grobner)$**.

(%i1)   load(grobner)$

(%i2)   a:x^3+4*x^2+4*x;

(a) x^3+4x^2+4x

(%i3)   b:2*x^3+5*x^2+2*x;

(b) $2x^3+5x^2+2x$

(%i4)   poly_add(a, b, [x]);

(%o4) $3x^3+9x^2+6x$

poly_content (polynomial, [variables_list])

extracts the greatest common divisor of its coefficients for the list of variables. To use this function first call, **load(grobner)$**.

(%i1)	load(grobner)$
(%i2)	poly_content(−18*y+36*x+24*z^2,[x,y,z]);
(%o2)	6

poly_depends_p (polynomial, variable, [variables_list])

poly_depends tests whether a polynomial depends on a variable. To use this function first call, **load(grobner)$**.

(%i1)	load(grobner)$
(%i2)	z:y−x$
(%i3)	poly_depends_p (−18*y+36*x+24*z^2,z,[x,y,z]);
(%o3)	false
(%i1)	load(grobner)$
(%i2)	poly_depends_p (−18*y+36*x+24*z^2,z,[x,y,z]);
(%o2)	true

poly_exact_divide (polynomial_1, polynomial_2, [variables])

divide a polynomial by another polynomial for the given list of variables. To use this function first call, **load(grobner)$**.

(%i1)	load(grobner)$
(%i2)	a*x^5+b*x^3;
(%o2)	ax^5+bx^3
(%i3)	−a*x^2+b*x^2;
(%o3)	$bx^2−ax^2$
(%i4)	poly_exact_divide (%o2,%o3,[−x]);
(%o4)	ax^3+bx

poly_expand (polynomial, [variables])

resolves polynomial into components from the list of variables given. To use this function first call, **load(grobner)$**.

(%i1)	load(grobner)$
(%i2)	poly_expand(((i−a)^2)*(i+b),[i]);
(%o2)	$i^3 + (b − 2a)i^2 + (a^2 − 2ab)i + a^2b$

(%i3)   poly_expand((((i–a)^2)*(i+b),[i,a,b]);

(%o3) $i^3 + bi^2 - 2ai^2 - 2abi + a^2i + a^2b$

(%i3)   poly_expand((((i–a)^2)*(i+b),[i,a]);

(%o3) $i^3 + bi^2 - 2ai^2 - 2abi + a^2i + a^2b$

(%i4)   poly_expand((((i–a)^2)*(i+b),[b]);

(%o4) $i^3 + b(i^2 - 2ai + a^2) - 2ai^2 + a^2i$

poly_gcd (polynomial_1, polynomial_2, [variables])

returns the greatest common divisor of polynomial_1, polynomial_2 from the list of variables. To use this function first call, **load(grobner)$**.

(%i1)   load(grobner)$
(%i2)   a:x^3+4*x^2+4*x;

(a) x^3+4x^2+4x

(%i3)   b:2*x^3+5*x^2+2*x;

(b) $2x^3+5x^2+2x$

(%i4)   poly_gcd(a, b, [x]);
(%o4) $-x^2 -2x$

poly_lcm (polynomial_1, polynomial_2, [variables])

returns the lowest common multiple of polynomial_1, polynomial_2 from the list of variables. To use this function first call, **load(grobner)$**.

(%i1)   load(grobner)$
(%i2)   a:x^3+4*x^2+4*x;

(a) x^3+4x^2+4x

(%i3)   b:2*x^3+5*x^2+2*x;

(b) $2x^3+5x^2+2x$

(%i4)   poly_lcm(a, b, [x]);

(%o4) $-2x^4-9x^3-12x^2-4x$

poly_multiply (polynomial_1, polynomial_2, [variables])

returns the product of polynomial_1, polynomial_2 from the list of variables. To use this function first call, **load(grobner)\$**.

(%i1)   load(grobner)\$

(%i2)   a:x^3+4*x^2+4*x;

(a) x^3+4x^2+4x

(%i3)   b:2*x^3+5*x^2+2*x;

(b) $2x^3+5x^2+2x$

(%i4)   poly_multiply(a, b, [x]);

(%o4) $2x^6+13x^5+30x^4+28x^3+8x^2$

poly_subtract (polynomial_1, polynomial_2, [variables])

subtracts polynomial_2 from polynomial_2 with the list of variables. To use this function first call, **load(grobner)\$**.

(%i1)   load(grobner)\$

(%i2)   a:x^3+4*x^2+4*x;

(a) x^3+4x^2+4x

(%i3)   b:2*x^3+5*x^2+2*x;

(b) $2x^3+5x^2+2x$

(%i4)   poly_subtract(a, b, [x]);

(%o4) $-x^3-x^2+2x$

polydecomp (polynomial, variable)

returns a list for polynomial after decomposing into the functional composition in terms of variable.

(%i1)   polydecomp (x^12+x^10, x);

(%o1) $[x^6+x^5, x^2]$

polygon ([[x1, y1], [x2, y2], [x3, y3],...])

draws polygons from draw2d function with the values x1,y1...

(%i1)   draw2d (polygon([[5,4],[9,2],[7,5],[3,7],[2,6]]));

(%o1)   [gr2d(polygon)]

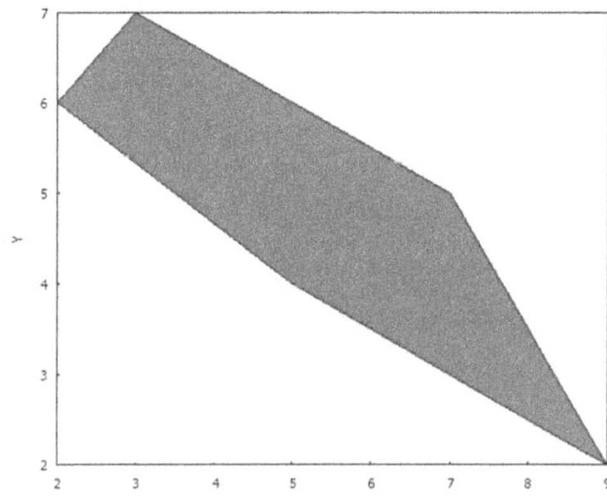

polynome2ele (polynomial, variable)

returns the list for the degree of the polynomial with the variable and elementary symmetric function of the roots of polynomial.

(%i1)   polynome2ele (3*x^3 – 4*x^2 + 6*x+10, x);

resolvante

generale

NOTE: To compile the system do load ("sym/compile");

0 errors, 0 warnings

(%o1) $[3,\frac{4}{3},2,-\frac{10}{3}]$

related function: ele2polynome – inverse of polynome2ele

ele2polynome (list for the degree of the polynomial, variable)

returns the polynomial from the list for the degree of the polynomial with the variable and elementary symmetric function of the roots of polynomial.

(%i1)   polynome2ele (3*x^3 – 4*x^2 + 6*x+10, x);

resolvante

generale

NOTE: To compile the system do load ("sym/compile");
0 errors, 0 warnings

(%o1) $\qquad [3, \frac{4}{3}, 2, -\frac{10}{3}]$

(%i2) $\qquad$ ele2polynome([3,4/3,2,–10/3], x);

(%o2) $\qquad x^3 - \frac{4x^2}{3} + 2x + \frac{10}{3}$

polynomialp (polynomial, [variables])

returns true if polynomial with the variables given as list.

(%i1) $\qquad$ polynomialp ((a+2)*(a–1), [a]);
(%o1) $\qquad$ true
(%i2) $\qquad$ polynomialp ((x + a)*(x–a), [a]);
(%o2) $\qquad$ false

polytocompanion (polynomial, variable)

return the companion matrix of polynomial.

(%i1) $\qquad$ polytocompanion (a*x^3+b*x^2-c*x, x);

(%o1) $\qquad \begin{bmatrix} 0 & 0 & 0 \\ 1 & 0 & \frac{c}{a} \\ 0 & 1 & -\frac{b}{a} \end{bmatrix}$

pop ([list])

returns the first element from the list.

(%i1) $\qquad$ i:[b*x^u,a*x^2,–c*x^–n];

(i) $\qquad [bx^u, ax^2, -\frac{c}{x^n}]$

(%i2) $\qquad$ pop (i);

(%o2) $\qquad bx^u$

posfun

declares a positive function.

(%i1) $\quad$ declare(b, posfun);
(%o1) $\quad$ done
(%i2) $\quad$ is(b(x)<0);

(%o2) false

(%i3) is(b(x)>0);

(%o3) true

position [points]

instructs the coordinates of the object's position with 3 numbered list. Default value: [0, 0, 0]

powerdisp

if it is set to true, output is displayed with its terms in order of increasing power.

(%i1)   powerdisp:true$

(%i2)   a^2+a^8+a^-3;

(%o2) $\frac{1}{a^3} + a^2 + a^8$

(%i3)   powerdisp:false$

(%i4)   a^2+a^8+a^-3;

(%o4) $a^8 + a^2 + \frac{1}{a^3}$

powerseries (expression, variable, point)

returns the power series for expression in the variable about the given point.

(%i1)   powerseries (log(x), x, a);

(%o1) $\left(\sum_{i2=0}^{\infty} \frac{a^{-i2-1}(-1)^{i2}(x-a)^{i2+1}}{i2+1} \right) + \log(a)$

powerset ({set},cardinality)

returns the set of all subsets of the given set.

(%i1)   powerset ({i, j, k});

(%o1)   {{},{i},{i,j},{i,j,k},{i,k},{j},{j,k},{k}}

(%i2)   powerset ({i, j, k},2);

(%o2)   {{i,j},{i,k},{j,k}}

pred

predicates (returns true or false) the given evaluation.

(%i1)   2<1,pred;

(%o1)   false

(%i2)   1<2,pred;

(%o2)   true

prev_prime (number)

returns the previous prime value for the given number.

(%i1)   prev_prime(31);

(%o1)   29

primep (number)

returns false, if the given number is a composite number or else returns true. Composite number – number that can be divided exactly by numbers other than 1 or itself.

(%i1)   primep (9);

(%o1)   false

(%i2)   primep (13);

(%o2)   true

primes (start, end)

returns the list of all primes from start to end.

(%i1)   primes(2, 21);

(%o1)   [2,3,5,7,11,13,17,19]

principal_components (matrix)

returns the principal components for a multivariate sample, which are used in multivariate statistical analysis to reduce the dimensionality of the sample. To use this function first call, load (descriptive).

(%i1)   load (descriptive);

(%o1)   "C:\maxima-5.38.1\share\maxima\5.38.1_5_gdf93b7
               b_dirty\share\descriptive\descriptive.mac"

(%i2)   matrix([1.0,15.6],[2.0,17.5],[3.0,36.6],[4.0,43.8],
               [5.0,58.2],[6.0,61.6],[7.0,65.2],[8.0,72.6],[9.0,98.9]);

$$(\%o2) \qquad \begin{bmatrix} 1.0 & 15.6 \\ 2.0 & 17.5 \\ 3.0 & 36.6 \\ 4.0 & 43.8 \\ 5.0 & 58.2 \\ 6.0 & 61.6 \\ 7.0 & 65.2 \\ 8.0 & 72.6 \\ 9.0 & 98.9 \end{bmatrix}$$

(%i3)   fpprintprec:4$
(%i4)   principal_components (%o2);

$$(\%o4) \qquad [[725.7,0.344], [99.95,0.04738], \begin{pmatrix} 0.09933 & 0.9951 \\ 0.9951 & -0.09933 \end{pmatrix}]$$

print (expression)

evaluates and displays expression.

(%i1)   for a:–3 thru 21 step 9 do print(a);

–3

6

15

(%o1)   done
(%i2)   print(expand((s-g)^–3))$

$$(\%o2) \qquad \frac{1}{s^3-3gs^2+3g^2s-g^3}$$

print_graph

print graph info.

Refer: dodecahedron_graph, tetrahedron_graph

printf (dest, "~string", expression)

returns formatted output for the expression given with a tilde followed by the string. If dest is set to true, then printf returns false. Some of the strings used are:

~%	new line
~&	fresh line
~t	tab
~$	monetary
~d	decimal integer
~b	binary integer
~o	octal integer
~br	base-b integer
~r	spell an integer
~f	floating point
~e	scientific notation
~h	bigfloat
(%o1)	printf(false, "~b", 8);
(%i1)	1000
(%i2)	printf(false, "~r", 231);
(%o2)	two hundred and thirty-one
(%i3)	printf(false, "~f", 67);
(%o3)	67.0

printfile ("file")   Refer: with_stdout

prints the output of the file specified.

product (expression, index, lower_limit, upper_limit);

evaluates expression between lower and upper limits with the index.

(%o1)	product(i^2, i, 2, 5);
(%i1)	14400 /* $2^2 \times 3^2 \times 4^2 \times 5^2$ */
(%o2)	product(x(i), i, 2, 5);
(%i2)	x(2)x(3)x(4)x(5)

properties (atom)

returns a list of properties associated with the atom.

(%o1)	product(i^2, i, 2, 5);
(%i1)	14400 /* $2^2 \times 3^2 \times 4^2 \times 5^2$ */
(%o2)	properties (%);
(%i2)	[system value]

psubst ([list], expression)

evaluates parallel substitutions for the given expression.

(%o1)   psubst ([b=a^2], (b)^3);

(%i1) a^6

ptriangularize (matrix, entry)

triangularize the matrix.

(%o1)   matrix([x,y],[1,−1])$

(%i2)   ptriangularize (%,y);

Proviso: $\{x\#0\}$

(%o2)
$$\begin{bmatrix} x & y \\ 0 & -\frac{y}{x} - 1 \end{bmatrix}$$

pui ([list], symmetric_polynomial, var)

decomposes the symmetric polynomial, in the variables in the list in terms of the power functions in the list. If values are missing in the list, formal values such as p1, p2 , etc. will be added.

(%o1)   pui;

(%i1)   pui

(%i2)   pui ([a,b,c], x*y, [x,y]);

resolvante

generale

NOTE: To compile the system do load ("sym/compile");

0 errors, 0 warnings

(%o2) $\dfrac{b^2-c}{2}$

(%i3)   pui ([a,b], x*y, [x,y]);

(%o3) $\dfrac{b^2-p2}{2}$

pui2comp (length, [list])

renders the list of complete functions with the length, in terms of the power functions given in the list.

(%i1)   pui2comp (2, [3,b,c]);

(%o1) $[3, b, \dfrac{c+b^2}{2}]$

similar function **comp2pui(length, [list]), comp2ele(length, [list])**

(%i1)	comp2pui (2, [3,b,c]);
(%o1)	$[3, b, 2c - b^2]$
(%i1)	comp2ele(2, [3,b,c]);
(%o1)	$[3, b, b^2 - c]$

pui2polynome (polynomial, [list])

returns the polynomial variable whose power functions of the root are given in the list.

(%i1)   polynome2ele (4*b^2 +5*b^3 + 6*b - 7, b);

resolvante

generale

NOTE: To compile the system do load ("sym/compile");

0 errors, 0 warnings

$$(\%o1) \qquad [3, -\frac{4}{5}, \frac{6}{5}, \frac{7}{5}]$$

push (item, [list])

returns the item item to the list and returns a new list.

(%i1)	d:[-c,y];
(d)	[-x,y]
(%i2)	push (a^b+c, d);
(%o2)	$[c + a^b, -c, y]$

put (atom, value, indicator)   qput (atom, value, indicator)

assigns the given value to the atom.rem removes the effect of put.

qput is same as put, but arguments are quoted.

(%i1)	put (x, (a+b)^3, c);
(%i2)	get(x,c);
(%o2)	$(b + a)^3$

pv (intrest_rate, future_value, period)

estimates present value of the money, from the future value for the given interest rate (not in percent) and number of periods in months. To use this function first call, **load(finance)**.

(%i1)   load(finance)$

(%i2)	pv(0.010,100000,1); Refer: fv
(%o2)	99009.900990099
(%i3)	fv(0.010,100000,1);
(%o3)	100000

qrange ([list] or [matrix])

returns interquartilic range (difference between the third and first quartiles). To use this function first call, **load (descriptive).**

(%i1)	load (descriptive);
(%o1)	"C:\maxima-5.38.1\share\maxima\5.38.1_5_gdf93b7
	b_dirty\share\descriptive\descriptive.mac"
(%i2)	[1, 2, 3, 4, 5, 6, 7, 8]$
(%i3)	qrange (%);
(%o3)	$\dfrac{7}{2}$

qty (dimensional quantity)

returns the nondimensional part of a dimensional quantity. To use this function first call, **load("ezunits")$.**

(%i1)	load ("ezunits")$
(%i2)	b:10`A *2 `s$
(%i3)	qty(b);
(%o3)	20

quadrilateral([x1, y1], [x2, y2], [x3, y3], [x4, y4])
draws a quadrilateral.

(%i1)	draw2d(quadrilateral([2,2],[3,3],[4,−1],[3,−3]))$

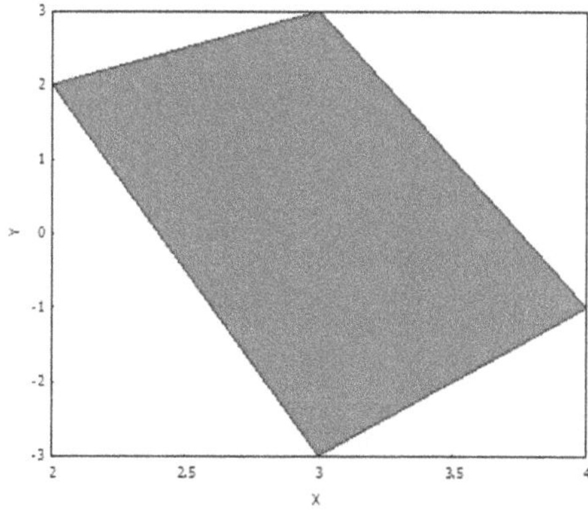

quantile ([list] or [matrix])

returnsp-quantile. To use this function first call, **load (descriptive).**

(%i1)	load (descriptive);
(%o1)	"C:\maxima-5.38.1\share\maxima\5.38.1_5_gdf93b7 b_dirty\share\descriptive\descriptive.mac"
(%i2)	[1, 2, 3, 4, 5, 6, 7, 8]$
(%i4)	quantile (%o2,3/4);quantile (%o2,1/4);
(%o3)	$\dfrac{25}{4}$
(%o4)	$\dfrac{11}{4}$

quit ()

terminates the Maxima session.

quotient (polynomial_1, polynomial_2)

returns quotient or divides polynomial_1 by polynomial_2.

(%i1)	2*x^6+13*x^5+30*x^4+28*x^3+8*x^2;
(%o1)	$2x^6 + 13x^5 + 30x^4 + 28x^3 + 8x^2$
(%i2)	x^3+4*x^2+4*x;
(%o2)	$x^3 + 4x^2 + 4x$
(%i3)	quotient (%o1, %o2);
(%o3)	$2x^3 + 5x^2 + 2x$
(%i4)	quotient (7, 3);
(%o4)	2

radcan (expression)

simplifies expression, which contain logs, exponentials, and radicals.

(%i1)	expand((j+i)^3);
(%o1)	$j^3 + 3ij^2 + 3i^2j + i^3$
(%i2)	log(%)$
(%i3)	radcan (%);
(%o3)	$3\log(j+i)$

radexpand

if it is set to true, it simplifies radicals.

(%i1) radexpand:true$

(%i2) sqrt (64*a^4);

(%o2) $8a^2$

(%i3) radexpand:fale$

(%i4) sqrt (64*a^4);

(%o4) $\sqrt{64a^4}$

radius (graph)

returns the radius of the graph. To use this first call, **load (“graphs”)$**.

(%i1) load (“graphs”)$

(%i2) cycle_graph(8)$

(%i3) draw_graph(%);

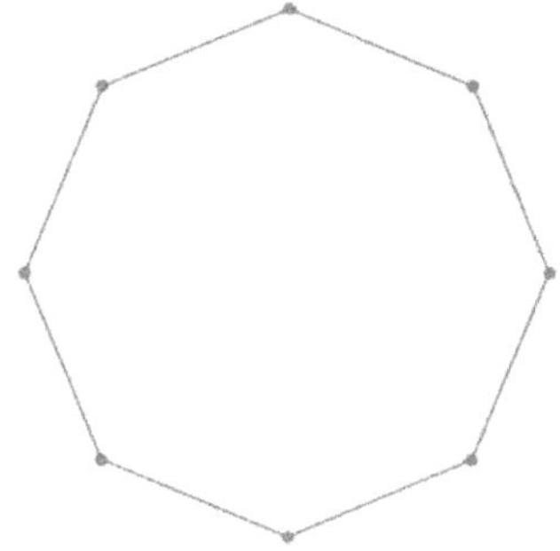

(%o3) done

(%i4) radius(%o2);

(%o4) 4

random(number)

returns random number less than or equal to given positive number.

(%i1) random(2.01); /* float */

(%o1) 1.83675729522192

(%i2) random(201);

(%o2) 28

random_discrete_uniform (integer, sample_size)

returns a random discrete uniform list for a positive integer at the given sample size. To use this function first call, **load(distrib)$.**

(%i1)	load(distrib)$
(%i2)	random_discrete_uniform (82,6);
(%o2)	[79,71,55,21,21,11]

random_exp (number,k)

returns an exponential random variate for the given size. To use this function first call, load(distrib)$.

(%i1)	load(distrib)$
(%i2)	random_exp (2.1,3);
(%o2)	[0.3626460538697, 0.1858992869583658,0.4574883375112974]

random_graph (vertices, edges)

returns a random graph for the given vertices and edges (probability). To use this function first call, **load ("graphs")$.**

(%i1)	load ("graphs")$
(%i2)	random_graph (8, 4);
(%o2)	GRAPH(8 vertices, 28 edges)
(%i3)	draw_graph(%);

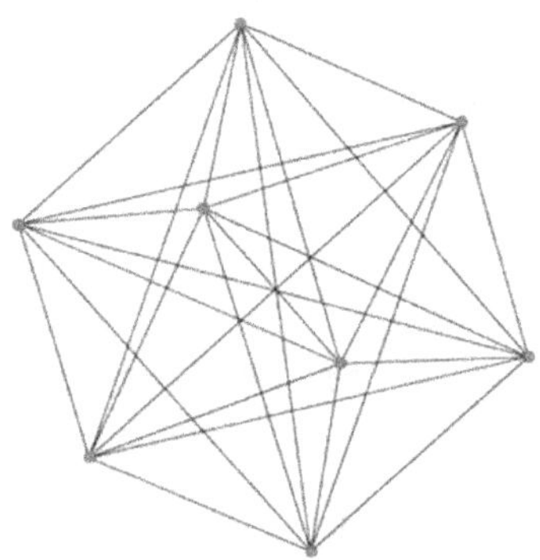

(%o3)	done

random_tree (vertices)

returns a random tree for the given vertices. To use this function first call, **load ("graphs")$**.

(%i1)	load ("graphs")$
(%i2)	random_tree (21);
(%o2)	GRAPH(21 vertices, 20 edges)
(%i3)	draw_graph(%);

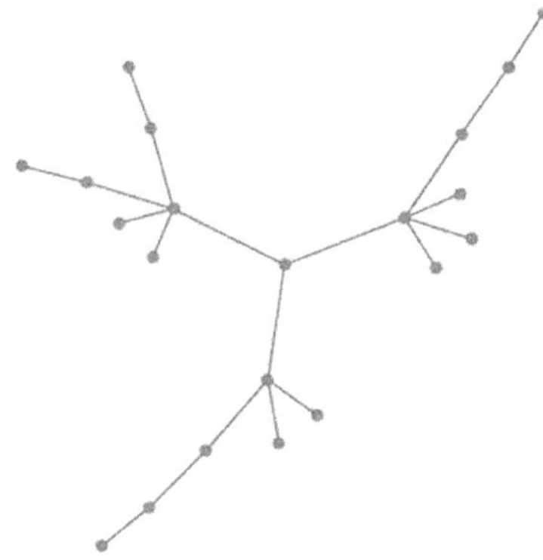

(%o3)	done

range ([list] or [matrix])

returns the difference between the extreme values. To use this function first call, **load (descriptive)$**.

(%i1)	load (descriptive)$
(%i2)	range ([6.2,2.8,1.3,7.8,2.5,4.1,0.2]);
(%o2)	7.6 /* 7.8 – 0.2 */

rank (matrix)

returns the rank of the matrix.

(%i1)	rank(matrix([0,4,5],[0,7,8],[8,9,0]));
(%o1)	3

rassociative

used with declare for right-associative property.

(%i1)	declare (i, rassociative);
(%i2)	i(i(x, y), i(y));
(%o2)	i(x,i(y,y))

rat (expression, variable)

converts expression into canonical form by expanding and combining over a common denominator and cancelling the greatest common divisor of the numerator and denominator and also converting floating point numbers to rational numbers

(%i1) $\qquad$ r^5-5*n*r^4+10*n^2*r^3-10*n^3*r^2+5*n^4*r-n^5;

(%o1) $\qquad$ $r^5-5nr^4+10n^2r^3-10n^3r^2+5n^4r-n^5$

(%i2) $\qquad$ r^2-2*n*r+n^2;

(%o2) $\qquad$ $r^2-2nr+n^2$

(%i3) $\qquad$ %o1/%o2;

(%o3) $\qquad$ $\dfrac{r^5-5nr^4+10n^2r^3-10n^3r^2+5n^4r-n^5}{r^2-2nr+n^2}$

(%i4) $\qquad$ rat(%,r,n);

(%o4) $\qquad$ $-n^3 + 3rn^2 - 3r^2n + r^3$

ratcoef (expression, variable)

returns the coefficient of the expression.

(%i1) $\qquad$ r^5-5*n*r^4+10*n^2*r^3-10*n^3*r^2+5*n^4*r-n^5;

(%o1) $\qquad$ $r^5 - 5nr^4 + 10n^2r^3 - 10n^3r^2 + 5n^4r - n^5$

(%i2) $\qquad$ ratcoef (%,n);

(%o2) $\qquad$ $-5r^4$

ratdenom (expression)

returns the denominator from a rational expression.

(%i1) $\qquad$ z*n^-r/(i*sin(z)*r);

(%o1) $\qquad$ $\dfrac{z}{in^r r\,\sin(z)}$

(%i2) $\qquad$ ratdenom(%);

(%o2) $\qquad$ $in^r r\,\sin(z)$

ratdenomdivide

if ratdenomdivide is set to true, ratexpand expands a ratio in which the numerator is a sum into a sum of ratios.

$(\%i1)$ k: (b^2 + d)/(a^3 +c);

(k) $\dfrac{d+b^2}{c+a^3}$

$(\%i2)$ ratdenomdivide: true\$

$(\%i3)$ ratexpand (k);

$(\%o3)$ $\dfrac{d}{c+a^3} + \dfrac{b^2}{c+a^3}$

$(\%i4)$ ratdenomdivide: false\$

$(\%i5)$ ratexpand (k);

$(\%o5)$ $\dfrac{d+b^2}{c+a^3}$

ratdiff (expression, x)

differentiates the rational expression with respect to variable.

$(\%i1)$ b:x^3+4*x/x^4-a*x;

$(\%o1)$ $x^3 - ax + \dfrac{4}{x^3}$

$(\%i2)$ ratdiff (b, x);

$(\%o2)$ $\dfrac{3x^6 - ax^4 - 12}{x^4}$

ratepsilon

default value: $2.0e^{-15}$

ratexpand(expression)

expands expression by multiplying products of sums or exponentiated sums or combining fractions over a common denominator, cancelling the greatest common divisor of the numerator and denominator.

$(\%i1)$ (x^-4+x^3+3*y/(x^2+y));

$(\%o1)$ $\dfrac{3y}{y+x^2} + x^3 + \dfrac{1}{x^4}$

$(\%i2)$ ratexpand (%);

$(\%o2)$ $\dfrac{y}{x^4y+x^6} + \dfrac{1}{x^2y+x^4} + \dfrac{x^3y}{y+x^2} + \dfrac{3y}{y+x^2} + \dfrac{x^5}{y+x^2}$

ratinterpol ([matrix], degree_ of_numerator)

returns a rational interpolator for the data matrix or list from the degree of numerator. To use this function first call, **load(interpol)$**.

(%i1)   load(interpol)$

(%i2)   x:matrix([2.1,6.5], [3.1,8.5], [3.4,9.1], [5.2,12.7],
             [6.5,15.3], [8.2,18.7], [8.5,19.3]);

(x)
$$\begin{bmatrix} 2.1 & 6.5 \\ 3.1 & 8.5 \\ 3.4 & 9.1 \\ 5.2 & 12.7 \\ 6.5 & 15.3 \\ 8.2 & 18.7 \\ 8.5 & 19.3 \end{bmatrix}$$

(%i3)   ratinterpol(x,2);

(%o3) $\dfrac{2x^2+\frac{43x}{10}+\frac{23}{10}}{x+1}$

(%i3)   ratinterpol(x,1);

(%o3) $2x + \dfrac{23}{10}$

rationalize (float number)

converts all floats into rational numbers.

(%i1)   rationalize (0.75*x);

(%o1) $\dfrac{3x}{4}$

ratnumer (expression)

returns the numerator of the expression,

(%i1)   (n^-r/j^-k);

(%o1) $\dfrac{j^k}{n^r}$

(%i2)   ratnumer(n^-r/j^-k);

(%o2) j^k

ratnump (iinteger)

returns true for integer or ratio of integers.

(%i1)	ratnump (3/4);
(%o1)	true
(%i2)	ratnump (0.75)
(%o2)	true

ratp_coeffs (expression, variable)

returns the list of powers and coefficients for the variable. To use this function first call, **load("ratpow")$**.

(%i1)	load("ratpow")$
(%i2)	ratp_coeffs(–4*x^5+7*x^2,x);
(%o2)	[[5,–4],[2,7]]

ratp_hipow (expression, variable)

returns the highest power of the variable in the expression. To use this function first call, **load("ratpow")$**.

(%i1)	load("ratpow")$
(%i2)	ratp_hipow(–4*x^6+7*x^8,x);
(%o2)	8

ratp_lopow (expression, variable)

returns the lowest power of the variable in the expression.To use this function first call, **load("ratpow")$**.

(%i1)	load("ratpow")$
(%i2)	ratp_lopow(–4*x^6+7*x^8,x);
(%o2)	6

ratsimp (expression)

simplifies the expression and its subexpressions.

(%i1)	k: (i^(0.5 *x) + 1)^2*(i^(x/2) – 1)^2/(i^x – 1);

$$(k) \qquad \frac{\left(i^{\frac{x}{2}}-1\right)^2 \left(i^{0.5x}+1\right)^2}{i^x-1}$$

(%i2)   ratsimp (k);   Refer:fullratsimp

(rat: replaced 0.5 by 1/2 = 0.5)

(%o2) $\dfrac{i^{2x}-2i^{x}+1}{i^{x}-1}$

ratsubst (y, x, expression)

returns the expression after substituting 'y' for 'x'.

(%i1)   ratsubst (x, x^3, (x^4*x^2));

(%o1) x^2

read (expression)

evaluates and prints the expression or string.

(%i1)   b:2*x$

(%i2)   read("value of c is:", c:b/x);

value of c is: 2

read_list("File Location")

reads and loads the list from the location.

To assign data for 'x' from the notepad file (.txt) with a data coloumn.

(%i1)   x: read_list ("F:/Experiment/Data/potential_data.txt");

read_matrix("File Location")

reads and loads the matrix from the location.

Keep a notepad (.txt) file with data in coloumns.

x: read_matrix ("F:/Experiments/Data/amp_potential_data.txt");

readchar ("string", value)

returns part of string from the mentioned value by using make_string_input_stream.

(%i1)   make_string_input_stream("wxMaxima", 2);

(%o1)   Stream [CHARACTER]

(%i2)   readchar(%o1);

(%o2)   x

readline ("string", start_value, end_value)

returns part of string from start to before the end value by using make_string_input_stream.

(%i1)	make_string_input_stream("wxMaxima", 2,6);
(%o1)	Stream [CHARACTER]
(%i2)	readline (%o1);
(%o2)	xMax

readonly (expression)

reads the expression or string without evaluation.

| (%i1) | b:5$ |
| (%i2) | read("enter expression to evaluate:"); |

enter expression to evaluate4*b

| (%o2) | 20 |
| (%i3) | readonly("enter expression to evaluate:"); |

enter expression to evaluate3*b

| (%o2) | 3b |

realpart (expression)   imagpart (expression)

returns the real part of the expression and the opposite function: **imagpart**, which returns the real part of the expression.

(%i1)	realpart (x+y*%i);
(%o1)	x
(%i2)	imagpart (x+y*%i);
(%o2)	y

realroot (expression, variable)

returns the real root of the expression for the variable.

| (%i1) | realroot(x^2+x–6,x, –1,3); |
| (%o1) | [x=–3,x=2] |

rearray (name, dimension)

changes the dimensions of an array.

(%i1)	array (k, 5);	/* array named 'k' for 5 elements */
(%o1)	k	
(%i2)	arrayinfo (k);	

(%o2)	[declared,1,[5]]
(%i3)	rearray (k, 7);
(%o3)	k
(%i4)	arrayinfo (k);
(%o4)	[declared,1,[7]]

rectangle ([x$_{maximum}$,y$_{maximum}$], [x$_{minimum}$,y$_{minimum}$])

draws a rectangle with [xmaximum,ymaximum], [xminimum,yminimum].

| (%i1) | draw2d(rectangle([5,2],[−3,−1])); |

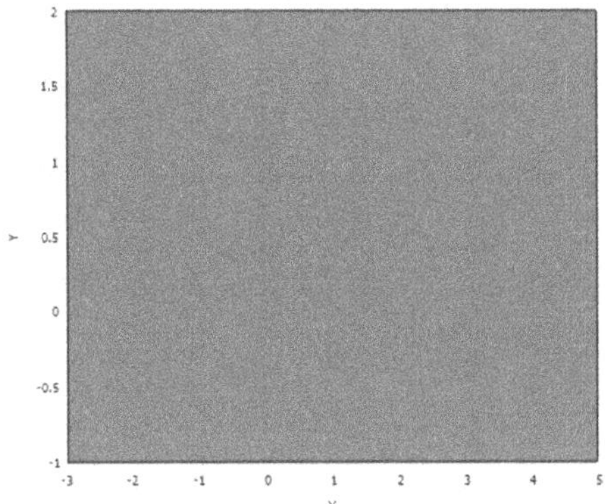

rectform (expression)

evaluates expression containing real and imaginary values.

(%i1)	rectform(sqrt(2)*%e^(%i*%pi/4));
(%o1)	%i+1
(%i2)	(sqrt(2)*%e^(%i*%pi/4));

$$(\%o2) \qquad \sqrt{2}\left(\frac{\%i}{\sqrt{2}} + \frac{1}{\sqrt{2}}\right)$$

rem (atom, indicator)   Refer: put

removes the assigned value to the atom. It removes the effect of put.

(%i1)	put (x, (a+b)^3, c);
(%i2)	get(x,c);
(%o2)	$(b+a)^3$
(%i3)	rem(x,c)
(%o3)	done
(%i4)	get(x,c);
(%o4)	false

remainder (expression_1, expression_2)

returns remainder for the division of expression_1 by expression_2.

(%i1)	remainder(x^5+x^2, x^3+x);
(%o1)	x^2+x
(%i2)	remainder(8,3);
(%o2)	2

remarray (all)

removes array and frees the storage of array.

(%i1)	array (k, 5); /* array named 'k' for 5 elements */
(%o1)	k
(%i2)	fillarray (k, [j/i, x*i, i/j,(x+i),j*y]);
(%o2)	k
(%i3)	listarray(k);
(%o3)	[j/i,ix,i/j,x+i,jy,jy]
(%i4)	remarray(k)
(%o4)	[k]
(%i5)	listarray(k);
(%o5)	listarray: argument must be an array; found: k
	-- an error. To debug this try: debugmode(true);

rembox (expression, label)

removes the box in the expression for the given label.

(%i1)	k: ((a–b)/2)+((x+a)/2)+((b–x)/2);
(k)	$\dfrac{x+a}{2}+\dfrac{b-x}{2}+\dfrac{a-b}{2}$
(%i2)	dpart (k,1,0); Refer: dpart
(%o2)	$\left[\dfrac{x+a}{2}\right]+\dfrac{b-x}{2}+\dfrac{a-b}{2}$
(%i3)	rembox (%);
(%o3)	$\dfrac{x+a}{2}+\dfrac{b-x}{2}+\dfrac{a-b}{2}$

remfunction (function)   **remfunction (all)**

removes the function definitions. remfunction (all) removes all the function definitions.

(%i1)	f(x):=x^2+2$
(%i2)	f(3);
(%o2)	11
(%i3)	remfunction(f);
(%o3)	[f]
(%i4)	f(3);
(%o4)	f(3)

remove_constvalue (constant)   Refer: declare_constvalue

removestheconstant value already declared. To use this function first call, **load(ezunits).**

(%i1)   load ("ezunits")$

(%i2)   declare_constvalue (p, 10 `m / sec);

(%o2) $10\,\grave{}\,\dfrac{m}{sec}$ /* Note: ` is prefixed */

(%i3)   time:(600 `m)/ p;

(time) $\dfrac{600\,\grave{}}{p}\,m$

(%i4)   constvalue (%);

(%o4)   60 ` sec

(%i5)   remove_constvalue (p);

(%o6)   done

(%i3)   time:(600 `m)/ p;

(time) $\dfrac{600\,\grave{}}{p}\,m$

(%i4)   constvalue (%);

(%o4) $\dfrac{600\,\grave{}}{p}\,m$

remove_dimensions (units, dimension)

removes the previously assigned fundamental dimensions. To use this function first call, **load(ezunits)\$**.

(%i1)	load ("ezunits")\$
(%i1)	fundamental_dimensions;
(%o2)	[length, mass, time, current, temperature, quantity, luminous_ intensity]
(%i3)	declare_fundamental_dimensions (dollar, rupee);
(%o3)	done
(%i4)	fundamental_dimensions;
(%o4)	[length, mass, time, current, temperature, quantity, luminous_intensity,dollar,rupee]
(%i5)	remove_fundamental_dimensions (dollar, rupee);
(%o5)	done
(%i6)	fundamental_dimensions;
(%o6)	[length, mass, time, current, temperature, quantity, luminous_intensity]

remove_fundamental_units (units, dimension)

reverts the previously assigned fundamental units. To use this function first call, **load(ezunits)\$**.

(%i1)	load ("ezunits")\$
(%i2)	fundamental_dimensions;
(%o2)	[length, mass, time, current, temperature, quantity, luminous_intensity]
(%i3)	declare_fundamental_dimensions (dollar, rupee);
(%o3)	done
(%i4)	fundamental_dimensions;
(%o4)	[length, mass, time, current, temperature, quantity, luminous_intensity, dollar, rupee]
(%i5)	declare_fundamental_units (rupee, dollar);
(%o5)	[rupee]
(%i6)	dimensions (70 \` rupee/dollar);
(%o6)	$\dfrac{rupee}{dollar}$
(%i7)	remove_fundamental_units (rupee, dollar);
(%o7)	[false. false]

(%i8)	dimensions (70 `rupee/dollar);
(%o8)	$\dfrac{dimensions(rupee)}{dimensions(dollar)}$

rempart (expression, [parts])

removes the parts from the expression. To use third function first call, **load(functs) $.**

(%i1)	load(functs)$
(%i2)	expand((i–j+n)^2);
(%o2)	$n^2 - 2jn + 2in + j^2 - 2ij + i^2$
(%i4)	rempart(%,[1,4]); /*removes 1 to 4 parts */
(%o4)	$i^2–2ij$

rename_file (file1, file2)

renames file file1 to file2

rest (expression, n)

returns expression with first 'n' elements removed if 'n' is positive and its last 'n' elements removed if 'n' is negative.

(%i1)	expand((i–j+n)^2);
(%o1)	$n^2 - 2jn + 2in + j^2 - 2ij + i^2$
(%i2)	rest(%,3);
(%o2)	$j^2 - 2ij + i^2$
(%i3)	rest(%o1,–3);
(%o3)	$n^2 - 2jn + 2in$

resultant (polynomial_1, polynomial_2, variable)

returns resultant of two polynomials eliminating the variable.

(%i1)	expand((i+6)*(i+3));
(%o1)	$i^2+9i+18$
(%i2)	resultant(%o1,(i+2),i);
(%o2)	4
(%i3)	expand((i+5)*(i+6));

(%o3)	$i^2+11i+30$
(%i4)	resultant(%o3,(i+2),i);
(%o4)	12

return (value)

returns the evaluated value in logical programming.

| (%i1) | for a:–3 thru 26 step 6 do display(a*b); |

–3b

3b

9b

15b

21b

(%o1)	done
(%i2)	for a:–3 thru 26 step 6 do if a=9 then return(a*b);
(%o2)	9b

reveal (expression, integer_depth)

replaces parts of expression at the integer depth.

Sums and differences are replaced by Sum(n) where n is the number of operands of the sum.

Products are replaced by Product(n) where n is the number of operands of the product.

Exponentials are replaced by Expt.

Unary negation is replaced by Negterm.

Lists are replaced by List(n) where n ist the number of elements of the list.

(%i1)	g:expand((n–r)^3);
(%o1)	$-r^3 + 3nr^2 - 3n^2r + n^3$
(%i2)	reveal (g, 1);
(%o2)	Sum(4)
(%i3)	reveal (g, 2);
(%o3)	Negterm+Product(3)+Negterm+Expt
(%i4)	reveal (g, 3);
(%o4)	$-\text{Expt}+3n\text{Expt}-\text{Product}(3)+n^3$

reverse ([list])

reverses the order of the members of the list.

(%i1)   reverse ([n^–2,r^–3,m*6,k^2]);

(%o1) $[k^2, 6m, \frac{1}{r^3}, \frac{1}{n^2}]$

revert (expression, variable)revert2 (expression, variable,value)

return the reverse of the expression, Taylor series for the variable at the given value. To use this function first call, **load ("revert")$**.

(%i1)   k: taylor (1/(x+1), x, 0, 4);

(k) $1 - x + x^2 - x^3 + x^4 + \cdots$

(%i2)   load ("revert")$

(%i3)   revert (taylor (1/(x+1), x, 0, 4),x);

(%o3)/R/ $x^4 - x^3 + x^2 - x$

(%i4)   s:expand((a+2)*(c+3));

(s)   ac+2c+3a+6

(%i5)   revert (s,a);

(%o5) $\dfrac{a}{c+3}$

(%i6)   revert2 (taylor (1/(x+1), x, 0, 4),x,4);

(%o6) $-x + (1 - x)^4 + (1 - x)^3 + (1 - x)^2 + 1$

(%i7)   revert (s,a,4);

(%o7) $\dfrac{-2c+a-6}{c+3}$

rhs (expression)

returns the right-hand side of the expression.

(%i1)   (r^g)*(s^n) = (j+k)^3;

(%o1) $r^g s^n = (k+j)^3$

(%i2)   expand(rhs(%));

(%o2) $k^3+3jk^2+3j^2k+j^3$

rmdir (directory)

remove the specified directory

rmxchar

changes the character displayed as the right delimiter for a matrix from the default '['.

(%i1)   x: matrix ([j, i^2], [u/i, j*k]);

(x) $\begin{bmatrix} j & i^2 \\ \frac{u}{i} & jk \end{bmatrix}$

(%i2)   rmxchar: "|"$

(%i3)   x: matrix ([j, i^2], [u/i, j*k]);

(x) $\begin{matrix} [j & i^2| \\ [\frac{u}{i} & jk| \end{matrix}$

rncombine (expression)

simplifies the sum expression by combining the terms with the same denominator into a single term. To use this function first call, **load (rncomb)$**.

(%i1)   load (rncomb)$
(%i2)   b:(x*t/3)+(y*i/4)–(e*x/(2*r))–(z*n/2);

(b) $-\frac{nz}{2}+\frac{iy}{4}+\frac{tx}{3}-\frac{ex}{2r}$

(%i3)   rncombine (b);

(%o4) $\frac{-6nz+3iy+4tx}{12}-\frac{ex}{2r}$

romberg (expression, variable, lower_limit, upper_limit)

returns numerical integration by Romberg's method from, lower_limit, upper_limit. To use this function first call, **load (rncomb)$**.

(%i1)   load (rncomb)$
(%i2)   romberg (0.5*x^2, x, 2.5,4.5);
(%o2)   12.58333333333333

rootscontract (expression)

returns products of roots into roots of products from expresssion.

(%i1)   (sqrt(i)*j^(3/2));

(%o1) $\sqrt{i}\,j^{\frac{3}{2}}$

(%i2)   rootscontract ((sqrt(x)*y^(3/2)));

(%o2) $\sqrt{ij^3}$

round (number)

returns the closest integer.

(%i1)   round (2.4);

(%o1)   2

(%i2)   round (2.7);

(%o2)   3

row (matrix, m)

returns the mth row of the matrix.

(%i1)   M: matrix ([−a,3*y,u], [2*y,e,i*t],[n*c,v,m*e]);

(%o1) $\begin{bmatrix} -a & 3y & u \\ 2y & e & it \\ cn & v & em \end{bmatrix}$

(%i2)   row (M, 2);

(%o2) $[2y \quad e \quad it]$

rowswap (matrix, i,j)

swap the rows 'i' and 'j' in the matrix.

(%i1)   M: matrix ([−a,3*y,u], [2*y,e,i*t],[n*c,v,m*e]);

(%o1) $\begin{bmatrix} -a & 3y & u \\ 2y & e & it \\ cn & v & em \end{bmatrix}$

(%i2)   rowswap (M,1,3);

(%o2) $\begin{bmatrix} cn & v & em \\ 2y & e & it \\ -a & 3y & u \end{bmatrix}$

rreduce (f, [List])

Refer:rreduce

extends the binary function 'f' to the list.

(%i1)	rreduce (f, [a, b, c]);
(%o1)	f(a,f(b,c))
(%i2)	lreduce (f, [a, b, c]);
(%o2)	f(f(a,b),c)

run_testsuite ([options])

run the Maxima test suite and it has optional keywords to run the test. display_all: Display all tests.display_known_bugs: Displays tests that are marked as known bugs. Time: Display time information.

(%i1)   run_testsuite(display_known_bugs=true);

/* runs tests and executes problems one by one with the error */

same_xy

if it is set to true, the scales used in the 'x' and 'y' axes will be the same, in 2d or 3d plots.

(%i1)   plot2d (2*x^2, [x, –8, 8], [xtics, –7,1,7],[ytics, 0,15, 120],[axes, solid],grid2d,[**same_xy, true**],[label, ["m", 6, 15]],[xlabel, "Time (s)"], [ylabel, "Temperature (k)"])$

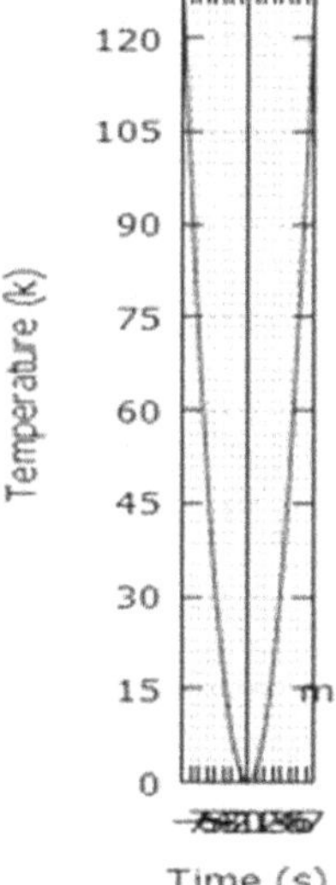

(%i1) plot2d (2*x^2, [x, –8, 8], [xtics, –7,1,7],[ytics, 0,15, 120],[axes, solid],grid2d,[**same_xy, false**],[label, ["m", 6, 15]],[xlabel, "Time (s)"], [ylabel, "Temperature (k)"])$

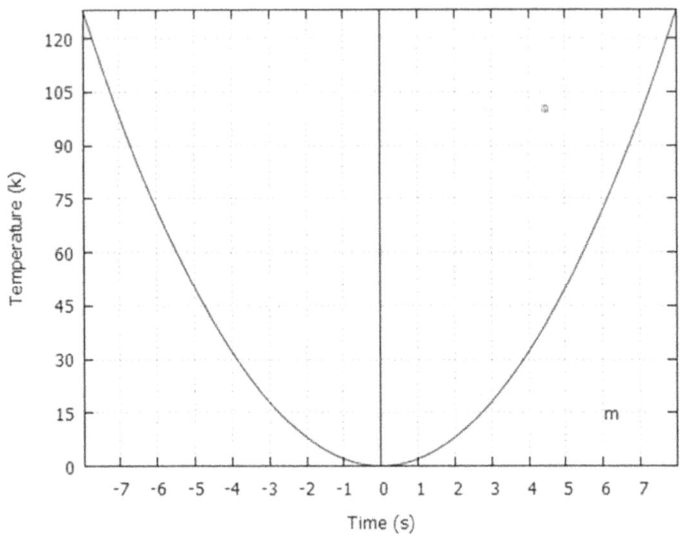

same_xyz

same as 'same_xy' function but for 3d plots.

(%i1) plot3d(1/(1+x^2+y^2),[x,-4,4],[y,-3,3],
[same_xyz, true])$

$$1/(y^2+x^2+1)$$

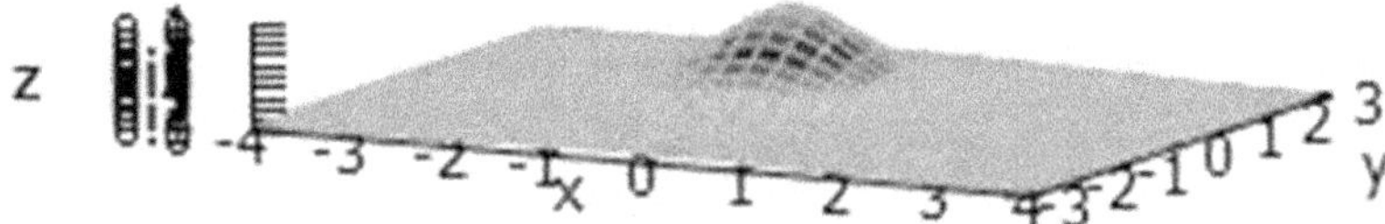

(%i1)   plot3d(1/(1+x^2+y^2),[x,–4,4],[y,–3,3],
[same_xyz, false])$

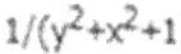

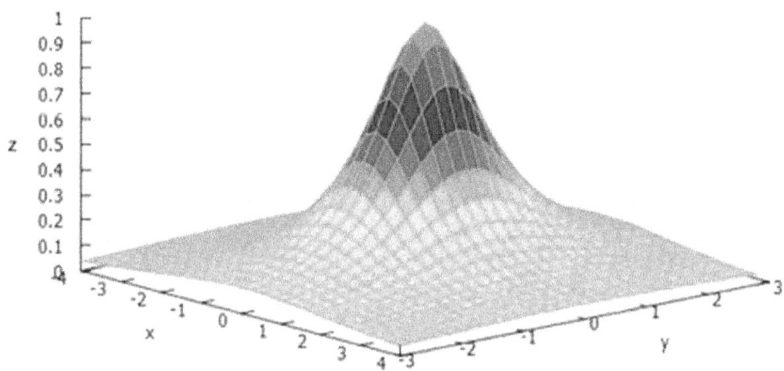

save (filename, values, functions)

stores the file with the given filename and values. The saved file may be loaded by load (filename).

saving (rate,amount,number)

returns the tableof values at periodic saving with the amountand number of periods at the given intrest rate. To use this function first call, **load(finance)$**.

(%i1)   load(finance)$
(%i2)   saving(0.1,1000,12)$

(%o2)

"n"	"Balance"	"Interest"	"Payment"
0.000	0.000	0.000	0.000
1.000	46.763	0.000	46.763
2.000	98.203	4.676	46.763
3.000	154.787	9.820	46.763
4.000	217.029	15.479	46.763
5.000	285.495	21.703	46.763
6.000	360.808	28.549	46.763
7.000	443.652	36.081	46.763
8.000	534.780	44.365	46.763

9.000	635.021	53.478	46.763
10.000	745.287	63.502	46.763
11.000	866.579	74.529	46.763
12.000	1000.000	86.658	46.763

scalar   Refer: scalarp

to declar the scalar function as declare(expression, scalar).

scalarp (expression)

returns true if expression is scalar.

(%i1)	declare(i, scalar);
(%o1)	done
(%i2)	scalarp (i);
(%o2)	true
(%i3)	scalarp (n);
(%o3)	false

scanmap (function, expression)

recursively applies function to expression, in a top down manner.

(%i1)	a*y^2+a−a*c;
(%o1)	ay^2-ac+a
(%i2)	scanmap(factor,%);
(%o2)	$a(y^2-c+1)$
(%i3)	i*(a−c)^3;
(%o3)	$(a-c)^3$
(%i4)	scanmap(expand,%);
(%o4)	$-c^3i + 3ac^2i − 3a^2ci + a^3i$

scatterplot ([list] or matrix, options)

returns scatter plot for the given list or matrix with the plotting options. To use this function first call, load ("descriptive")\$ and load ("distrib")\$.

(%i1)	load ("descriptive")\$load("distrib")\$

(%i3)   scatterplot(matrix([1,7],[2,10],[3,17],[4,28],[5,43],[6,62]
               [7,85], [8,112],[9,143])), xrange = [−1,10], yrange = [0,150],
               point_type = filled_circle, xtics = 0.5, ytics = 15);

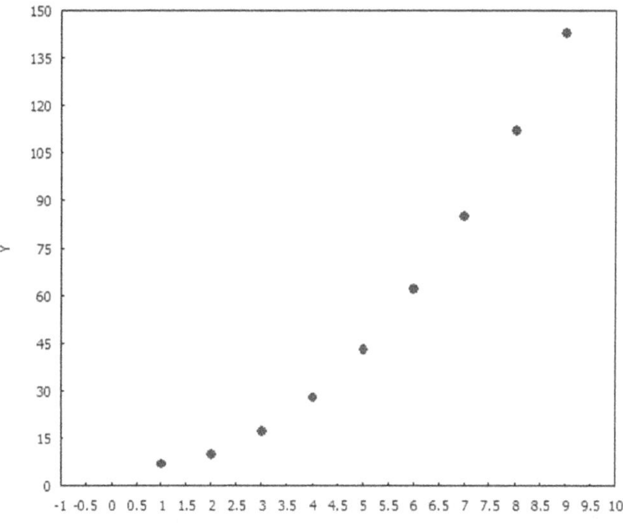

sconcat (arguments)

concatenates arguments.

(%i4)   i:6.3;j:8.6;

               a:sconcat (i, j/2);

(i)   6.3
(j)   8.6
(a)   6.34.3

scopy ("string")

returns a copy of string as a new string.

(%i1)   a:scopy("wxMaxima");
(a)   wxMaxima
(%i2)   stringp(a);
(%o2)   true
(%i3)   stringp(wxMaxima);
(%o3)   false

sdowncase ("STRING", start, end)

returns lowercase of the given string from start to end.

(%i1)   sdowncase ("WXMAXIMA",1,3);

(%o1)   wxMAXIMA

sec(value)

returns secant for the given value. To use tignometric function it is better to call, **load(ntrig)$**.

(%i1)   load(ntrig);

(%o1)   "C:\maxima-5.38.1\share\maxima\5.38.1_5_gdf93b7

               b_dirty\share\trigonometry\ntrig.mac"

(%i2)   sec(0.5);

(%o2)   1.139493927324549

sech(value)

returns hyperbolic secant for the given value. To use tignometric function it is better to call, **load(ntrig)$**.

(%i1)   load(ntrig);

(%o1)   "C:\maxima-5.38.1\share\maxima\5.38.1_5_gdf93b7

               b_dirty\share\trigonometry\ntrig.mac"

(%i2)   sech(0.5);

(%o2)   0.886818883970074

second (expression)

returns the second part of the expression which may be an element of a list, second row of a matrix or second term of a sum etc.

(%i1)   b:matrix([j,n*i,n^2],[-4*x, -3/u, -3*z]);

(b) $\begin{bmatrix} j & in & n^2 \\ -4x & -\dfrac{3}{u} & -3z \end{bmatrix}$

(%i2)   second(%);

(%o2) $[-4x, -\dfrac{3}{u}, -3z]$

sequal ("string_1", "string_2")

returns true if string_1 and string_2 contain the same sequence of characters.

(%i1)	sequal ("wxMaxima", "WXMAXIMA");
(%o1)	false
(%i2)	sequal ("wxMaxima", "wxMaxima");
(%o2)	true

sequalignore ("string_1", "string_2")

returns true if string_1 and string_2 contain the same alphabets or characters unlike the function sequal .

(%i1)	sequalignore ("wxMaxima", "WXMAXIMA");
(%o1)	true

set_draw_defaults (options)

sets user defined graphics options as default.

(%i1)   set_draw_defaults(xrange = [–1,10], yrange = [0,150], point_type = filled_circle, xtics = 0.5, ytics = 15,color = red, grid=true)$

(%i2)   scatterplot(matrix([1,7],[2,10],[3,17],[4,28],[5,43],[6,62], [7,85], [8,112],[9,143]));

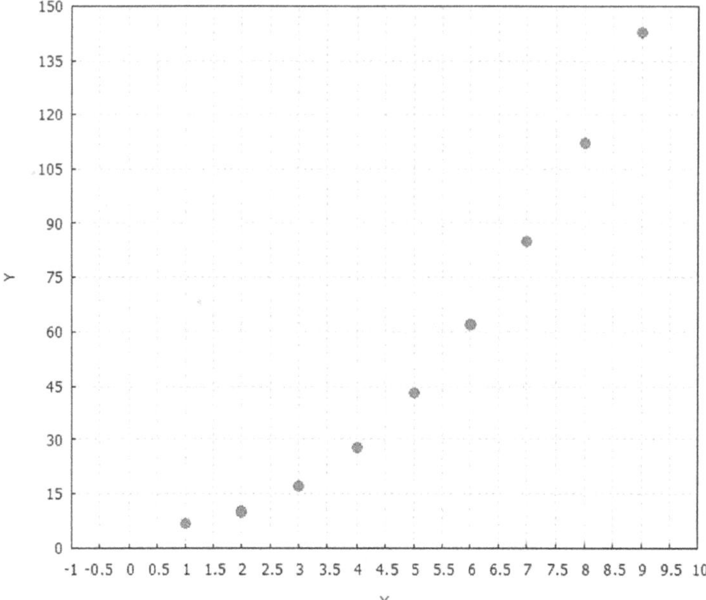

(%o2) [gr2d(points)]

set_partitions ({set}, number)

returns the set of all partitions at the given number.

(%i1)	set_partitions ({–n,k,–g}, 2);
(%o1)	{{{–g},{k,–n}},{{–g,k},{–n}},{{–g,–n},{k}}}
(%i2)	set_partitions ({–n,k,–g, m}, 3);
(%o2)	{{{–g},{k},{m,–n}},{{–g},{k,m},{–n}},{{–g},{k,–n},{m}},
	{{–g,k},{m},{–n}},{{–g,m},{k},{–n}},{{–g,–n},{k},{m}}}

setdifference (a, b)

returns a set with elements in the set 'a' that are not in the set 'b'.

(%i1)	setdifference (
	{–1,n,–g,–r,s,4,–a,k,–3,0},{2,b,–a,ss,7,8,jj,k});
(%o1)	{–3,–1,0,4,–g,n,–r,s}

setelmx (element, row, coloum, matrix)

returns the matrix by substituting the element at the specified (row, coloumn) [th]position in the given matrix.

(%i1)	b:matrix([j,n*i,n^2],[–4*x, –3/u, –3*z]);

$$(b) \qquad \begin{bmatrix} j & in & n^2 \\ -4x & -\dfrac{3}{u} & -3z \end{bmatrix}$$

(%i2)	setelmx (k^j, 1, 2, b);

$$(\%o2) \qquad \begin{bmatrix} j & k^j & n^2 \\ -4x & -\dfrac{3}{u} & -3z \end{bmatrix}$$

setequalp (x, y)

returns true if sets 'x' and 'y' have the same elements.

(%i1)	setequalp ({i,j,k}, {k,i,j});
(%o1)	true
(%i2)	setequalp ({n,i,j}, {k,i,j});
(%o2)	false

setify ([list])

returns a set from the elements of the list

(%i1)   setify ([–n,n,s,n,k,j,kk]);
(%o1)   {j,k,kk,–n,n,s}

setp ({set})

returns true for a set.

(%i1)   setp{j,k,kk,–n,n,s}
(%o1)   true

setunits ([unit_list])

to set units based on default values. To use this function first call, **load(unit)\$**.

(%i1)   load("unit")\$
(%i2)   N;   /* Newton */

(%o2) $\dfrac{kgm}{s^2}$

(%i3)   milligram*centimeter/minute;

(%o3) $\dfrac{1}{6000000000}\dfrac{kgm}{s}$

(%i4)   setunits([milligram,centimeter,minute]);

(%o4) done
(%i5)   2*N;

(%o5) $720000000000\dfrac{\%\%\,mg\,cm}{\%min^2}$

sexplode (string)

returns the list of characters in string. To use this function first call, **load(stringproc)\$**.

(%i1)   load(stringproc)\$
(%i2)   sexplode ("Its wxMaxima");   Refer: charlist
(%o2)   [I,t,s, ,w,x,M,a,x,i,m,a]
(%i3)   sexplode ("2x7im");
(%o3)   [2,x,7,i,m]

shortest_path (from, to, graph)

returns the shortest path in between two points in the graph. To use this function first call, **load("graphs")$**.

(%i1)	load ("graphs")$
(%i2)	cycle_graph(8)$
(%i3)	draw_graph(%);

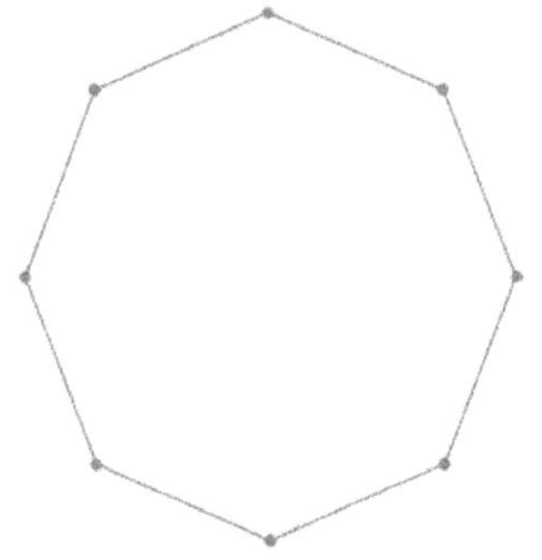
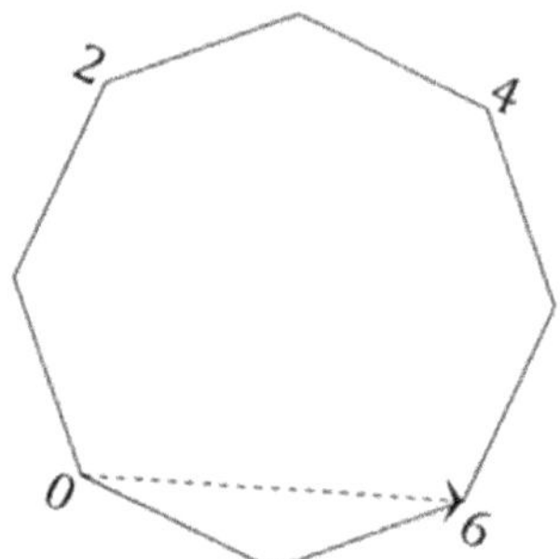

(%o3)	done
(%i4)	shortest_path(0, 6,%o2);
(%o4)	[0,7,6]

shortest_weighted_path (from, to, graph)

returns the length between two points. To use this function first call, **load("graphs")$**.

(%i1)	load ("graphs")$
(%i2)	cycle_graph(8)$
(%i3)	draw_graph(%);

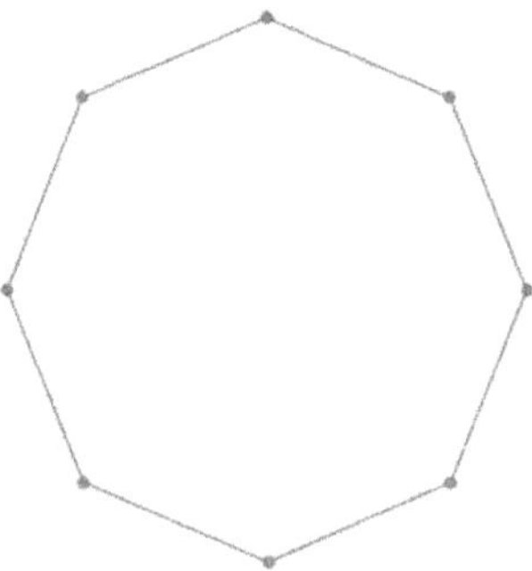

(%o3)	done
(%i4)	shortest_weighted_path (0, 6,%o2);
(%o4)	[2,[0,7,6]]

(%i5)   shortest_weighted_path (0, 5,%o2);
(%o5)   [3,[0,7,6,5]]

showratvars (expression)

returns a list of the canonical rational expression variables for the given expression. Related function: **ratvars (expression)**

(%i1)   (n^-r)+(j/r);

(%o1) $\dfrac{j}{r} + \dfrac{1}{n^r}$

(%i2)   showratvars ((n^-r)+(j/r));

(%o2) $[j, n^r, r]$

(%i3)   ratvars ((n^-r)+(j/r));

(%o3) $[\dfrac{r+jn^r}{n^r r}]$

showtime

if it is set to true, computation time is printed for each output.

(%i1)   showtime:true$
Evaluation took 0.0000 seconds (0.0000 elapsed) using 80 bytes. (%i2)
expand(((i–j)^3);
Evaluation took 0.0000 seconds (0.0020 elapsed) using 10.469 KB.

(%o2) $-j^3 + 3ij^2 - 3i^2j + i^3$

(%i3)   expand(((i–j)^2);
Evaluation took 0.0000 seconds (0.0000 elapsed) using 8.320 KB.

(%o3) $j^2 - 2ij + i^2$

(%i4)   %o2/%o3;
Evaluation took 0.0000 seconds (0.0000 elapsed) using 1.328 KB.

(%o4) $\dfrac{-j^3+3ij^2-3i^2j+i^3}{j^2-2ij+i^2}$

sign (expression)

returns the sign of the expression: pos (positive), neg (negative), zero, pz (positive or zero), nz (negative or zero), pn (positive or negative), or pnz (positive, negative, or zero).

(%i1)   sign((%i)^2);

(%o1)   neg

(%i1)   sign(-1*(%i)^2);

(%o1)   pos

similaritytransform (matrix)   simtran (matrix)

returns similarity transform of the matrix. To use this function first call, **load ("eigen")$**.

(%i1)   load ("eigen")$

(%i2)   m:matrix([2,1],[-1,1]);

(%o2) $\begin{bmatrix} 2 & 1 \\ -1 & 1 \end{bmatrix}$

(%i3)   simtran (%);

(%o3) $[[[-\frac{\sqrt{3}\%i-3}{2}, \frac{\sqrt{3}\%i+3}{2}], [1,1]], [[[\frac{1}{\sqrt{2}}, -\frac{\sqrt{3}\%i+1}{2^{\frac{3}{2}}}]],$

$[[\frac{1}{\sqrt{2}}, \frac{\sqrt{3}\%i-1}{2^{\frac{3}{2}}}]]]]]$

sin(x)

returns sine value for angle 'x' expressed in radians.

(%i1)   sin(30),numer;

(%o1)   -0.9880316240928618

sinh(value)

returns hyperbolic sine for the given value.

(%i1)   sinh(0.5);

(%o1)   0.5210953054937474

sinsert ("string", position)

returns a string by concatenationat the mentioned position.

(%i1)   x:"wxima"$

(%i2)   sinsert("max",x,3);

(%o2)	"wxmaxima"
(%i3)	sinsert("max",x,4);
(%o3)	"wximaxma"

sinvertcase ("string", start, end)

returns string with character start to end is inverted.

(%i1)	sinvertcase("wxMaxima");
(%o1)	WXmAXIMA
(%i2)	sinvertcase("wxMaxima",1,5);
(%o2)	WXmAxima

skewness (list or matrix)   Refer: pearson_skewness

returns skewness coefficient for the list or matrix. To use this function first call, **load (descriptive)\$**.

(%i1)	load (descriptive)\$
(%i2)	[15.6,17.5,36.6,43.8,58.2,61.6,65.2,72.6,98.9]\$
(%i3)	skewness (%), numer;
(%o3)	0.1239051579025224
(%i4)	[a,b,c]\$
(%i5)	skewness (%o4), numer;

$$(\%o5) \quad \frac{\sqrt{3}\left(\left(c-\frac{c+b+a}{3}\right)^3+\left(b-\frac{c+b+a}{3}\right)^3+\left(a-\frac{c+b+a}{3}\right)^3\right)}{\left(\left(c-\frac{c+b+a}{3}\right)^2+\left(b-\frac{c+b+a}{3}\right)^2+\left(a-\frac{c+b+a}{3}\right)^2\right)^{\frac{3}{2}}}$$

(%i6)	[a,b]\$
(%i7)	skewness (%), numer;

$$(\%o7) \quad \frac{\sqrt{2}\left(\left(b-\frac{b+a}{2}\right)^3+\left(a-\frac{b+a}{2}\right)^3\right)}{\left(\left(b-\frac{b+a}{2}\right)^2+\left(a-\frac{b+a}{2}\right)^2\right)^{\frac{3}{2}}}$$

slength ("string")

returns the number of characters in the string including spaces.

(%i1)	slength("wx Maxima");
(%o1)	9

smake (number, character)

Rreturns a string for the given number with the character.

(%i1)   smake(6,"@");

(%o1)   @@@@@@

smax (list or matrix)

returns maximum value in the list or a list containing the maximum values of the coloumns in the matrix.To use this function first call, **load (descriptive)$**.

(%i1)   load (descriptive)$

(%i2)   matrix([21,2,1], [1,31,8], [1,23,1]);

(%o2) $\begin{bmatrix} 21 & 2 & 1 \\ 1 & 31 & 8 \\ 1 & 23 & 1 \end{bmatrix}$

(%i3)   smax(%);

(%o3)   [21,31,8]

smin (list or matrix)

returns minimum value in the list or a list containing the minimum values of the coloumns in the matrix. To use this function first call, **load (descriptive)$**.

(%i1)   load (descriptive)$

(%i2)   matrix([21,2,-1], [1,31,8], [41,-31,1]);

(%o2) $\begin{bmatrix} 21 & 2 & -1 \\ 1 & 31 & 8 \\ 41 & -31 & 1 \end{bmatrix}$

(%i3)   smin(%);

(%o3)   [1,-31,-1]

smismatch (string_1, string_2)

returns the position of the first character of string_1 at which string_1 and string_2 differ if no mismatch then returns false.

(%i1)   smismatch("wxMaxima", "wxmaxima");

(%o1)   3

solve (expression, variable)

important function in programming and it solves the expression for the variable from the expression. Expressions and variables can also be given as list.

(%i1)   solve([x+y=−1, 3*x−y=−11], [x,y]);
(%o1)   [[x=−3,y=2]]
(%i2)   solve([2*x=4*y], [x,y]);
(%o2)   [[x=2%r1,y=%r1]]
(%i3)   solve((x^3−27=0),x);

(%o3) $$\left[x = \frac{3^{\frac{3}{2}}\%i-3}{2}, x = -\frac{3^{\frac{3}{2}}\%i+3}{2}, x = 3\right]$$

some (predicate, expression)

returns true if the predicate is true for one or more given arguments.

(%i1)   some("<",[1,2,3],[3,4,5]);
(%o1)   true
(%i2)   k:2*3$some("=",[6], [k]);
(%o2)   true

sort([list], predicate)

sorts a list as per predicate.

(%i1)   sort([1.65,2.31,−3.41,−4.13],ordergreatp);
(%o1)   [2.31,1.65,−3.41,−4.13]
(%i2)   sort([abc,bac,cab,bca,cba,acb],orderlessp);
(%o2)   [abc,acb,bac,bca,cab,cba]

space

retuns space character.

split (string, delim)

returns the list with unparsed string from delimiter.

(%i1)   split("wxXmMaxima","Xm");
(%o1)   [wx,Maxima]

sposition ("character", "string")

returns the number of position of the first character in string.

(%i1)   sposition ("x", "wxMaxima");

(%o1)   2

sprint (expressions)

evaluates the expressions one by one and returns it.

(%i1)   for i:0 thru 5 do sprint(oddp(i))$

false true false true false true /* 0 1 2 3 4 5 → check for odd */

sqfr (expr)

returns square-free polynomial factors of degree one.

(%i1)   expand((x–2)^2*(x+3)^2);

(%o1) $x^4 + 2x^3 - 11x^2 - 12x + 36$

(%i2)   sqfr(%o1);

(%o2) $(x^2 + x - 6)^2$

(%i3)   factor(%o1);

(%o3) $(x - 2)^2 (x + 3)^2$

sqrt (value)

returns square root for the value.

(%i1)   sqrt(%i);

(%o1) $1.0(-1)^{1/4}$

sqrtdispflag

if it is false, returns display with exponent ½. Default value:true.

(%i1)   sqrtdispflag:true$

(%o1)   sqrt(x);

(%i2) $\sqrt{x}$

(%o2)   sqrtdispflag:false$

(%i3)   sqrt(x);

(%o3) $x^{1/2}$

sremove ("character", "string", start, end)

returns the string by removing the character from start to end.

(%i1)	sremove("x","wxMaxima");
(%o1)	wMaima
(%i2)	sremove("x","wxMaxima",1,3);
(%o2)	wMaxima

sremovefirst ("character", "string)

returns the string by removing the character at very first position.

(%i1)	sremovefirst("x","wxMaxima");
(%o1)	wMaxima

sreverse ("string")

returns the string with all the characters reversed.

(%i1)	sreverse("wxMaxima");
(%o1)	amixaMxw

ssearch ("character", "string", start, end)

returns the position of the character in the string from start to end.

(%i1)	ssearch("x","wxMaxima",1,7);
(%o1)	2

ssort ("string", test)

returns the string with all characters in an order. test mode used are:

clessp, clesspignore, cgreaterp, cgreaterpignore, cequal, cequalignore.

(%i1)	ssort("Symbolic wxMaxima");
(%o1)	MSaabciilmmmowxxy
(%i2)	ssort("Symbolic wxMaxima", cgreaterp);
(%o2)	yxxwommliicbaaSM
(%i3)	ssort("Symbolic wxMaxima", clessp);
(%o3)	MSaabciilmmowxxy

ssubst (new, old, "string", start, end)

returns a string after substituting new character for old from start to end of the string.

(%i1)   ssubst("am","is", "I is wxMaxima. I is wrong.");

(%o1)   I am wxMaxima. I am wrong.

(%i2)   ssubst("am","is", "I is wxMaxima. I is wrong.",1,5);

(%o2)   I am wxMaxima. I is wrong.

ssubstfirst (new, old, "string", start, end)

returns a string after substituting new character at the first position for old from start to end of the string.

(%i1)   ssubstfirst ("am","is", "I is wxMaxima. I is wrong.");

(%o1)   I am wxMaxima. I is wrong.

standardize ([list] or matrix)

subtracts each element of a list or row of the matrix from mean and divides by standard deviation. To use this function first call, **load(descriptive)$**.

(%i1)   load (descriptive)$

(%i2)   standardize([a,b,c]);

(%o2)

$$\left[\frac{\sqrt{3}\left(a-\frac{c+b+a}{3}\right)}{\sqrt{\left(c-\frac{c+b+a}{3}\right)^2+\left(b-\frac{c+b+a}{3}\right)^2+\left(a-\frac{c+b+a}{3}\right)^2}}, \right.$$

$$\frac{\sqrt{3}\left(b-\frac{c+b+a}{3}\right)}{\sqrt{\left(c-\frac{c+b+a}{3}\right)^2+\left(b-\frac{c+b+a}{3}\right)^2+\left(a-\frac{c+b+a}{3}\right)^2}},$$

$$\left. \frac{\sqrt{3}\left(c-\frac{c+b+a}{3}\right)}{\sqrt{\left(c-\frac{c+b+a}{3}\right)^2+\left(b-\frac{c+b+a}{3}\right)^2+\left(a-\frac{c+b+a}{3}\right)^2}} \right]$$

(%i3)   standardize([i,j,k,l]);

(%o3)
$$\frac{2\left(i-\frac{l+k+j+i}{4}\right)}{\sqrt{\left(l-\frac{l+k+j+i}{4}\right)^2+\left(k-\frac{l+k+j+i}{4}\right)^2+\left(j-\frac{l+k+j+i}{4}\right)^2+\left(i-\frac{l+k+j+i}{4}\right)^2}},$$

$$\frac{2\left(j-\frac{l+k+j+i}{4}\right)}{\sqrt{\left(l-\frac{l+k+j+i}{4}\right)^2+\left(k-\frac{l+k+j+i}{4}\right)^2+\left(j-\frac{l+k+j+i}{4}\right)^2+\left(i-\frac{l+k+j+i}{4}\right)^2}},$$

$$\frac{2\left(k-\frac{l+k+j+i}{4}\right)}{\sqrt{\left(l-\frac{l+k+j+i}{4}\right)^2+\left(k-\frac{l+k+j+i}{4}\right)^2+\left(j-\frac{l+k+j+i}{4}\right)^2+\left(i-\frac{l+k+j+i}{4}\right)^2}},$$

$$\frac{2\left(l-\frac{l+k+j+i}{4}\right)}{\sqrt{\left(l-\frac{l+k+j+i}{4}\right)^2+\left(k-\frac{l+k+j+i}{4}\right)^2+\left(j-\frac{l+k+j+i}{4}\right)^2+\left(i-\frac{l+k+j+i}{4}\right)^2}}$$

(%i4)   standardize([1,2,3,4]);

(%o4) $[-\frac{3}{\sqrt{5}},-\frac{1}{\sqrt{5}},\frac{1}{\sqrt{5}},\frac{3}{\sqrt{5}}]$

stardisp

if it is true, multiplication is displayed by *. Default value: false.

(%i1)   stardisp:false$
(%i2)   c*a
(%o2)   ac
(%i3)   stardisp:true$
(%i4)   c*a
(%o4)   a*c

starplot(data,options)

returns star plot for the given data for the given options. To use this function first call, **load ("descriptive")$**.

(%i1)   load ("descriptive")$
(%i2)   x:[1,2,3,4,5,6,7,8,9]$y:[7,10,17, 28,43,62,85,112,143]$

(%i3)   starplot(x, y,   stars_colors = [red,orange], sample_keys = ["Volt","Ampere"],star_center=[2,6],star_radius=13, proportional_axes = xy, line_width=4)$

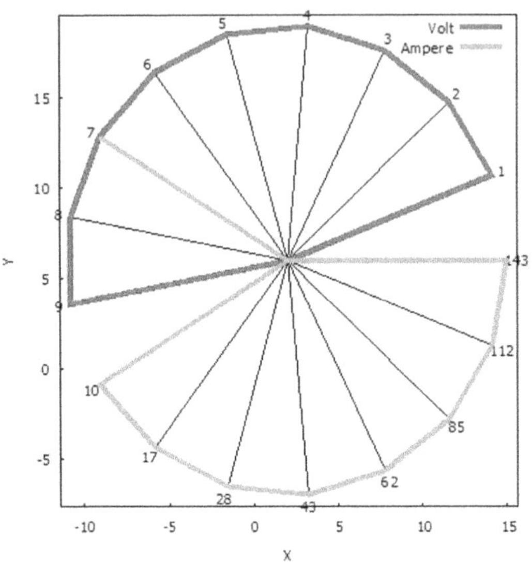

stats_numer

if it is set to true, returns statistical functions in floating point numbers, else returns in symbolic and rational formats. Default value: true. To use this function first call, **load("stats")$**.

status (feature)

returns a list of system features such as Lisp version, operating system type, etc.

(%i1)   status (feature);

(%o1)   [cl,mk-defsystem,readline,regexp,syscalls,i18n,loop,

compiler,clos,mop,clisp,ansi-cl,common-lisp,lisp\=cl,

interpreter,sockets,generic-streams,logical-pathnames,

screen,ffi,gettext,unicode,base-char\=character,

pc386,win32]

std (data)

returns the square root of the variance for the given data of list or matrix. To use this function first call, **load ("descriptive")$**.

(%i1)   load ("descriptive")$

(%i2)   x: matrix ([1,–3], [2, 6], [3,–1],[–4,–3]);

$$(\%o2)\qquad \begin{bmatrix} 1 & -3 \\ 2 & 6 \\ 3 & -1 \\ -4 & -3 \end{bmatrix}$$

(%i3)   std (x);

$$(\%o3)\qquad [\frac{\sqrt{29}}{2},\frac{\sqrt{219}}{4}]$$

(%i4)   var(x)   /* variance */

$$(\%o4)\qquad \left[\frac{29}{4},\frac{219}{16}\right]$$

step

important command in logical programming to change the periodic values.

(%i1)   for a:–3 thru 26 step 4 do display(a);

a=–3

a=1   /* step increase by 4 up to a maximum 26 */

a=5

a=9

a=13

a=17

a=21

a=25   /* do loop breaks as condition becomes false, (25+4)>26 */

(%o1)   done

strim ("character", "string")

returns a string by removing the characters in both ends.

(%i1)   strim ("/" , "/symbolic wxMaxima computations/");

(%o1)   symbolic wxMaxima computations

strimr ("character", "string")

returns a string by removing the characters in the right end.

(%i1)   strim ("/" , "/symbolic wxMaxima computations/");

(%o1)   /symbolic wxMaxima computations

stringdisp

if it is set to true, strings are displayed within double quote marks.

Default value: false

(%i1)   stringdisp: true$

(%i2)   "wxMaxima for symbolic computations";

(%o2)   "wxMaxima for symbolic computations"

(%i3)   stringdisp: false$

(%i4)   "wxMaxima for symbolic computations";

(%o4)   wxMaxima for symbolic computations

stringp ("string")

returns true for a string.

(%i1)   b: "wxMaxima"$

(%i2)   stringp(b);

(%o2)   true

(%i3)   stringp(a);

(%o3)   false

sublis ([list], expression)

evaluates parallel substitutions for the given expression.

(%o1)   sublis ([b=a^2], (b)^3);

(%i1) a^6

sublist ([list], condition)

returns the list of elements, if the given condition is true or else returns [].

(%i1)   i:[2,2.1,1,3,–4.13,8.2,6.2,8.5,5.8]$

(%i2)   sublist (i, floatnump); /* returns float numbers */

(%o2)   [2.1,–4.13,8.2,6.2,8.5,5.8]

(%i3)   sublist (i, integerp);   /* returns integers */

(%o3)   [2,1,3]
(%i4)   sublist (%o2, integerp);
(%o4)   []

submatrix (row,Matrix, coloumn)

returns a matrix after deleting specified rows and/or columns.
(%i1)   x: matrix ([i, j, q], [k,l,t], [m,-n,-r]);

$$(\%o1) \qquad \begin{bmatrix} i & j & q \\ k & l & t \\ m & -n & -r \end{bmatrix}$$

(%i2)   submatrix (3,x,2);

$$(\%o2) \qquad \begin{bmatrix} i & q \\ k & t \end{bmatrix}$$

(%i3)   submatrix (1,x);

$$(\%o2) \qquad \begin{bmatrix} k & l & t \\ m & -n & -r \end{bmatrix}$$

subset ([list], condition)

returns the set of elements, if the given condition is true or else returns {}.
(%i1)   i:{2,2.1,1,3,-4.13,8.2,6.2,8.5,5.8}$
(%i2)   subset (i, floatnump);   /* returns float numbers */
(%o2)   {-4.13,2.1,5.8,6.2,8.2,8.5}
(%i3)   subset (i, integerp);   /* returns integers */
(%o3)   {1,2,3}
(%i4)   subset (%o2, integerp);
(%o4)   {}

subsetp (subset, set)

returns true if and only if the subset is in the given set.
(%i1)   i:{2,2.1,1,3,-4.13,8.2,6.2,8.5,5.8}$
(%i2)   subset (i, floatnump);
(%o2)   {-4.13,2.1,5.8,6.2,8.2,8.5}
(%i3)   subsetp (%o2, %o1)
(%o3)   true

subst (new_value, old_value, expression)

substitutes new value for old value in the expression.

(%i1)   c:a^2+x$

(%i2)   subst(b,a,c);

(%o2) $x+b^2$

substring ("string", start, end)

returns the string from start to end position.

(%i1)   substring ("wxMaxima", 2, 6);

(%o1)   xMax

subvar (subscripted expression)

evaluates the specified subscripted expression.

(%i1)   a:b^−2$subvar (a, k);

(%o1) $\left(\dfrac{1}{b^2}\right)_k$

sum (expression)

returns sum of the expression.

(%i1)   sum (k^2+1, k, 2, 6);

(%o1)   95   /* 5+10+17+26+37 */

supcase ("string", start, end)

returns the string from start to end with uppercase letters.

(%i1)   supcase("wxmaxima",3);

(%o1)   wxMAXIMA

(%i2)   supcase("wxmaxima",3,4);

(%o2)   wxMaxima

symbolp (character)

returns true if the character is a symbol.

(%i1)   symbolp(95.2876);

(%o1)   false

(%i2)   symbolp(%i);

(%o2)   true

symmdifference({set_1, set_2})

returns the symmetric difference between sets.

(%i1)   symmdifference({2,x,y,z},{8,x,y,k});
(%o1)   {2,8,k,z}

tab

can be used for tab character.

take_inference (position, object)   Refer:inference_result

returns the value for the position stored in object from the inference result. To use this function first call, **load(inference_result)$**.

(%i1)   load(inference_result)$

(%i3)   b: 3$ h: 2$ /* b = base; h = height */

(%i4)   inference_result("Rectangle", ['base=b, 'height=h,
               'area=b*h,'perimeter=2*(b+h)],[1,2,4,3]);

$$
(\%o4) \quad \begin{bmatrix} \text{Rectangle} \\ \text{base} = 3 \\ \text{height} = 2 \\ \text{perimeter} = 10 \\ \text{area} = 6 \end{bmatrix}
$$
               /* [1,2,4,3] refers display order */

                              /* perimeter displayed at 3rd */

(%i5)   take_inference('base,%o4);
(%o5)   3
(%i6)   take_inference(4,%o4);
(%o6)   10   /* 4th value defined at %i4, refers perimeter */

tan(x)

returns tangent value for angle 'x' expressed in radians.

(%i1)   tan(30),numer;
(%o1)   −6.405331196646276

tanh(value)

returns hyperbolic tangent for the given value.

(%i1)   tanh(0.5);
(%o1)   0.4621171572600097

taylor (expression, varible, point, n)

expands the expression with Taylor or Laurent series with the variable at the point, containing the terms (variable – point)^n.

(%i1)	taylor $(1/(x+1)$, x, 0, 6);
(%o1)	$1 - x + x^2 - x^3 + x^4 - x^5 + x^6 + ...$

taylorinfo (expression)

returns information about the Taylor series in the given expression.

(%i1)	taylor $(1/(x+1)$, x, 0, 6);
(%o1)	$1 - x + x^2 - x^3 + x^4 - x^5 + x^6 + ...$
(%i2)	taylorinfo (%);
(%o2)	$[[x,0,6]]$

taylorp (expression)

returns true if the expression is a Taylor series or else returns false.

(%i1)	taylor $(1/(x+1)$, x, 0, 6);
(%o1)	$1 - x + x^2 - x^3 + x^4 - x^5 + x^6 + ...$
(%i2)	taylorp (%o1);
(%o2)	true

taytorat (expression)

converts expression from taylor form to canonical rational expression form.

(%i1)	taylor $(1/(x+1)$, x, 0, 6);
(%o1)	$1 - x + x^2 - x^3 + x^4 - x^5 + x^6 + ...$
(%i2)	taytorat (%o1);
(%o2)/R/	$x^6 - x^5 + x^4 - x^3 + x^2 - x + 1$

tcl_output ([list])

prints elements of a list enclosed by { }, as the Tcl/Tk programming.

(%i1)	tcl_output ([2, 8, 4, 5, 6], 1, 4)$
(%o1)	{2.000000000 6.000000000
}	/*arranged in order and returns the result */

test_mean ([list], options)

performs mean t-test for the given list. To use this function first call,

load ("stats")$.

The output may show the following results:

mean_estimate: the sample mean.

conf_level: confidence level selected by the user.

conf_interval: confidence interval for the population mean.

method: inference procedure.

hypotheses: null and alternative hypotheses to be tested.

statistic: value of the sample statistic used for testing the null hypothesis.

distribution: distribution of the sample statistic, together with its parameter(s).

p_value: p-value of the test.

(%i1)   load("stats")$

(%i2)   test_mean([3.1,2.3,2.1,4.3,4.4,7.2,5.8,8.5,
               4.1,4.3],'conflevel=0.95);

```
MEAN TEST
mean_estimate = 4.61
conf_level = 0.95
```

(%o2)
```
conf_interval = [3.14649717584353,6.07350282415647]
method = Exact t − test. Unknown variance.
hypotheses = H0: mean = 0 , H1: mean # 0
statistic = 7.125742666799893
distribution = [student_t, 9]
```
$p_{value} = 5.50994234527202310^{-5}$

tex (expression)

prints Tex format.

(%i1)   integrate((x^−3), x);

(%o1) $-{1 \over 2x^2}$

(%i2)   tex(%);

$$-{{1}\over{2\,x^2}}$$

(%o2)   false

tex1 (expression)

returns string in TeX output for the given expression.

(%i1)   integrate((x^–3), x);

(%o1) $-\dfrac{1}{2x^2}$

(%i2)   tex(%);

(%o2)   -{{1}\over{2\,x^2}}

texput (atom, "string")

assigns Tex output form, string to the atom.

(%i1)   texput (a, "/kj");

(%o1)   /kj

(%i2)   tex(a);

$$/kj$$

(%o2)   false

thru

important function in statements for doing iterations. Basic algorithm with 'thru' for using 'do'in iterations are:

for variable: initial_value step increment thru limit do body.

for variable: initial_value step increment while condition do body.

(%i1)   for a: –3 thru 26 step 4 do display(a);

a=–3

a=1   /* step increase by 4 up to a maximum 26 */

a=5

a=9

a=13

a=17

a=21

a=25   /* do loop breaks as condition becomes false, (25+4)>26 */

time (%o1, %o2, %o3, ...)

returns list of times in seconds, to compute the output.

(%i1)   x:0$while (x^2–5<=0) do (x:x+0.00001)$

               time(%o1,%o2);

(%o3)   [0.0,15.1164969]

timedate()

returns date and time at GMT time zone.

(%i1)   timedate () ;

(%o1) 2017–11–2623:21:24+05:30

title [title, "text"]

displays title for plot.

(%i1)   x:[1,2,3,4,5,6,7,8,9]$y:[7,10,17,28,43,62,85,112,143]$

               plot2d([discrete,x,y],[title,"ChartTitle"],[xlabel,"Time
               (s)"],[ylabel, "Potential (V)"])$

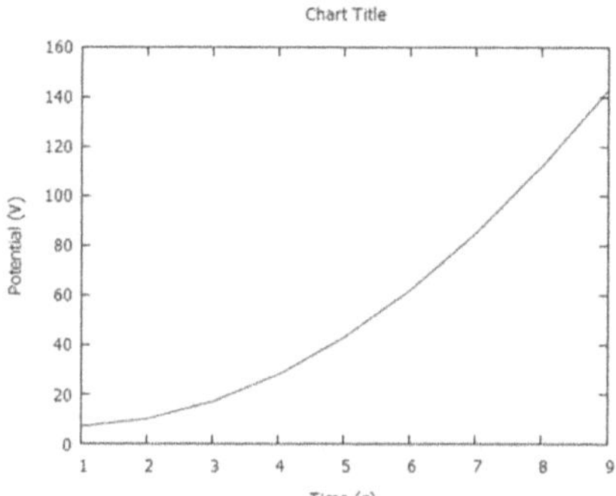

tldefint (expression, x, lower_limit, upper_limit)   Refer: ldefint

returns the definite integral of expression with respect to 'x' between the upper limit 'b' and the lower limit 'a'.

(%i1)   tldefint (2*x^4, x, a, b);

(%o1) $\dfrac{2b^5}{5} - \dfrac{2a^5}{5}$

(%i2)   tldefint ((2*x)^4, x, a, b);

(%o3) $\dfrac{16b^5}{5} - \dfrac{16a^5}{5}$

toeplitz ([coloumn], [row])

returns Toeplitz matrix with the list of column and row.

(%i1)   toeplitz([2,3],[i,y,z]);

(%o1) $\begin{bmatrix} 2 & y & z \\ 3 & 2 & y \end{bmatrix}$

tokens ("string", 'test)

returns a list of tokens from string based on the test arguement. Test arguments are: constituent, alphacharp, digitcharp, lowercasep, uppercasep, charp, characterp, alphanumericp

(%i1)   tokens("Symbolic wxMaxima",'uppercasep);

(%o1)   [S,M]

tpartpol (symmetric_form, [variables])   Refer: partpol

tests if the polynomial is symmetric with the variables of the list.

(%i1)   part2cont ([[i^−3−2*b, 5, 2]], [j, k]);

resolvante

generale

NOTE: To compile the system do

load("sym/compile");

0 errors, 0 warnings

(%o1) $\left(\frac{1}{i^3} - 2b\right) j^5 k^2$

(%i2)   partpol(%,[j,k]);

(%o2) $[[\frac{1}{i^3} - 2b, 5, 2]]$

(%i3)   tpartpol(%o1,[j,k]);

(%o3)   MANQUE DES ELEMENTS DE L\'ORBITE

tracematrix (matrix)

returns the sum of the diagonal elements (trace) of a matrix. To use this function first call, **load(functs)$**.

(%i1)   load(functs)$

(%i2)   matrix([i^−n,−n, t], [u, v^k, −g/r], [m^s, k*j, −r/n])

(%o2) $\begin{bmatrix} \frac{1}{i^n} & -n & t \\ u & v^k & -\frac{g}{r} \\ m^s & jk & -\frac{r}{n} \end{bmatrix}$

(%i3)   tracematrix (%);

(%o3) $v^k - \frac{r}{n} + \frac{1}{i^n}$

transparent

if it is set to true, polygons are unfilled and becomes transparent. Default value: false. By fill_color command, given color can be filled.

(%i1)   draw2d(line_width=2, fill_color=orange, polygon([[3,0], [6,0],[4.5,4.5]]), transparent=true, line_width=5, polygon ([[6,0],[9,0],[7.5,4.5]]))$ Refer: draw2d

/* two polygons first is filled with orange, second is transparent */

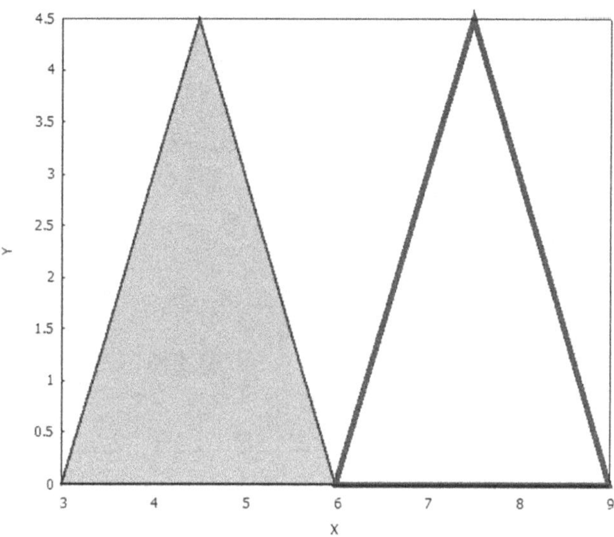

transpose (matrix)

returns the transpose of the matrix.

(%i1)   matrix([i^-n,-n, t], [u, v^k, -g/r], [m^s, k*j, -r/n])

(%o1)
$$\begin{bmatrix} \dfrac{1}{i^n} & -n & t \\ u & v^k & -\dfrac{g}{r} \\ m^s & jk & -\dfrac{r}{n} \end{bmatrix}$$

(%i2)   transpose(%);

(%o2)
$$\begin{bmatrix} \dfrac{1}{i^n} & u & m^s \\ -n & v^k & jk \\ t & -\dfrac{g}{r} & -\dfrac{r}{n} \end{bmatrix}$$

tree_reduce (function, {set} or [list])

extends the binary function to an n-aray function of a set or list.

(%i1)   tree_reduce (f, {i, j, k});

(%o1)   f(f(i,j),k)

treillis (integer)   Refer: ltreillis; lgtreillis

returns the list of partitions for integer.

(%i1)   treillis (4);

(%o1)   [[4],[3,1],[2,2],[2,1,1],[1,1,1,1]]

(%i2)   ltreillis (4, 5);

(%o2)   [[4,0,0,0,0],[3,1,0,0,0],[2,2,0,0,0],[2,1,1,0,0],[1,1,1,1,0]]

(%i3)   lgtreillis (4, 2);

(%o3)   [[3,1],[2,2]]

treinat ([partition])

retruns the list of partitions inferior to the given list of partition.

(%i1)   treinat ([1, 1, 1, 1]);

(%o1)   [[5],[4,1],[3,2],[3,1,1],[2,2,1],[2,1,1,1],[1,1,1,1,1]]

(%i2)   treinat ([1, 3]);

(%o2)   [[4],[3,1],[2,2],[1,3]]

(%i3)   treinat ([2, 2]);

(%o3)   [[4],[3,1],[2,2]]

(%i4)   treinat ([6, 2]);

(%o4)   [[8],[7,1],[6,2]]

(%i5)   treinat ([2, 6]);

(%o5)   [[8],[7,1],[6,2],[5,3],[4,4],[3,5],[2,6]]

triangle ([x1,y1], [x2,y2], [x3,y3])

draws a triangle for the specified coordianates [x1,y1], [x2,y2] and [x3,y3] using draw2d function.

(%i1)   draw2d(triangle([3,3],[4,3],[3.5,4]))$

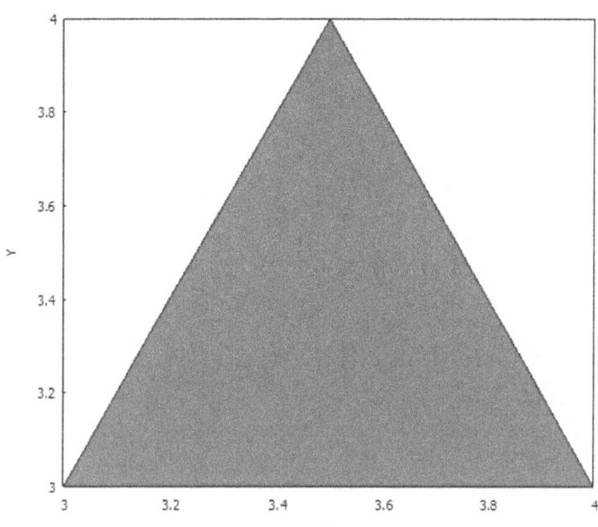

triangularize (matrix)

returns upper triangular form of the matrix as Gaussian elimination.

(%i1)   matrix ([a,b], [c,d]);

(%o1) $\begin{bmatrix} a & b \\ c & d \end{bmatrix}$

(%i2)   triangularize (%);

(%o2) $\begin{bmatrix} a & b \\ 0 & ad - bc \end{bmatrix}$

(%i3)   matrix ([a,b,c], [d,e,f], [g,h,i]);

(%o3) $\begin{bmatrix} a & b & c \\ d & e & f \\ g & h & i \end{bmatrix}$

(%i4)   triangularize (%);

(%o4) $\begin{bmatrix} a & b & c \\ 0 & ae - bd & af - cd \\ 0 & 0 & (ae - bd)i + (cd - af)h + (bf - ce)g \end{bmatrix}$

trigexpand (expression)

expands trigonometric or hyperbolic functions of sums of angles in the given expression.

(%i1)	trigexpand(sin(x+y));
(%o1)	cos(x)sin(y)+sin(x)cos(y)
(%i2)	trigexpand(sin(2*x));
(%o2)	2cos(x)sin(x)
(%i3)	trigexpand(cos(2*x));
(%o3)	$\cos(x)^2 - \sin(x)^2$
(%i4)	trigexpand(tan(x+y));

$$(\%o4) \qquad \frac{\tan(y)+\tan(x)}{1-\tan(x)\,\tan(y)}$$

(%i5)	trigexpand(tan(2*x));

$$(\%o5) \qquad \frac{2\,\tan(x)}{1-\tan(x)^2}$$

triginverses

if it is set to all, simplifies of the composition of trigonometric and hyperbolic functions with their inverse functions.

(%i1)	atan(x) /* inverse tangent function */
(%i2)	tan(%)
(%o2)	x
(%i3)	triginverses:all$
(%i4)	atan(tan(x));
(%o4)	x

trigrat (trigonometric expression)

returns canonical quasilinear form of a trigonometric expression.

(%i1)	trigexpand(sin(x+y));
(%o1)	cos(x)sin(y)+sin(x)cos(y)
(%i2)	trigrat(cos(x)*sin(y)+sin(x)*cos(y));
(%o2)	sin(y+x)
(%i3)	trigrat(tan(y)+sin(x));

$$(\%o3) \qquad \frac{\sin(y+x)-\sin(y-x)+2\,\sin(y)}{2\,\cos(y)}$$

trigreduce (expression, variable)

combines products and powers of trigonometric or hyperbolic sin's and cos's of the varaible into those of multiples of variable.

(%i1)   trigexpand(cos(2*x));
(%o1) $\cos(x)^2-\sin(x)^2$

(%i2)   trigreduce(%,x);

(%o2) $\dfrac{\cos(2x)+1}{2}+\dfrac{\cos(2x)}{2}-\dfrac{1}{2}$

related function: poissimp

poissimp

(%i1)   trigexpand(cos(2*x));
(%o1) $\cos(x)^2-\sin(x)^2$
(%i2)   poissimp(%);
(%o2) $\cos(2x)$
(%i3)   trigexpand(sin(x+y));
(%o3) $\cos(x)\sin(y)+\sin(x)\cos(y)$
(%i4)   poissimp(%);
(%o4) $\sin(y+x)$

trigsimp (expression)

with the identities, $\sin(x)^2 + \cos(x)^2 = 1$ and $\cosh(x)^2 - \sinh(x)^2 = 1$ simplify tan, sec, etc., to sin, cos, sinh, cosh expression.

(%i1)   trigexpand(cos(2*x));
(%o1) $\cos(x)^2-\sin(x)^2$
 (%i2)   trigsimp(%);
(%o2) $2\cos(x)^2-1$

(%i3)   trigexpand(tan(2*x));

(%o3) $\dfrac{2\tan(x)}{1-\tan(x)^2}$

(%i4)   trigsimp(%);

(%o4) $\dfrac{2\cos(x)\sin(x)}{2\cos(x)^2-1}$

(%i5)   sinh(x)^2-cosh(x)^2;

(%o5)	$\sinh(x)^2-\cosh(x)^2$
(%i6)	trigsimp(%);
(%o6)	-1

truncate (number)

returns the closest integer not greater than the given number.

Similar functions are: ceiling (number) and floor(number).

ceiling (number)

return the least integer that is greater than or equal to the given number.

floor(number)   Refer: floor

returns the largest integer less than or equal to the given number.

(%i1)	x:31.00000001$
(%i2)	truncate(x);
(%o2)	31
(%i3)	ceiling(x);
(%o3)	32
(%i4)	floor(x);
(%o4)	31
(%i5)	z:31.9999999999
(%i6)	truncate(z);
(%o6)	31
(%i7)	ceiling(z);
(%o7)	32
(%i8)	floor(z);
(%o8)	31

ttyoff

if it is set to true, output expressions are not displayed but output expressions are computed and assigned labels. Default value: false.

(%i1)	integrate(x^3,x);	
(%o1)	$\dfrac{x^4}{4}$	
(%i2)	ttyoff:true;	
(%i3)	integrate(x^3,x);	/* no output display */
(%i4)	%o3*x;	

(%i5)   print(%o4);

(%i6)   ttyoff:false;

(%o6)   false

(%i7)   print(%o4);

(%o7) $\dfrac{x^5}{4}$

ueivects(matrix)   **uniteigenvectors (matrix)**   Refer: eivects

returns eigenvectors of the matrix. The first sublist is eigenvalues, and the other sublists are the unit eigenvectors. To use this function first call, **load ("eigen")\$**.

(%i1)   load ("eigen")\$

(%i2)   M:matrix([1,2],[4,3]);

(M) $\begin{bmatrix} 1 & 2 \\ 4 & 3 \end{bmatrix}$

(%i3)   ueivects (M);

(%o3) $[[[5,-1],[1,1]],[[[\tfrac{1}{\sqrt{5}},\tfrac{2}{\sqrt{5}}]],[[\tfrac{1}{\sqrt{2}},-\tfrac{1}{\sqrt{2}}]]]]$

union ({sets})

returns the union of the sets.

(%i1)   i:{a,b,c}\$j:{c,e,f}\$k:{a,g,h}\$

(%i2)   union (i,j,k);

(%o2)   {a,b,c,e,f,g,h}

unique ([list])

returns the unique elements of the list.

(%i1)   k:[a−c,b,a−a,c/c];

(k)   [a−c,b,0,1]

(%i2)   unique (k);

(%o2)   [0,1,b,a−c]

unitp (expression)

returns true if the expression is a literal dimension. To use this function first call, **load (ezunits).**

(%i1)	load ("ezunits")$
(%i2)	declare_constvalue (p, 10 ` m / sec);

$$(\%o2) \qquad 10 \ ` \ \frac{m}{sec}$$

(%i3)	unitp(%);
(%o3)	true

units (expression)

returns the units of a dimensional quantity in the expression, or returns 1 if it is non-dimensional. To use this function first call, **load (ezunits)$.**

(%i1)	load ("ezunits")$
(%i2)	declare_constvalue (p, 10 ` m / sec);

$$(\%o2) \qquad 10 \ ` \ \frac{m}{sec}$$

(%i3)	units(%);

$$(\%o3) \qquad \frac{m}{sec}$$

(%i4)	fundamental_units (1 `C/s);	/* C = Coulomb */
(%o4)	A	/* Ampere second */
(%i5)	units(%);	
(%o5)	1	

unitvector (matrix)   uvect (matrix)

returnsunit vector of the matrix. To use this function first call, **load ("eigen")$.**

(%i1)	load ("eigen")$
(%i2)	M:matrix([1,2],[4,3])$
(%i3)	unitvector(M);

$$(\%o3) \qquad \begin{bmatrix} \frac{1}{3} & \frac{1}{\sqrt{2}} \\ 1 & \frac{3}{\sqrt{17}} \end{bmatrix}$$

(%i4)   N:matrix([a,b],[c,d]);

(N) $\begin{bmatrix} a & b \\ c & d \end{bmatrix}$

(%i5)   unitvector(N);

(%o5) $\begin{bmatrix} \dfrac{a}{\sqrt{bc+a^2}} & \dfrac{b}{\sqrt{bd+ab}} \\ \dfrac{c}{\sqrt{cd+ac}} & \dfrac{d}{\sqrt{d^2+bc}} \end{bmatrix}$

unknown (expression)

returns true if the expression is not recognized.

(%i1)   notequal (a, b)$

(%i2)   is(a=b);

(%o2)   false

(%i3)   is(a>b);

(%o3)   unknown

unless

evaluates / iterates till the condition is satisfied.

(%i1)   for p: 2 unless p > 6 do (x:p^2, p+1, display(x));

x=4

x=9

x=16

x=25

x=36

(%o1)   done

(%i1)   for p: 2 unless p >= 6 do (x:p^2, p+1, display(x));

x=4

x=9

x=16

x=25   /* as condition is >= */

(%o1)   done

unorder()   Refer: ordergreat and orderless

disables the order created by the commands ordergreat or orderless.(%i1)
expand((i–j+n)^3);

(%o1) $n^3 - 3jn^2 + 3in^2 + 3j^2n - 6ijn + 3i^2n - j^3 + 3ij^2 - 3i^2j + i^3$

(%i2)   ordergreat(i,n);
(%o2)   done
(%i3)   expand((i–j+n)^3);
(%o3) $i^3 + 3ni^2 - 3ji^2 + 3n^2i - 6jni + 3j^2i + n^3 - 3jn^2 + 3j^2n - j^3$

(%i4)   unorder();
(%o4)   [n,i]
(%i5)   expand((i–j+n)^3);
(%o5) $n^3 - 3jn^2 + 3in^2 + 3j^2n - 6ijn + 3i^2n - j^3 + 3ij^2 - 3i^2j + i^3$

unsum (f,n)   Refer: sum

returns the first backward difference $f(n) - f(n - 1)$ and it is the inverse of the
function, sum.   Related functions are: sum, nusum.

nusum (expression, variable, i_0, i_1)

returns indefinite hypergeometric summation for the expression with respect
to the variable.

(%i1)   sum (k^2, k, k+0, k+2);
(%o1) $(k+4)^2+(k+2)^2+k2$
(%i2)   unsum(%, k);
(%o2)   6k+9
(%i3)   nusum (k^2, k, k+0, k+2);
(%o3) $3k^2+6k+5$
(%i4)   unsum(%, k);
(%o4)   3(2k–1)+(2×3)

uppercasep (character)

returns true if character is uppercase.

(%i1)	uppercasep ("w");
(%o1)	false
(%i2)	uppercasep ("W");
(%o2)	true

values

returns list of user allocated variables.

(%i1)	a:3.1$ b:8.25$ c:-3.41$
(%i2)	values;
(%o2)	[a,b,c]

vandermonde_matrix([List])

returns Vandermondematrix for the given list.

(%i1)	vandermonde_matrix ([a,b,c,d]);

$$(\%o1) \quad \begin{bmatrix} 1 & a & a^2 & a^3 \\ 1 & b & b^2 & b^3 \\ 1 & c & c^2 & c^3 \\ 1 & d & d^2 & d^3 \end{bmatrix}$$

(%i2)	vandermonde_matrix ([1,2,3,4]);

$$(\%o2) \quad \begin{bmatrix} 1 & 1 & 1 & 1 \\ 1 & 2 & 4 & 8 \\ 1 & 3 & 9 & 27 \\ 1 & 4 & 16 & 64 \end{bmatrix}$$

var (data)

returns the variance for the given data of list or matrix. To use this function first call, **load ("descriptive")$**.

(%i1)	load ("descriptive")$
(%i2)	var ([a,b,c,d]);

$$(\%o2) \quad \frac{\left(d-\frac{d+c+b+a}{4}\right)^2+\left(c-\frac{d+c+b+a}{4}\right)^2+\left(b-\frac{d+c+b+a}{4}\right)^2+\left(a-\frac{d+c+b+a}{4}\right)^2}{4}$$

(%i3)	var ([1,2,3,4]);

$$(\%o3) \quad \frac{5}{4}$$

(%i4)   var (matrix([a,b],[c,d]));

(%o4) $$[\frac{\left(c-\frac{c+a}{2}\right)^2+\left(a-\frac{c+a}{2}\right)^2}{2},\frac{\left(d-\frac{d+b}{2}\right)^2+\left(b-\frac{d+b}{2}\right)^2}{2}]$$

vector ([x,y], [dx,dy])

draws vector with draw2d or draw3d function.

(%i1)   draw2d(xrange = [0,10], yrange= [0,10],
          vector([2,5],[8,2]));

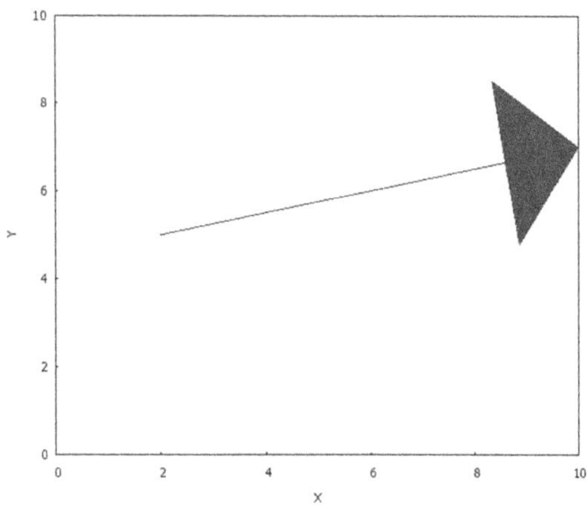

(%i1)   draw3d(vector([0,0,0],[8,1,5]));

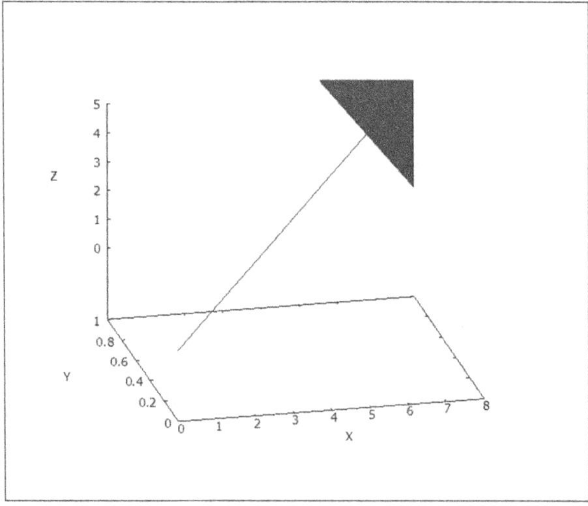

vertex_distance (from, to, graph)   Refer:shortest_path

returns the length of the shortest path in between two points in the graph whereas the function **shortest_path** returns, the shortest path in between two points in the graph. To use this function first call, **load("graphs")\$**.

(%i1)   load ("graphs")\$
(%i2)   cycle_graph(8)\$
(%i3)   draw_graph(%);

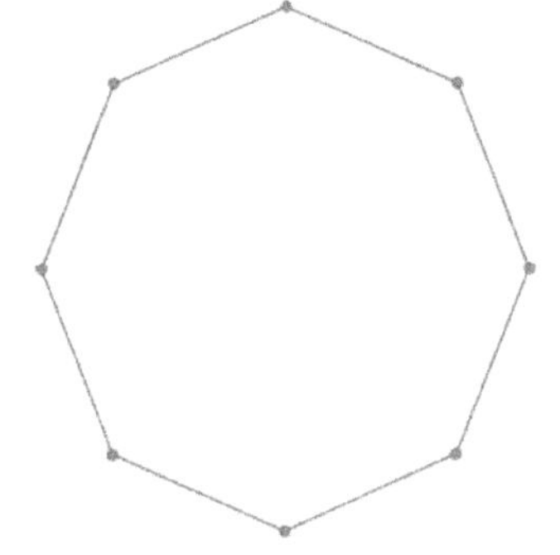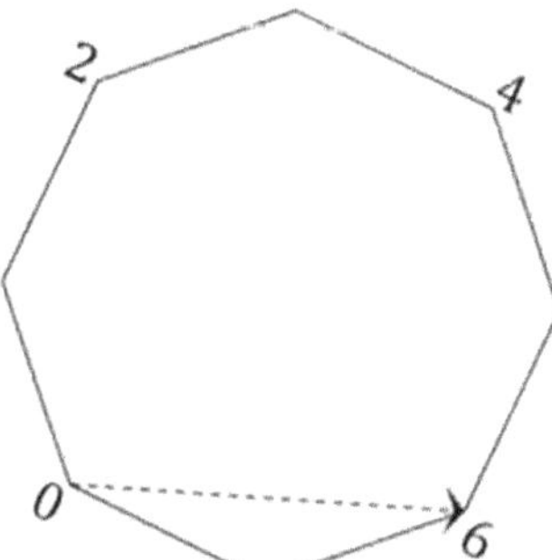

(%o3)   done
(%i4)   shortest_path(0, 6,%o2);
(%o4)   [0,7,6]
(%i5)   vertex_distance(0, 6,%o2);
(%o5)   2   /* 0 → 7 = 1 unit, 0 → 7 → 6 = 2 units */

vertex_eccentricity (point, graph)
returns the eccentricity of the vertex in the graph. To use this function first call, **load("graphs")\$**.

(%i1)   load ("graphs")\$
(%i2)   cycle_graph(8)\$
(%i3)   draw_graph(%);
(%o3)   done   →
(%i4)   vertex_eccentricity(0, %o2);
(%o4)   4   /* opposite unit distance */
(%i5)   vertex_eccentricity(4, %o2);
(%o5)   4   /* maximum distance between vertices */

Related functions: vertex_connectivity,min_vertex_cut, vertices

vertex_connectivity (graph)

returns the vertex connectivity of the graph.

(%i6)   vertex_eccentricity(4, %o2);

(%o6)   2   /* maximum distance between vertices */

min_vertex_cut(graph)

returns the minimum vertex cut in the graph.

(%i7)   min_vertex_cut (%o2);

(%o7)   [6,0]   /* maximum distance between vertices */

vertices (graph)

returns the list of vertices in the graph.

(%i8)   vertices(%o2);

(%o8)   [7,6,5,4,3,2,1,0]

view = [x_angle, z_angle]

angles, in degrees, to view direction for a 3D plot by rotation, first angle is for vertical rotation along 'x' axis, in the range and the second angle is for horizontal rotation along 'z' axis, in the range [0, 360].Default value: [60,30].

(%i1)   draw3d(view=[130, 60], explicit(x^2+y^2,x,–1,1,
               y,–1,1));

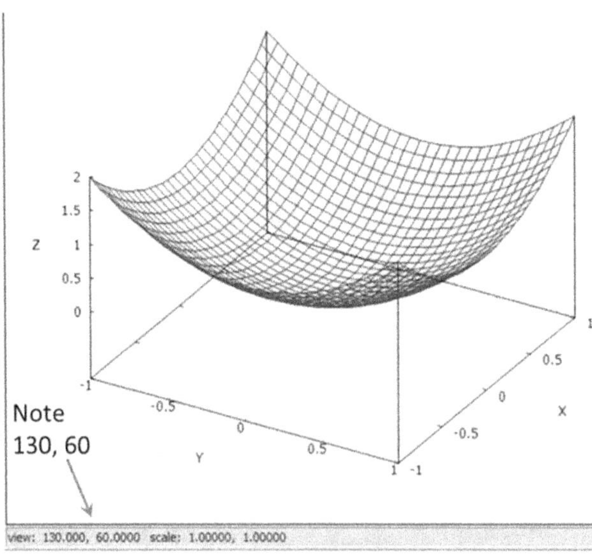

(%i2)   draw3d (view = [289,62], explicit(x^2+y^2,x,–1,1,
              y,–1,1));

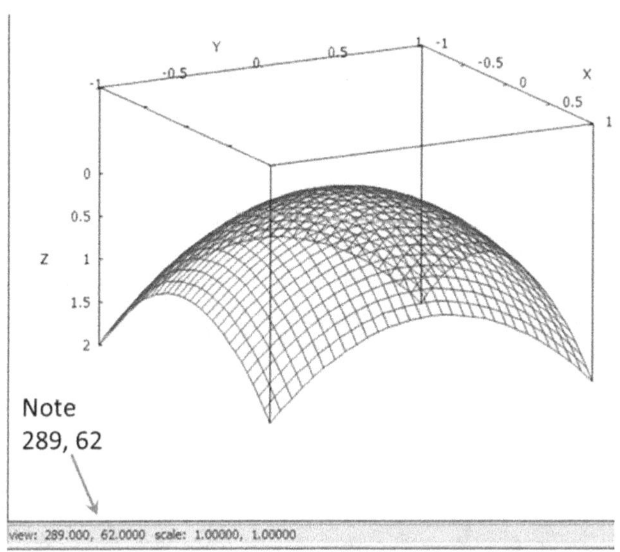

wheel_graph (n)

returns the wheel graph with n+1 vertices. To use this function first call, **load("graphs")$**.

(%i1)   load ("graphs")$
(%i2)   wheel_graph (8);
(%o2)   GRAPH(9 vertices, 16 edges)
(%i3)   draw_graph(%);

(%t3)   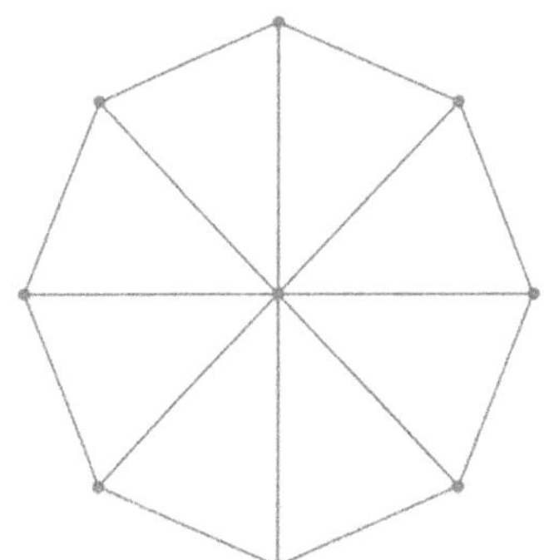

(%o3)   done

while

important function in statements for doing iterations.

(%i1)   i:2; while (i^2-2<=36) do (i: i+1, print(i−1));

(i)   2   /* i = 2+1; $3^2-2 < 36$ */

2

3

4

5   /* i = 5+1; $6^2-2 < 36$ */

6   /* do loop breaks as condition becomes false;
                            $7^2-2 < 36$ */

(%o1)   done

(%i2)   x:9; while (x^2−16>0) do (x: x−1, display(x));

(x)   9   /* iteration to find $\sqrt{16}$ */

x=8

x=7

x=6

x=5

x=4

(%i2)   done

wired_surface

if it is set to true, the draw3d plot function displays grid based graph. Default
value: false. Related function: enhanced3d.

(%i1)   draw3d(enhanced3d   =   [x,y,x],   wired_surface   =   false,
             explicit(x^2+y^2, x,-2,2,y,-2,2)) $

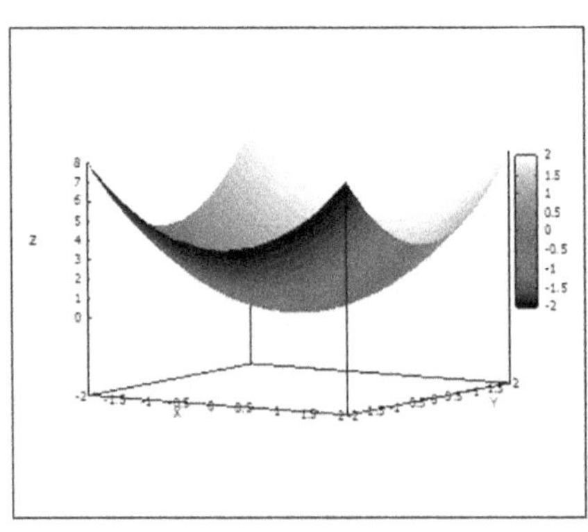

(%i1)   draw3d(enhanced3d   =   [x,y,x],   wired_surface   =   true,
             explicit(x^2+y^2, x,-2,2,y,-2,2)) $

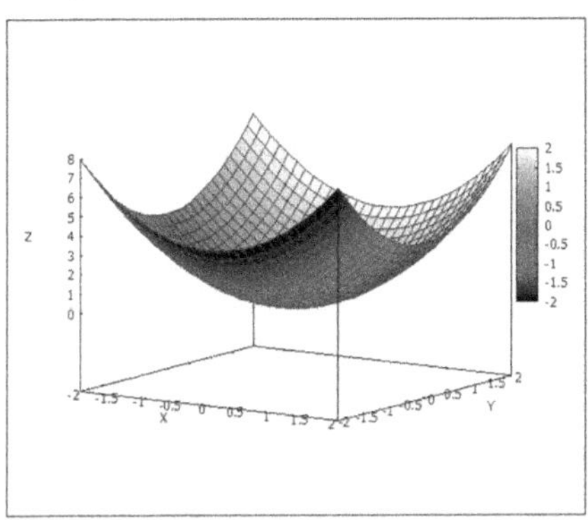

with_stdout ("file", expression)

evaluates expression and writes the output to the file name specified. By
printfile("file") command output can be displayed.

(%i1)   with_stdout ("string", for i:2 thru 6 do print("j=" ,i+1))$

(%i2)   printfile ("string")$

j=3

j=4

j=5

j=6

j=7

write_data ([data], "drive/folder/filename.extension")

writes the given data as list or matrix to the destination path as given by file
name.

(%i1)   write_data([b,c,d,a],"E:/experiment/sample.txt")$

/* In this the list the data, *b, c, d, a* are stored in the folder named *experiment* at
E: drive with the filename *sample.txt* as text file. */

writefile ("drive/folder/filename.extension")

writes the transcript to the destination path as given by file name. The
interaction between user and wxMaxima is recorded in this file.

(%i1)   writefile("E:/experiment/sample.txt")$

#<OUTPUT BUFFERED FILE-STREAM CHARACTER E:\experiment\sample.
txt>

/*text file named *sample.txt* is opened by wxMaxima to transcript, in the folder named *experiment* at *E:* drive. */

x [x, minimum, maximum]   y [y, minimum, maximum]

specifies minimum and maximum values for 'x' and 'y' in plotting.

(%i1)   plot2d (x^3, [x, –8, 8]) $

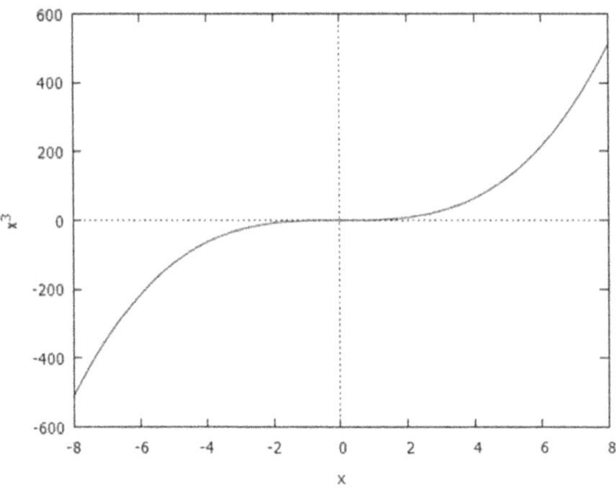

(%i1)   plot2d (y^3, [y, –8, 8]$

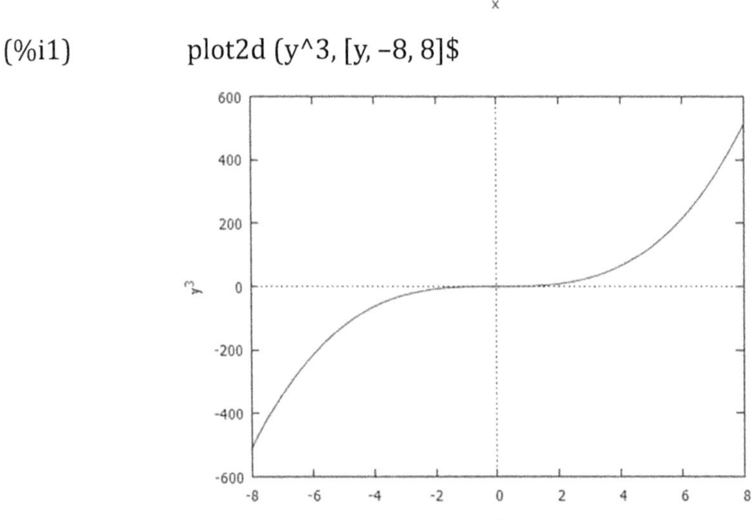

xaxis   yaxis   xaxis_color   yaxis_color

if it is true, axis will be shown with specifications. Default value: false.

(%i1)   draw2d (explicit(x^3, x, −8, 8), xaxis= true, yaxis=true, xaxis_color=red, yaxis_color = orange)$

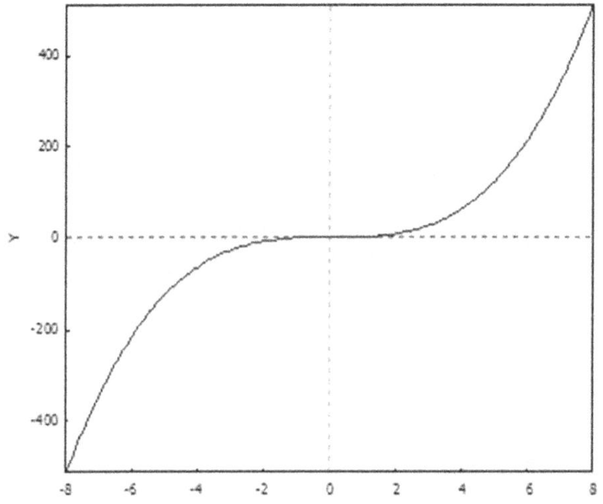

(%i1)   draw2d (explicit(x^3, x, −8, 8), xaxis= false, yaxis= true)$

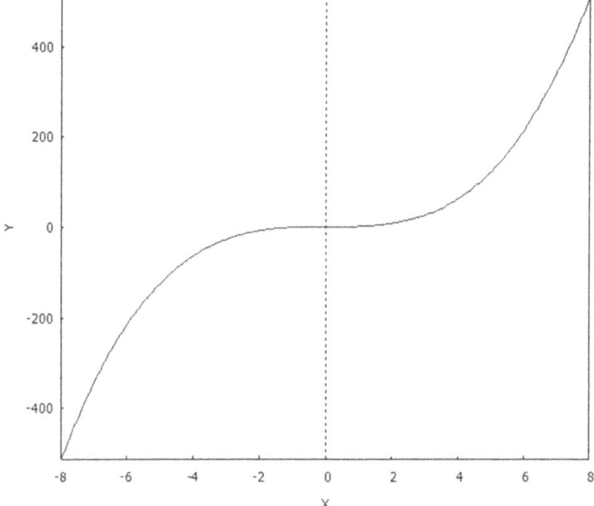

xaxis_width   **yaxis_width**

fixes width of the axis value.

(%i1)   draw2d (explicit (x^3, x, –8, 8), xaxis= true, yaxis=true, xaxis_
              width = 8, yaxis_width = 2)$

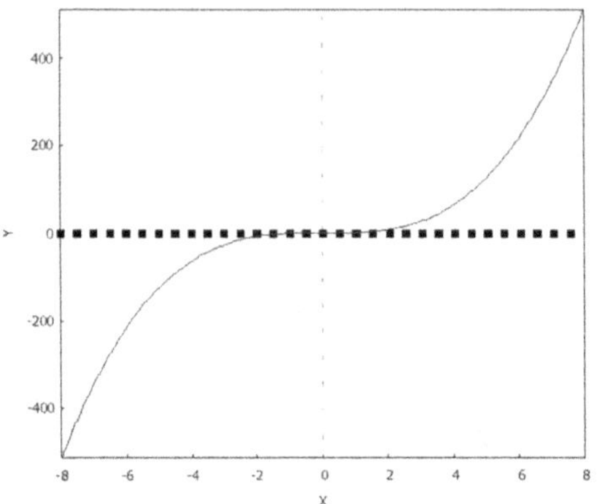

xlabel [xlabel, "string"]   **ylabel [ylabel, "string"]**

labels the given string to the 'x' and 'y' axes.

(%i1)   plot2d (x^3, [x, –8, 8], [xlabel, "x-function"],
              [ylabel, "y-function"])$

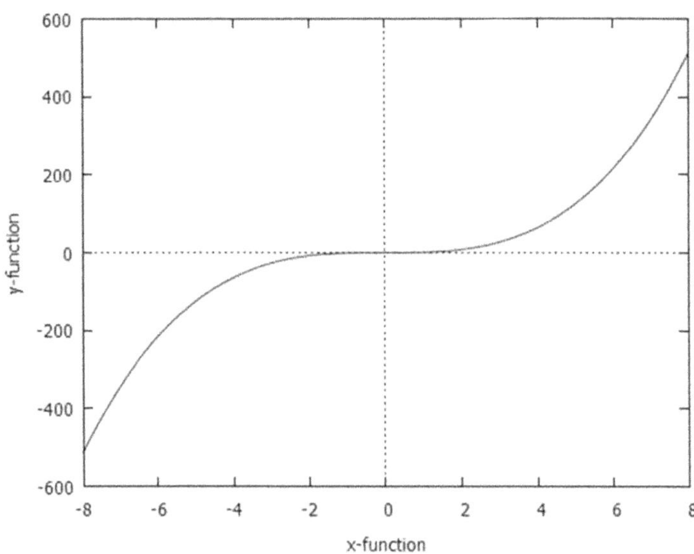

xrange =[minimum, maximum]   yrange = [minimum, maximum]

sets the minimum and maximum range for 'x' and 'y' axes. Default value: auto.

(%i1)   draw2d (explicit(x^3, x, –8, 8), xrange = [–20,20],
             yrange = [–600, 600])$

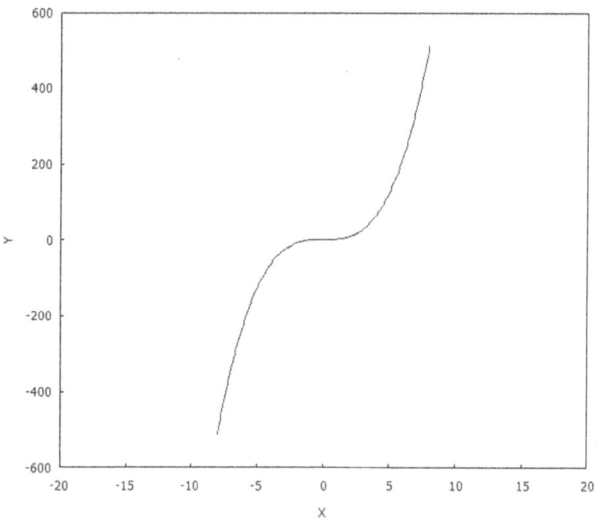

xtics[xtics,minimum, interval, maximum]
ytics[ytics, minimum, interval, maximum]

fixes axis-tic value from minimum to maximum at the given interval.

(%i1)   plot2d (x^3, [x, –8, 8], [xtics, –8, 2, 8],
             [ytics, –500, 50, 500])$

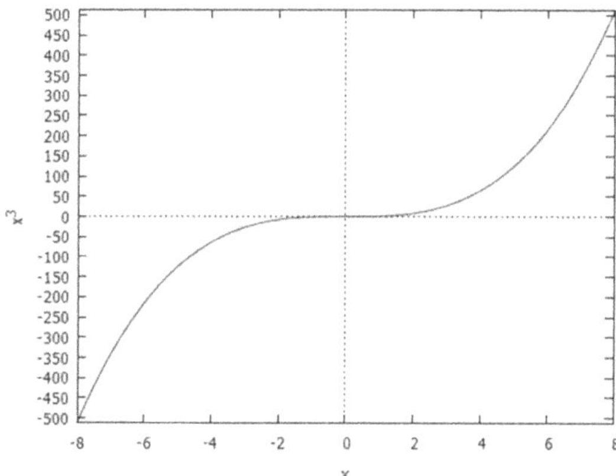

xreduce (f, [List])   Refer: lreduce

extends the binary function 'f' to the list.

(%i1)   xreduce (f, [n,j]);

(%o1)   f(n,j)

yaxis   [y, minimum, maximum]

in plot3d function, it is one of the independent variable for 'y' axis.

(%i1)   plot3d (x^3, [x, –8, 8],[y, –600, 600])$

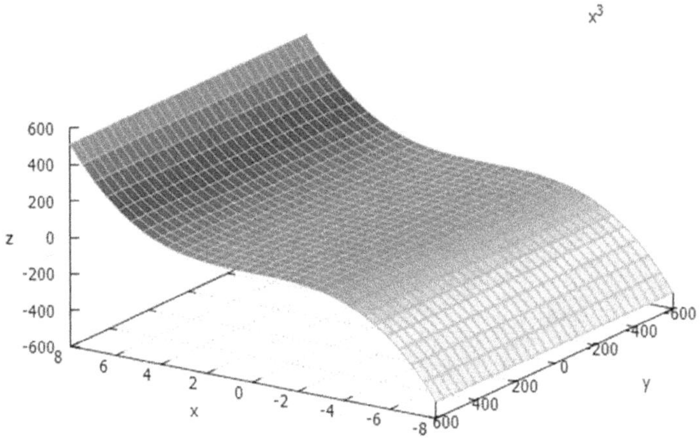

xu_grid = value, yv_grid= value

coordinates number in second variable in 3d plot. Default value: 30

(%i1)   draw3d (xu_grid = 10, yv_grid = 20, explicit (x^3, x, –8, 8, y, –800, 800))$

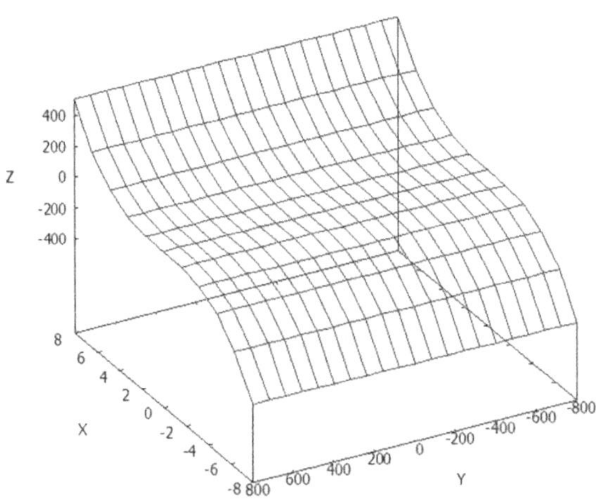

(%i1)   draw3d (xu_grid = 5, yv_grid = 10, explicit (x^3, x, –8, 8, y, –800, 800))$

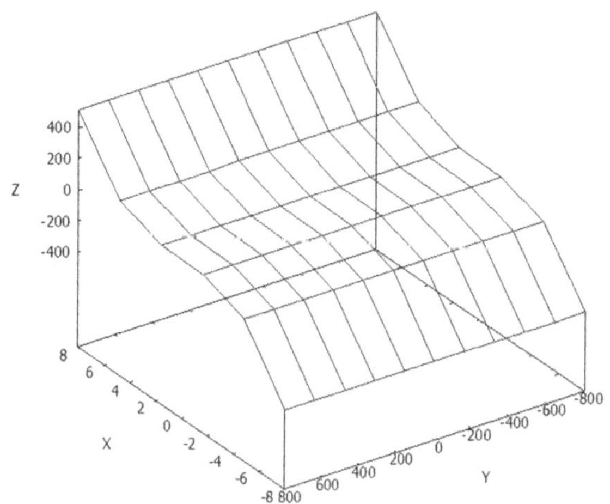

yx_ratio [yx_ratio, value]

refers the ratio between vertical and horizontal axes in 2d plot.

(%i1)   plot2d (x^3, [x, –8, 8], [yx_ratio, 2]);

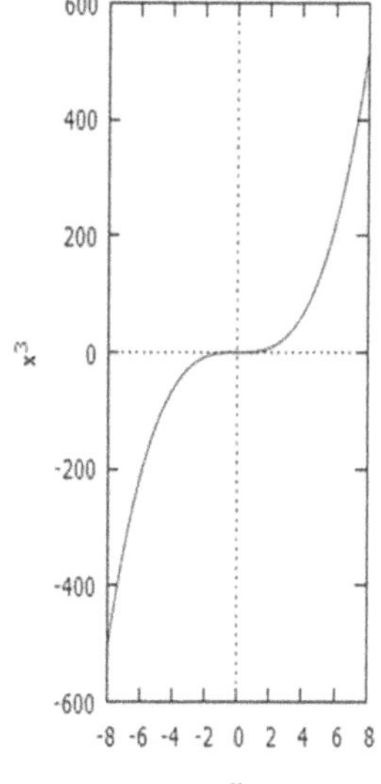

(%i1)   plot2d (x^3, [x, –8, 8], [yx_ratio, 0.5]);

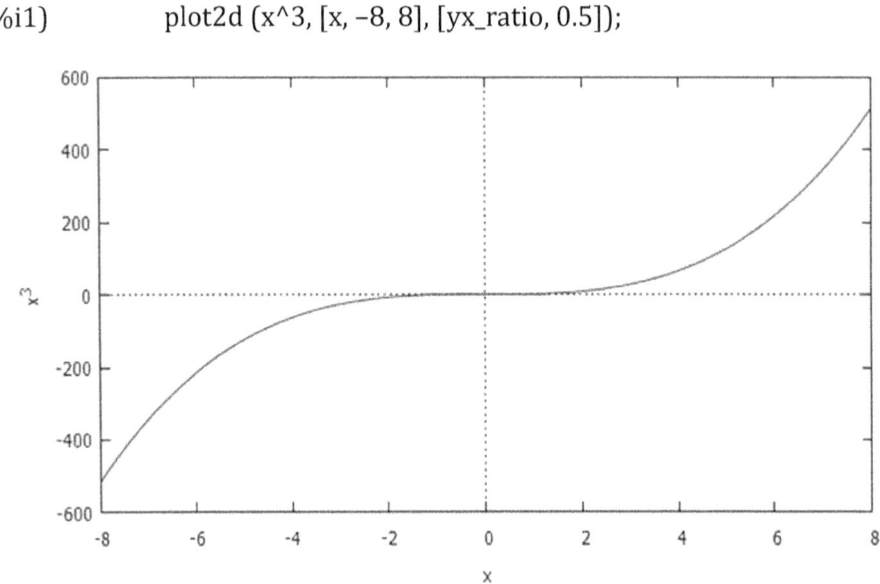

z [z, minimum, maximum]

specifies minimum and maximum values for 'z' axis in 3D plotting.

(%i1)   plot3d (x^3, [x, –8, 8],[y, –600, 600], [z, –1000, 1000])$

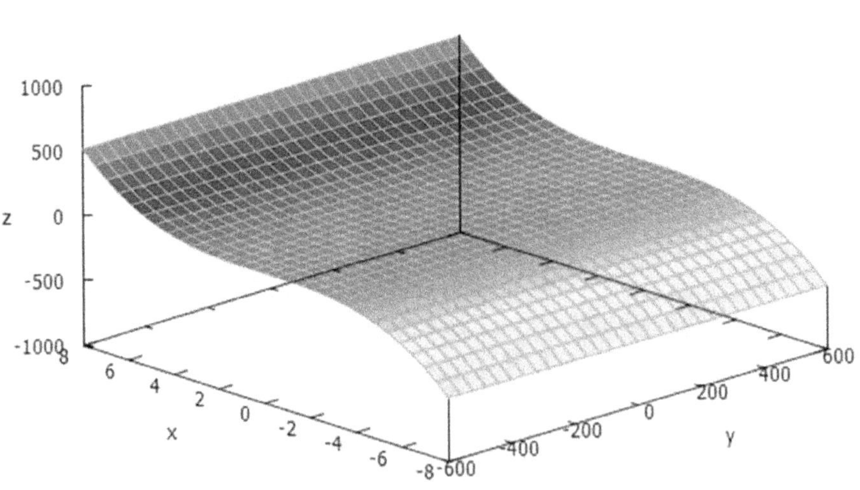

zaxis_width

fixes width of the 'z' axis.

(%i1)   draw3d (explicit (x^3, x, –8, 8, y, –800, 800), xaxis = true, xaxis_
             width = 1, yaxis = true, yaxis_width = 3,

             zaxis =true,   zaxis_width = 6)$

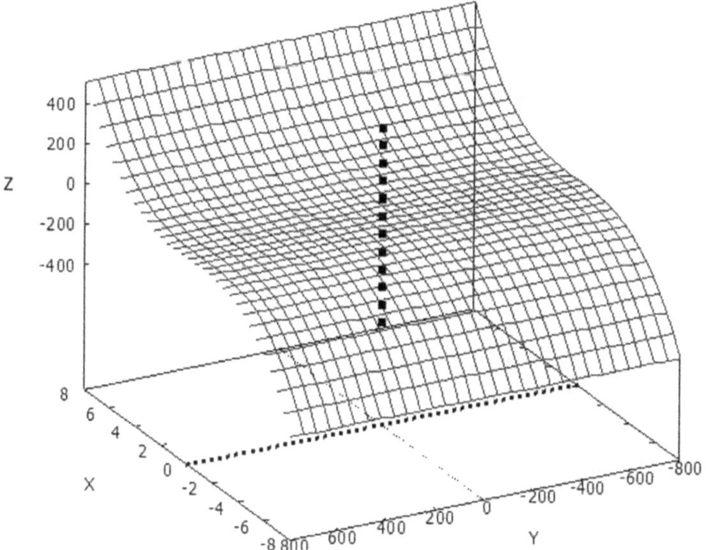

zeroequiv (expression, variable)

returns true, if the expression is equivalent to zero with reference to variable, or else returns false or dont know.

(%i1)   expand((r–3)^2);

(%o1) r^2-6r+9

(%i2)   zeroequiv((r^2–6*r+9)–(r–3)^2, r);

(%o2)   true

(%i3)   expand((r–n)^2);

(%o3) $r^2-2nr+n^2$

(%i4)   zeroequiv((r^2–2*n*r+n^2)–(r–n)^2, r);

(%o4)   dontknow

zerofor (matrix)   Refer: identfor

returns a zero matrix that has the same shape as the matrix.

(%i1)   matrix ([2^n, i,4], [–a, uy,r]);

(%o1)
$$\begin{matrix} 2^n & i & 4 \\ -a & uy & r \end{matrix}$$

(%i2)   zerofor (%);

0 errors, 0 warnings

(%o2)
$$\begin{bmatrix} 0 & 0 & 0 \\ 0 & 0 & 0 \end{bmatrix}$$

zeromatrix (row_value, coloumn_value)

returns a matrix with the given row and column values with all elements are equal to zero.

(%i1)   zeromatrix (2, 3);

(%o1)
$$\begin{bmatrix} 0 & 0 & 0 \\ 0 & 0 & 0 \end{bmatrix}$$

zeromatrixp (matrix)

returns true if a matrix with the given row and coloumn values with all elements are zero.

(%i1)   zeromatrix (2, 3);

(%o1)
$$\begin{bmatrix} 0 & 0 & 0 \\ 0 & 0 & 0 \end{bmatrix}$$

(%i2)   zeromatrixp(%);
(%o2)   true
(%i3)   matrix ([0, i, 0], [0, 0, 0])$
(%i4)   zeromatrixp(%o3);
 (%o4)   false

zlabel [zlabel, "string"]

labels the given string to the 'z' axis in 3D plot.

(%i1)   plot3d (x^3, [x, −8, 8],[y, −600, 600],[z, −1000, 1000], [xlabel, "x-label"], [ylabel, "y-label"],[zlabel, "z-label"])$

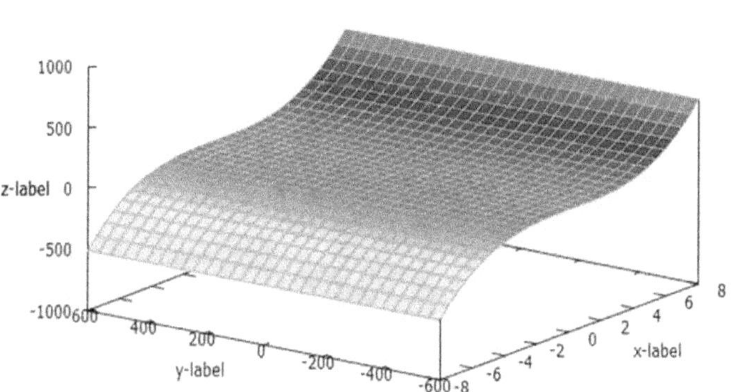

zrange =[minimum, maximum]

sets the minimum and maximum range for 'z' axis.

Default value: auto.

(%i1)   draw3d (explicit(x^3, x, −8, 8, y, −1000, 1000), xrange = [−20,20], yrange = [−600, 600], zrange =[−800, 800])$

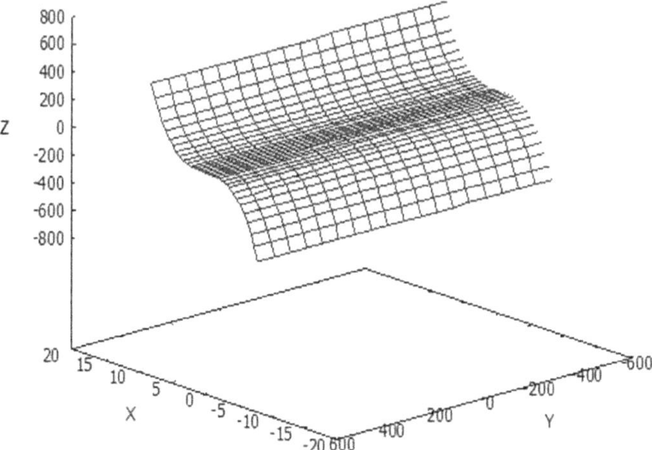

ztics [ztics, minimum, interval, maximum]   Refer: xtics and ytics

fixes 'z' axis value from minimum to maximum at the given interval.

It is specified along with 'xtics' and 'ytics' values.

(%i1)   plot3d (x^3, [x, –8, 8],[y, –600, 600],[z, –150, 150],[xtics, –12, 2, 12],[ytics, –500, 100, 500],[ztics, –100, 50, 100])$

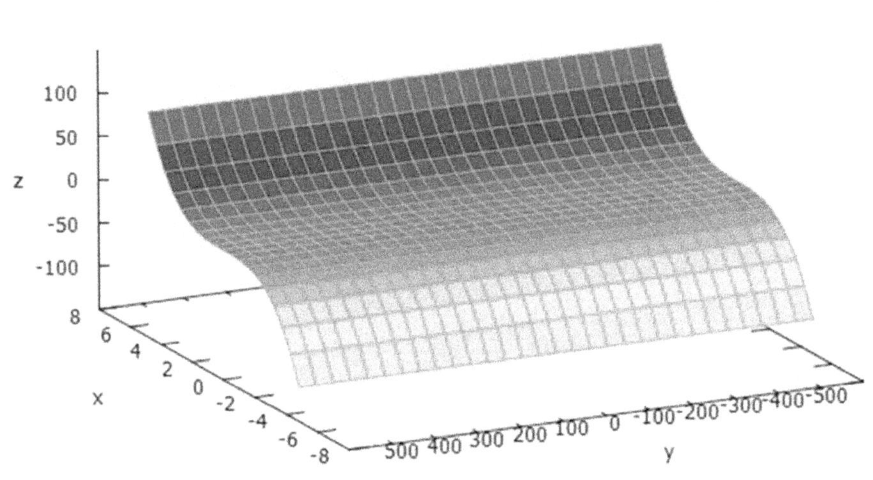

www.ingramcontent.com/pod-product-compliance
Lightning Source LLC
LaVergne TN
LVHW011003200726
843509LV00011B/965